HTML ARTISTRY:

MORE THAN CODE

http://www.htmlartistry.com

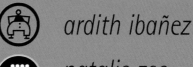 *ardith ibañez*

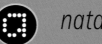 *natalie zee*

CONTENTS AT A GLANCE

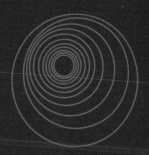

HTML ARTISTRY: MORE THAN CODE

International Standard Book Number: 0-156830-454-4

Library of Congress Catalog Card Number: 97-80763

Printed in the United States of America

This book was produced digitally by Macmillan Computer Publishing and manufactured using computer-to-plate technology (a film-less process) by GAC, Indianapolis, Indiana.

First Printing: May 1998

00 99   4   3   2

Trademarks

Executive Editor:
Alicia Buckley

Managing Editor:
Brice Gosnell

NEW RIDERS PUBLISHING

The staff of New Riders Publishing is committed to bringing you the best computer books. What our readers think of New Riders is important to our ability to serve our customers. If you have any comments, no matter how great or how small, we'd appreciate your taking the time to send us a note.

You can reach New Riders Publishing at the following:

New Riders Publishing
201 W. 103rd Street
Indianapolis, Indiana 46290

Acquisitions Editor
Michelle Reed

Development Editors
Jennifer Eberhardt
Laura Frey

Project Editor
Kevin Laseau

Copy Editor
San Dee Phillips

Technical Editor
Steve Mulder

Production Team
Marcia Deboy
Michael Dietsch
Jennifer Earhart
Cynthia Fields
Maureen West

Indexer
Christine Nelsen

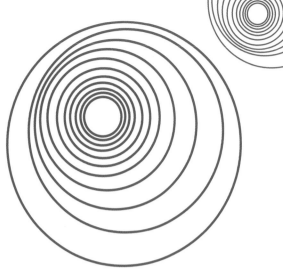

about the authors

ARDITH IBAÑEZ

Today, I provide creative direction for Akimbo Design (http://www.akimbodesign.com), a San Francisco Web design studio. Our clients include Macromedia, Inc., Columbia TriStar Interactive, California Pizza Kitchen, MGM, and PhotoDisc. I have also co-authored the Web design books, *HTML Web Magic* and *Creating Killer Interactive Web Sites*. Four years ago, I never thought I would be designing Web sites. I was designing flyers, restaurant menus, T-shirts, posters, and postcards. I was painting on found objects and creating collages with my illustrations and photographs. I was working as a sculptor's apprentice working with cast acrylics. I was binding my own books. Computers and scanners intimidated me. I finally became interested in the Web because I saw the opportunity to create a mobile and inexpensive portfolio of my work.

My very first Web site, I'm ashamed to say, was frightful! This "site" was actually just one long page of images and HTML text captions centered against a corrugated metal background tile. In some places, I naively used <blink> text because of what I thought was "cool." (It was the only Web animation available at the time.) I had abandoned all my design sensibilities to throw every possible HTML trick into one page.

Today, my philosophy and approach to design for the Web has changed dramatically. I found that successful Web sites come from a dedication to design shaped around content. I try to stay away from bells and whistles (and blinky text) just for the sake of using them. I focus on the story of the site and make sure that all the elements of the site point back to it.

And most of all, I try to have fun with every project or else the end result becomes spiritless and ordinary. I see the Web and the computer as alternative outlets for the same creative juices that inspired my earlier print designs and paintings. I try not to surrender all my time and attention to the computer monitor and digital image. I try to go back to my roots. I faithfully keep a scrapbook of sketches and ordinary doodads that catch my attention—postcards, wrappers, postal stamps, letters from friends. Here, I can explore ideas and illustrate my vision freely. I can make "mistakes" and discover more ideas and perhaps solutions for my design work. Having fun and creating meaningful designs also means getting out there and living! It's important to me to spend time with family and friends and relax. There's more to life than my own little Web designing universe. In order to contribute to society through my designs, I need to be able to experience what is important and meaningful to that society. *HTML Artistry* encapsulates the creative process and philosophy that I share with my partners and colleagues.

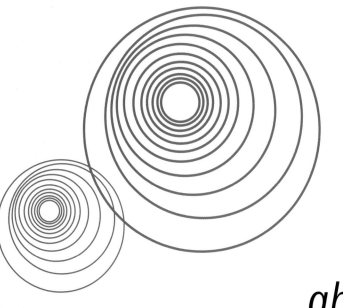

about the authors

NATALIE ZEE

My first Web site was back in college at U.C. Berkeley in early 1994 as a class experiment for a course in new media technologies. It was to be a learning resource for the class for our papers, group projects, and discussions. What was this HTML thing we had to learn? "Oh well", I thought, "I've gotta learn it to get a good grade in the class." There were no books on HTML yet, rather one person in the class learned it and gradually taught it to everyone. We all learned how to view source, modify pictures in Photoshop, and how to create animation with the `<blink>` tag. It was all so new. It was exciting.

Four years later, looking back at those prehistoric days before Netscape, before the big Web boom, behind all those gray pages, I can still remember that excitement. True, now those same Web pages look outdated. But the content is still there—the writings, discussions, and class projects that I can go back to and rediscover.

In terms of design, I never went to design school. The design and art part of my life was just always there. My father was an artist so he always encouraged me to draw, paint, and appreciate art. So growing up, I always found myself either drawing cartoons or fashion sketches. A strange combination, but I loved animation and fashion.

acknowledgements
and dedications

This book is dedicated to Benjamin and Miasma.

Ardith

This book is dedicated to life—enjoy it.

Natalie

We would like to send a shout out to all the Web designers, developers, and inspirational designers (and their assistants) who participated in the book. You all went out of your way to make this book a reality by sharing your time, materials, and ideas. Thanks also to the incredible staff at Macmillan—Laura Frey, Alicia Buckley, Michelle Reed, Steve Mulder—for believing in us and working with our crazy schedules.

Ardith Ibañez

I would like to thank my husband and business partner, Benjamin Rigby. Without his love, support, DHTML expertise, and googly eyes, this book would not have been possible. Not only did he help us edit and review our outlines and other materials to organize the book, but he painstakingly wrote all the techniques used in Chapters 5, 6, 8, and 9. That's love. True love. Thanks to our clients for giving us the opportunity to design Web sites of *HTML Artistry* and for being so patient with us during the process of writing this book—especially, Steve Shannon (Macromedia, Inc.), Ira Rubenstein and Terri Mathews (Columbia TriStar Interactive), Roxanne Ruben (California Pizza Kitchen), Ann Donovan (PhotoDisc), and the folks at Student Advantage. Of course, I must thank my family and friends for their encouragement, patience, and understanding—Mom and Papa, Mom and Dad, Arlene, Theo, Jess, Chris, Claudia, Julie Jo, Katie, Janxin, Elliot, Cindy, Olivia, Doria, Joanie, Kevin, and Belinda. Thank you for keeping us going and letting us use your TVs, VCRs, and computers to create our Web sites and to write this book. And last, but not least, thanks to Ms. Natalie Zee. It's an honor and a blast to work with her again on another book. (I miss working in the same office!) I am proud to have her as a friend and colleague.

Natalie Zee

Thank you to everyone, my family, friends, and clients, for putting up with my crazy work schedule and being so understanding and supportive of this project. I couldn't have done it without you. I'd especially like to thank my parents for always encouraging me to follow my dreams and pursue whatever makes me happy. Thanks also to Professor Howard Besser at U.C. Berkeley for introducing me to the Web and for his constant support. I couldn't have come up with new ideas for the book without the great help and feedback of Simon Smith. Thank you to Steve Shannon of Macromedia for being so patient and understanding when I was working on the book and not so much on the Dynamic HTML Zone. Also, to Jason Wolf, George Arriola, and Steve Zehngut for their assistance with "book stuff." Most of all, to my best friends, Karen, Paul, Maggie, and Eli for always making me laugh and for knowing the real me in the world outside of Web design. Finally, thanks to Ardith, the wonder designer and dear friend. From working at Macromedia to writing two books together, I am lucky to have someone I can work so well with and have fun with also. "Good Times."

table of contents

introduction

Why Read This Book

HTML Artistry: More Than Code leaps into new territory by exploring design and code techniques together. This book teaches you how to craft well-designed Web sites with a few simple tools—a good story or message, a strong sense for graphic design, and a solid understanding of HTML. If you search for the technical know-how to enhance the interactivity and functionality of your sites, this book is for you. If you dream about creating more compelling and aesthetically pleasing sites, this book is for you. If you always wondered what DHTML is and what it can do for you and your Web audience, this book is for you, too. If you feel as though you've seen and done everything there is to be seen and to be done on the Web, and you've run out of ideas, this book is *definitely* for you.

HTML Artistry is your guide to better Web design, made possible by HTML code—no plug-ins or fancy CGI scripts. This book discusses, explains, and encourages a multidisciplinary and cross-disciplinary approach to Web site development. First, we help you hone your design and programming skills by focusing on graphic design basics such as color, layout, typography—and HTML technology. Second, we share the insights of leading graphic designers working outside the context of the Web to give you a framework for what constitutes "good design" in general. Although the Web is a relatively new medium, you can still apply the same theories used in print, film, and television titles, CD and poster art, packaging, and public installations.

Overview

This book is divided into two parts. The first part of the book deals exclusively with classic HTML covering layouts, navigation, type effects, color, and customization through JavaScript coding. The second part covers dynamic HTML, going over layers, style sheets, interactivity, and animation. Because each chapter builds on previous chapters, we encourage you to go through the book in chronological order. However, we do invite you to skip around to the different Inspirational Design Models found between chapters. These feature spectacular designers working in various fields not necessarily related to the Web. They share their thoughts and experiences regarding what makes good design.

Each chapter provides the following:

- Full HTML code and examples

- Tips on how to achieve the right look for your Web site content

- Graphic techniques showing you the step-by-step process for creating the optimum graphics

- Case studies that spotlight certain Web developers and showcasing their thoughts and techniques on Web design

The companion Web site to this book, http://www.htmlartistry.com, is filled with examples from the book so you can see all the HTML in action. Also on the Web site, you can find great Web design resources as well as updates to the book. Most importantly, we hope that you will use this book not only as a reference guide to HTML but also as a starting ground to open yourself to your environment and how you can translate your daily inspirations into works of art on the Web.

Inspirational Design Models

When we design Web sites, we never just look at other Web sites. We watch TV, or go to the movies, or flip through dozens of magazines. Design is everywhere!

We thought it would be useful to include profiles of different designers working outside of the context of the Web because designers share the same issues. Whether it's designing a poster or designing a motion graphics piece, a designer addresses similar parameters and questions for each project—Who is the audience? How will this be used? What is the purpose? How can I communicate this idea? How can I be creative when I'm building this site for such a large corporation, for so many different people? How can I please everyone? How can I be expressive when I have such limited tools? What about technology? How do I start a design? When and where do I end?

The common thread between all nine designers? A love for and dedication to the art of visual communication.

As previously mentioned, between each chapter, we include interviews with different designers. Each designer has inspired us in some way and continues to inspire us. We hope you find some of the answers to these questions and find a way to apply them to your own Web designs..

PART 1:
Creating Web Sites with Classic HTML

We all heard that HTML is a programming language and not something created for design. We also heard of the many limitations of what it can do. Hey! Enough of what they say. HTML is here, so let's use it.

Designing with HTML can be both a challenging and rewarding experience. Don't be intimidated by it. The first part of the book covers classic HTML and prepares you, or refreshes your memory, before you dive into the world of Dynamic HTML in Part 2. We are here to help you think of HTML differently. It can be tricky, but it is an art form if you can use it in smart ways.

In Part 1, we grouped important Web design issues into separate chapters. From layouts, navigation, type effects, color, and personalization, we go over not only the specific HTML code, but also give you design and graphics techniques as well. Chapter 1, "Creating Compelling Layouts with Tables and Frames," covers both tables and frames, including how to make background images bleed and align along borderless frames. Chapter 2, "Designing Intuitive Navigation," discusses key issues in designing navigation from text links to rollover graphics. Chapter 3, "Type Effects: Enhancing Your Interface with Stunning Typography," goes over basic font attributes and lists (which will prepare you for Chapter 7's typography with style sheets). Chapter 4, "Color: Enjoying Unlimited Possibilities with a Limited Palette," shows you the unlimited possibilities you can achieve with a limited palette. Finally, Chapter 5, " Adding Sophistication and Interactivity with HTML and JavaScript," teaches you some of the basic JavaScript so that you can add a bit of technical sophistication and interactivity to your Web site.

We are here to tell you that "HTML is your friend." Remember that throughout this book. We put together some of what we think are the most widely used and smart HTML tricks we hope will inspire you to try on your own.

CHAPTER 1
CREATING COMPELLING LAYOUT WITH TABLES AND FRAMES

Creating a layout for your Web site can be one of the most challenging aspects of Web design. With so many different options, it can be hard to limit yourself to just one type of look for your site. But with the immediacy of the Web, changing your look can be a snap. Deciding to go with tables or frames for your site can depend upon a certain number of things such as the size of your site, how much information you need to present, or the specific audience or goal of the site.

In this chapter, you learn how to maximize your tables with graphics, colored backgrounds, and nested tables. Next, you'll move on to frames to discover some different frameset options, border control, and targeting frames. There is no simple answer, but this chapter shows you the many options that are before you and how you can maximize your site with the best layout to fit your needs.

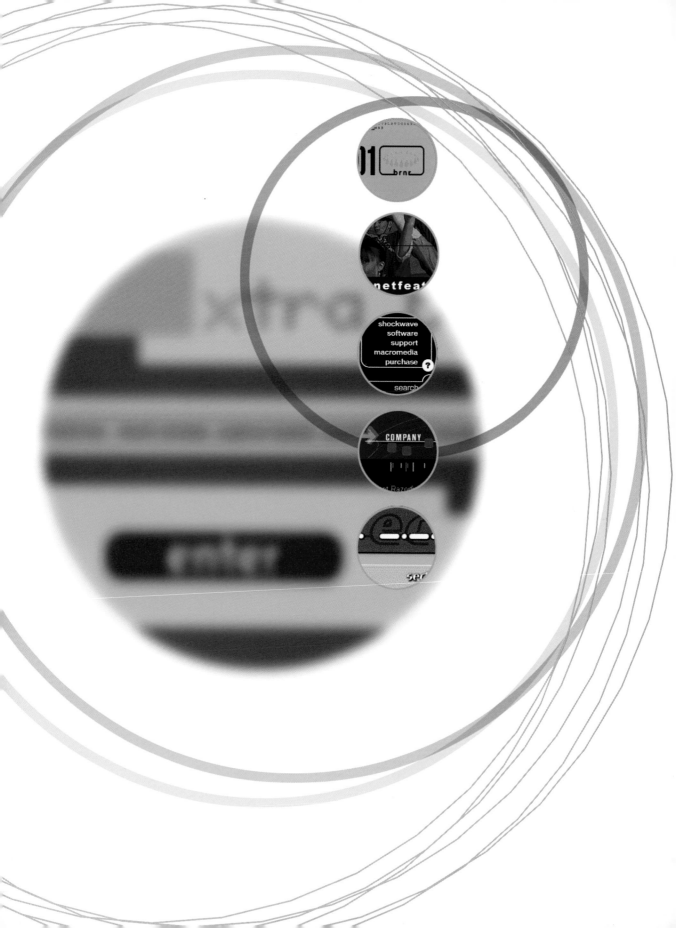

Tables

HTML tables were originally created for data, not for creating layout as it is widely used today. Because designers found limitations in HTML, tables were used at first to better align images and text, which soon found its way to aligning and formatting a whole page. Tables can get complicated and confusing with various table rows <TR> and table data <TD> cells, many of them nested within each other so that it's hard to distinguish your code. We'll go over some techniques on using tables for layout as well as learn a few tips so that you can organize your table data better. Figure 1.1 shows a basic nested table layout that is popular on the Web today.

Table for One

Start out by outlining the HTML code for just one table so that you can get a better idea in this chapter how to build upon it and create an effective layout.

```
<TABLE BORDER="2">
<TR>
<TD>This is cell #1</TD>
<TD>This is cell #2</TD>
</TR>
</TABLE>
```

With this simple one row, two data cell table, you can see how easy tables can be. Replace the generic data cell text with some graphics and text to better illustrate how to start a layout.

```
<TABLE BORDER="0">

<TR>
<TD><IMG SRC="tower.jpg"></TD>
<TD>The Eiffel Tower in Paris is one of the
most beautiful
places in the world to be.  Take an elevator
ride to the top and you'll see the River
Seine, Notre Dame, and the Louvre. When
you're done with the view, take a break in
one of the many outdoor cafes and treat
yourself to some excellent pastries and cof-
fee.</TD>
</TR>
</TABLE>
```

1.1

1.1   A simple table.

In this example (Figure 1.2), you can see how the graphic and text in the data cell can create some good alignment with the graphics and text. But there are a few problems with the table. With browser resizing, the text stretches out to the ends of the browser window as shown in Figure 1.3.

Always make sure when you have graphics in tables that the closing </TD> is flushed right up against the <IMG SRC> tag. Sometimes having a space or line break between them causes the browser to read it wrong and the table cell won't fit snug around the graphic.

In addition to the stretched text, align the text at the top with the graphic.

```
<TABLE WIDTH="300" BORDER="0">
<TR>
<TD VALIGN="top"><IMG SRC="tower.jpg"></TD>
<TD VALIGN="top">The Eiffel Tower in Paris
is one of the most beautiful places in the
world to be.  Take an elevator ride to the
top and you'll see the River Seine, Notre
Dame, and the Louvre. When you're done with
the view, take a break in one of the many
outdoor cafes and treat yourself to some
excellent pastries and coffee.</TD>
</TR>
</TABLE>
```

1.2

1.3

1.2   Graphics and text in a table.

1.3   Browser resizing causes the table to stretch.

Figure 1.4 created a fixed width table and aligned the text with the top of the graphic with the VALIGN property. You can also set widths of <TD> cells as well and VALIGN your graphic or text with either top, or bottom (the default is middle).

Cellpadding and cellspacing properties also give you some control as you use tables for layout. *Cellspacing* is control over the padding of the table borders—how thick or thin they are. *Cellpadding* is the space in pixels between the item in the <TD> cell and the table borders. This is illustrated in Figure 1.5.

```
<TABLE BORDER="2" CELLPADDING="4" CELLSPAC-
ING="6">
<TR>
<TD>This is cell #1</TD>
<TD>This is cell #2</TD>
</TR>
<TR>
<TD>This is cell #3</TD>
<TD>This is cell #4</TD>
</TR>
</TABLE>
```

As you can see by modifying the cellpadding and cellspacing, you can gain better formatting control over your table layout.

Colored Tables

Coloring tables can be a great way to separate information, blend your graphics to a different background, and create different shapes. You can color the whole table or individual table data cells by using the bgcolor attribute and the color's hexadeximal number in your code like this:

```
<TABLE BORDER="2">
<TR>
<TD BGCOLOR="#FF0033">This is cell #1</TD>
<TD BGCOLOR="#FF6666">This is cell #2</TD>
</TR>
<TR>
<TD BGCOLOR="#FF3399">This is cell #3</TD>
<TD BGCOLOR="#FFCCCC">This is cell #4</TD>
</TR>
</TABLE>
```

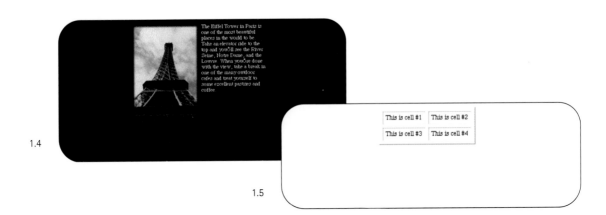

1.4

1.5

1.4   Fixed width table.

1.5   Cellpadding and cellspacing.

Figure 1.6 shows a sample of some colored table data cells in different colors to illustrate how the colors work. You can also color an entire table by using the same bgcolor attribute in the opening <TABLE> tag like this: <TABLE BGCOLOR="#000000">.

But for more complex action, use colored tables within your layout to separate text and graphics. Figure 1.7 shows a colored table that takes on different colors and shapes to create an almost graphical screen.

To achieve this look, the page is organized in three tables. There is the top table that contains the xtra bold logo graphic. In order to create the overlapping squares, the table is divided into three columns. When creating colored tables, it is important to have cellpadding and cellspacing both equal to zero so that there are no gaps between the color spaces. Tables that have no content (images or text) have
s to create space within the table data cell.

```
<TABLE BORDER="0" CELLPADDING="0"
CELLSPACING="0">
<TR>
<TD WIDTH="175" HEIGHT="20"><BR></TD>
<TD WIDTH="30" HEIGHT="20"
BGCOLOR="#CCCC33"><BR></TD>
<TD WIDTH="275" HEIGHT="20"
BGCOLOR="#CCCC33"><BR></TD>
</TR>

<TR>
<TD WIDTH="175" HEIGHT="60"
BGCOLOR="#999933"><BR></TD>
<TD WIDTH="40" HEIGHT="60"
BGCOLOR="#999933"><BR></TD>
<TD WIDTH="275" HEIGHT="60"
BGCOLOR="#CCCC33"><IMG SRC="images/xtra.gif"
WIDTH="275" HEIGHT="60" ALT="Xtra Bold"></TD>
</TR>

<TR>
<TD WIDTH="175" HEIGHT="20"><BR></TD>
<TD WIDTH="40" HEIGHT="20"
BGCOLOR="#CCCC33"><BR></TD>
<TD WIDTH="275" HEIGHT="20"
BGCOLOR="#CCCC33"><BR></TD>
</TR>
</TABLE>
```

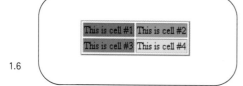

1.6

1.7

1.6　Colored table cells.

1.7　Using colored tables to design layouts with funky shapes.

This is illustrated better in Figure 1.8 where the table borders are turned so you can see the column and row separations.

Next is the middle small striped banner. Again it is divided into three columns with the side columns having a small width of 5 so that it creates the over-all outline of brown around the other stripes. In order to create pencil thin lines, we used a single pixel transparent gif as the content for the table data cell.

```
<TABLE BORDER="0" CELLPADDING="0"
CELLSPACING="0">
<TR>
<TD WIDTH="5" HEIGHT="4"
BGCOLOR="#663300"><IMG
SRC="images/pixel.gif"></TD>
<TD WIDTH="485" HEIGHT="4"
BGCOLOR="#663300"><IMG
SRC="images/pixel.gif"></TD>
<TD WIDTH="5" HEIGHT="4"
BGCOLOR="#663300"><IMG
SRC="images/pixel.gif"></TD>
</TR>
```

```
<TR>
<TD WIDTH="5" HEIGHT="4"
BGCOLOR="#663300"><IMG
SRC="images/pixel.gif"></TD>
<TD WIDTH="485" HEIGHT="4"
BGCOLOR="#999933"><IMG
SRC="images/pixel.gif"></TD>
<TD WIDTH="5" HEIGHT="4"
BGCOLOR="#663300"><IMG
SRC="images/pixel.gif"></TD>
</TR>

<!-- light blue -->
<TR>
<TD WIDTH="5" HEIGHT="8"
BGCOLOR="#663300"><IMG
SRC="images/pixel.gif"></TD>
<TD WIDTH="485" HEIGHT="8"
BGCOLOR="#66CCCC"><IMG
SRC="images/pixel.gif"></TD>
<TD WIDTH="5" HEIGHT="8"
BGCOLOR="#663300"><IMG
SRC="images/pixel.gif"></TD>
</TR>
```

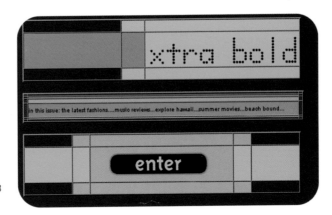

1.8

1.8   Table borders turned on.

```
<!-- orange -->
<TR>
<TD WIDTH="5" HEIGHT="25"
BGCOLOR="#663300"><IMG
SRC="images/pixel.gif"></TD>
<TD WIDTH="485" HEIGHT="25"
BGCOLOR="#FF6600"><FONT SIZE="1" FACE="arial,
helvetica, *"> in this issue: the latest
fashions....music reviews...explore
hawaii...summer movies...beach bound...</TD>
<TD WIDTH="5" HEIGHT="25"
BGCOLOR="#663300"><IMG
SRC="images/pixel.gif"></TD>
</TR>

<!-- yellow -->
<TR>
<TD WIDTH="5" HEIGHT="3"
BGCOLOR="#663300"><IMG
SRC="images/pixel.gif"></TD>
<TD WIDTH="485" HEIGHT="3"
BGCOLOR="#FFFF33"><IMG
SRC="images/pixel.gif"></TD>
<TD WIDTH="5" HEIGHT="3"
BGCOLOR="#663300"><IMG
SRC="images/pixel.gif"></TD>
</TR>

<TR>
<TD WIDTH="5" HEIGHT="4"
BGCOLOR="#663300"><IMG
SRC="images/pixel.gif"></TD>
<TD WIDTH="485" HEIGHT="4"
BGCOLOR="#663300"><IMG
SRC="images/pixel.gif"></TD>
<TD WIDTH="5" HEIGHT="4"
BGCOLOR="#663300"><IMG
SRC="images/pixel.gif"></TD>
</TR>
</TABLE>
```

Finally, the last table has again the overlapping shapes. This time there are five columns in the table so that the green rectangles on the left and right can appear as though they are overlapped with the main blue rectangle.

```
<TABLE BORDER="0" CELLPADDING="0"
CELLSPACING="0">
<TR>
<TD WIDTH="85" HEIGHT="20"><BR></TD>
<TD WIDTH="30" HEIGHT="20"
BGCOLOR="#66CCCC"><BR></TD>
<TD WIDTH="255" HEIGHT="20"
BGCOLOR="#66CCCC"><BR></TD>
<TD WIDTH="30" HEIGHT="20"
BGCOLOR="#66CCCC"><BR></TD>
<TD WIDTH="85" HEIGHT="20"><BR></TD>
</TR>

<TR>
<TD WIDTH="85" HEIGHT="60"
BGCOLOR="#CCCC33"><BR></TD>
<TD WIDTH="30" HEIGHT="60"
```

```
BGCOLOR="#CCCC33"><BR></TD>
<TD WIDTH="255" HEIGHT="60"
BGCOLOR="#66CCCC"><A HREF="main.html">
<IMG SRC="images/enter.gif" WIDTH="255"
HEIGHT="60" BORDER="0"  ALT="enter"></TD>
<TD WIDTH="30" HEIGHT="60"
BGCOLOR="#CCCC33"><BR></TD>
<TD WIDTH="85" HEIGHT="60"
BGCOLOR="#CCCC33"><BR></TD>
</TR>

<TR>
<TD WIDTH="85" HEIGHT="20"><BR></TD>
<TD WIDTH="30" HEIGHT="20"
BGCOLOR="#66CCCC"><BR></TD>
<TD WIDTH="255" HEIGHT="20"
BGCOLOR="#66CCCC"><BR></TD>
<TD WIDTH="30" HEIGHT="20"
BGCOLOR="#66CCCC"><BR></TD>
<TD WIDTH="85" HEIGHT="20"><BR></TD>
</TR>
</TABLE>
```

Nested Tables

In order to create compelling layout, you might find the need to have multiple tables within a larger one to gain better control. One problem with nested tables is that the larger they are, the longer they take to load. Your page won't show up until the final closing </TABLE> tag is read by the browser. Therefore, if you can, it's better to try and break up tables into sections. Make the first table small so that it can load quickly. This way, the user will always have something to see while the rest of the page loads.

Here's an example of code for a nested table:

```
<TABLE BORDER="2">
<TR>
<TD>this is data cell #1</TD>
<TD>
      <TABLE BORDER="2" bgcolor="#009999">
      <TR>
      <TD> this is the nested table cell
#1</TD>
      <TD>this is the nested table cell
#2</TD>
      </TR>
      </TABLE>
</TD>
</TR>
</TABLE>
```

As you can see, by inserting another table within a <TD></TD> tag, you can nest a complete table within the original table. Figure 1.9 shows the nested table in teal and has borders set to 2 to better illustrate the nesting effect.

Tables and Graphics: Break 'em Up!

Designers are finding a workaround when displaying big images. By cutting them up and putting them in tables, it gives the illusion that the image is loading faster than if it were one single, huge graphic. Also, you can section off areas in your graphic to either animate them or create individual links.

The netfeatures site (www.netfeatures.com) in Figure 1.10 uses a table grid to create a spectacular animated gif sequence. As a documentary site, art director and designer Hill Curtis wanted to give the page more movement and more mystery—not to mention a quicker download. "It became a moving portal into the documentary...giving the viewer a glimpse at what was inside, and hopefully drawing them in," explains Curtis.

Almost like those grids of television sets you see at department stores, each individual graphic is animated and changes the sequence, sometimes giving you a mixed array of a picture (see Figure 1.11 and Figure 1.12).

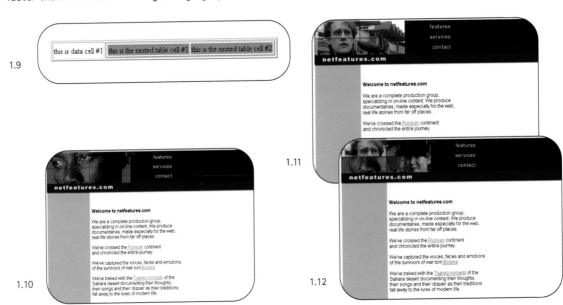

1.9

1.10

1.11

1.12

1.9   A nested table.

1.10   netfeatures.

1.11   A different animated sequence.

1.12   The mixing sequence.

The images are aligned in a grid that has two rows and two columns. Using the img low src attribute, each image loads with their static gif first (lt1.gif) before displaying the animated gif (lt.gif).

```
<IMG LOWSRC="images/lt1.gif"
SRC="images/lt.gif" WIDTH="153" HEIGHT="55"
BORDER="0">
```

Because the animated gifs are a bit more in file size, this ensures that the grid appears filled before the animation for each square begins. Each of the four <TD> cells contains the four corresponding <IMG SRC> code for each graphic.

```
<TABLE CELLPADDING=0 CELLSPACING=0 WIDTH=500
BORDER=0 >
<TR>
        <TD ALIGN="LEFT" VALIGN="TOP"
WIDTH="153" HEIGHT="55" >
<IMG LOWSRC="images/lt1.gif"
SRC="images/lt.gif" WIDTH="153" HEIGHT="55"
BORDER="0"></TD>
<TD ALIGN="LEFT" VALIGN="TOP" WIDTH="151"
HEIGHT="55" ><IMG LOWSRC="images/rt1.gif"
SRC="images/rt.gif" WIDTH="153" HEIGHT="55"
BORDER="0"></></TD>

</TR>
```

Here's the bottom two squares of the grid:

```
<TR>
        <TD ALIGN="LEFT" VALIGN="TOP"
WIDTH="153" HEIGHT="53" ><IMG
LOWSRC="images/lb1.gif" SRC="images/lb.gif"
WIDTH="153" HEIGHT="55" BORDER="0"></></TD>
<TD ALIGN="LEFT" VALIGN="TOP" WIDTH="151"
HEIGHT="53" ><IMG LOWSRC="images/rb1.gif"
SRC="images/rb.gif" WIDTH="153" HEIGHT="55"
BORDER="0"></></TD>
</TR>
</TABLE>
```

Again the overall effect of each square being an animated gif creates an interesting and different look.

Note:

When using images, it's a good idea to always define the width and height properties of the graphic. This enables the browser to read the file dimensions and reserve that space for your graphic. Your graphics load faster as a result.

By breaking up your graphics, you can not only create the illusion of a faster download, but you can also creatively use it to your advantage. Animate certain parts of it and try different image loading techniques such as 1-bit graphics for <IMG LOW SRC>. The possibilities are endless.

CASE STUDY:
MICHAEL FRENCH, DESIGNER,
BURNER NEW MEDIA

When you enter the BRNR (pronounced "burner") Web site (www.brnr.com), you never know what to expect (see Figure 1.13). Combining techno style graphics with technology savvy HTML tables and frames, designer Michael French is sometimes surprised at all the attention his site gets. "There isn't one unifying concept that holds brnr.com together because it started as a place for me to put random ideas," contemplates French.

Random or not, the different approach to layout and Web design has definitely made others notice. French takes an unconventional approach to designing for the Web and uses much of his experience of life and friends as inspirations for the work on his site. A graduate of Art Center in Pasadena, CA, French fell into the Web after taking one Web design class at the end of his senior year, not actually intending to make a career out of it. "By the end of that term, I was really excited about the fact that there was a design medium in which not everything had been done yet—and there certainly seemed to be a lot of room for improvement." He took a job right out of school for a Web design firm and now is working to build his own Web business with Burner New Media.

Needless to say, his design sense and style reflect not only an innovative approach to the Web but also (finally) present different solutions to technology with the x-periments area of the site. When asked about HTML tables and some possible solutions, French replied, "The unfortunate thing about tables is that we have to work with them at all. They're a really indirect way to do something that should be really direct (placing things where we want them). They can, however, be used to get around many of the Web's limitations that would otherwise affect a layout, so until a better system comes along, they're indispensable to a designer."

For the pure culture area of his site, French combines nested tables and animated gifs that are broken up to create an overall interactive look as shown in Figure 1.14.

As you can see from the code, the page is organized as a large table where the height is set to 100 percent so that the whole page centers vertically automatically, regardless of how much someone expands his browser window. The graphic is broken up into 13 irregular pieces with some animated and some not. These pieces are then fused together with a nested and borderless table.

```
<TABLE BORDER="0" CELLPADDING="0"
CELLSPACING="0" HEIGHT="100%">
<TR>
<TD>
        <TABLE BORDER="0" CELLPADDING="0"
CELLSPACING="0" WIDTH="600">
        <TR>
        <TD COLSPAN="5"><IMG BORDER=0
SRC="images/pureculture/1.gif" USEMAP="#top"
ISMAP TARGET="_top"></TD>
        </TR>
```

```
        <TR>
        <TD><IMG
SRC="images/pureculture/2.gif"></TD>
        <TD><A
HREF="mailto:info@brnr.com"><IMG BORDER="0"
SRC="images/pureculture/3.gif"></A></TD>
        <TD><IMG
SRC="images/pureculture/4.gif"></TD><TD><IMG
SRC="images/pureculture/4b.gif"></TD>
        <TD><A HREF="product.html"><IMG
BORDER="0"
SRC="images/pureculture/5.gif"></A></TD>
        </TR>

        <TR>
        <TD COLSPAN="3"><IMG
SRC="images/pureculture/6.gif"></TD>
        <TD VALIGN="top"
ALIGN="left"><NOBR><A
HREF="qa.html"><IMG BORDER="0"
SRC="images/pureculture/7.gif"></A>
        <IMG
SRC="images/pureculture/7b.gif"></NOBR></TD>
<TD VALIGN="top"><A HREF="product.html">
        <IMG BORDER="0" SRC=
"images/pureculture/8.gif"></A></TD>
        </TR>

        <TR>
        <TD COLSPAN="5"><A
```

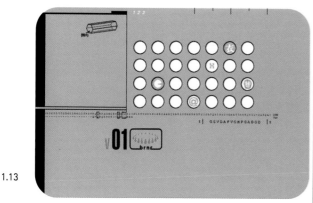

1.13

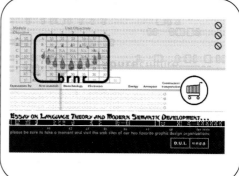

1.14

1.13   brnr.com home page.

1.14   Pure culture.

```
HREF="essay.html"><IMG SRC="images/purecul-
ture/9.gif" BORDER="0"></A></TD>
        </TR>

        <TR>
        <TD COLSPAN="5"><IMG
SRC="images/strip3.gif" WIDTH="600"
HEIGHT="13"></TD>
        </TR>

        <TR><TD COLSPAN="5"><IMG BORDER="0"
        SRC="images/pureculture/10.gif"
        USEMAP="#bottom" ISMAP
        TARGET="_top"></TD>
        </TR>
        </TABLE>
</TD>
</TR>
        </TABLE>
```

Figure 1.15 shows the page with borders turned on
to emphasize the different pieces and segments of
animation.

How does French think of all these cool and crazy
ideas that look so good? "All I know is that new ideas
don't come if you only look for them on the Web. I
think a lot of them hide in my shower." For the rest
of us, perhaps www.brnr.com will be all the inspiration we need.

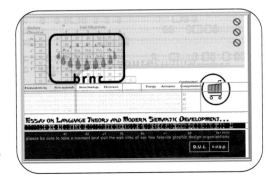

1.15

1.15   Table borders turned on.

Frames

When frames arrived on the Web design scene, there were a lot of mixed feelings among designers. It was confusing to design, not to mention the browser support was horrible in the early days. Now with the 4.0 browsers in effect, frames have become an effective solution for layout. Navigation can be inserted in a frame and not have to be reloaded each time you switch pages. Borderless frames provide a slick, seamless look between frame panels and eliminate the nasty default gray browser border. Frames are definitely a good idea! Figure 1.16 shows a more complex frameset on the Razorfish Web site.

Frames 101

To make some simple frame layouts, technically just remember that according to the layout and look your want, each frame is an individual HTML page. These individual pages work together much like a puzzle to form an overall look that is your layout, or *frameset*. Deciding upon which frameset look you want can be a difficult task as there are a wide variety of possibilities. This section focuses on some of the basics to help you maximize your frames as you work.

The <FRAME> tag simply enables you to reference your html file, name the specific frame, and define some of the other attributes such as scrolling, or resizing.

```
<FRAME SRC="yourpage.html" NAME="name of
frame" SCROLLING="auto¦none" NORESIZE>
```

Each <FRAME> tag is referenced within the <FRAMESET></FRAMESET> tag. This tag defines the layout such as how many rows and columns, and frame border specifications.

```
<FRAMSET ROWS="rowheight, %, *" COLS=
"colwidth, %, *">
```

The following are Frame attributes:

- NAME="namehere"   Frame name
- SRC="url"   Frame reference, location of HTML page for frame
- MARGINWIDTH="number"
- MARGINHEIGHT="number"
- SCROLLING="yes ¦ no ¦ auto"   Controls frame scrollbar
- NORESIZE   Frame is not resizeable by user
- FRAMEBORDER="no"   Borderless frame

1.16

1.16   Razorfish's frames Web site.

Figures 1.17 through 1.19 show some simple and popular two-frame layouts and their corresponding frameset code.

Figure 1.17 has a left side bar that can be used for navigation. The width of the side bar is determined in the frameset columns attribute. The browser reads the code in order from left to right, so by setting the first column number as 110, that means that 110 pixels over from the left of the browser, frame "red.html" will display. The wildcard "*" sign means that the second frame's (black.html) viewable area is determined by the browser. You can control whether a scrollbar is visible with the scrolling attribute. Setting it to "auto" means that a scrollbar's visibility is determined by the browser. Should the user need a scrollbar, one will be there.

The frameset code for Figure 1.17 is the following:

```
<FRAMESET COLS="110, *">
<FRAME SRC="red.html" NAME="side"
SCROLLING="auto">
<FRAME SRC="black.html" NAME="main"
SCROLLING="auto">
</FRAMESET>
```

Tip:

Sometimes, those scroll bars do get in the way of design. But always make sure that before you say "no" to scroll bars that you test and make sure on all monitor sizes that one isn't necessary. Otherwise, you'll have frustrated users who want to continue on an HTML page but can't because a scroll bar isn't present.

For Figure 1.18, the top frame becomes the navigation bar. This is great layout because you can have a larger main frame by having the navigation at the top. Now instead of reading columns, we define the number of rows for this layout. The top row is 80 pixels high and the rest defaults to the browser.

1.17

1.18

1.19

1.17   Side bar frame.

1.18   Top frame.

1.19   Bottom frame.

Here's the frameset code for Figure 1.18:

```
<FRAMESET ROWS="80, *">
<FRAME SRC="red.html" NAME="top"
SCROLLING="auto">
<FRAME SRC="black.html" NAME="main"
SCROLLING="auto">
</FRAMESET>
```

Figure 1.19 is just the inverse frame look of the previous one. It's a good look for creating a kiosk-like interface for the Web. Because the navigation is at the bottom, the main frame contains limited scrolling information or a good color contrast so that it is not difficult to read from top to bottom toward the bottom navigation bar.

The frameset code for Figure 1.19 is the following:

```
<FRAMESET ROWS="*, 80">
<FRAME SRC="black.html" NAME="main"
SCROLLING="auto">
<FRAME SRC="red.html" NAME="top"
SCROLLING="auto">
</FRAMESET>
```

With the varying options for framesets, you can coordinate your navigation and your content by the reliability of the fact that your navigation will always be present for your audience to use. What's even better is that you can lose the frame borders and create a seamless frame look as in Figure 1.20.

```
<FRAMESET FRAMEBORDER="no" BORDER="0" FRAME-
SPACING="0" ROWS="*, 80">
<FRAME SRC="black.html" NAME="main" MARGIN-
WIDTH="0" MARGINHEIGHT="0" SCROLLING="auto">
<FRAME SRC="red.html" NAME="top" MARGIN-
WIDTH="0" MARGINHEIGHT="0" SCROLLING="auto">
</FRAMESET>
```

By combining the border elements and margin-width/marginheight, you tighten up the layout and create a great seamless Web page layout. Framespacing works much like cellspacing in tables. This controls the space between each frame, hence each HTML page. By setting it to zero, the pages sit closer together and you lose the borders. MARGIN-WIDTH and MARGINHEIGHT for each <FRAME> tag perform double duty with the framespacing attribute and specify the top and bottom margins of each frame/HTML page. By setting them also to zero, they erase any visible space.

Tip:

Just in case users are visiting your site with a browser that doesn't support frames, you can use the <NOFRAMES></NOFRAMES> tag in your frame index page. Add the desired content between the tags and users who can't see frames will see something.

1.20

1.20 Borderless frames.

Nesting Frames

For more advanced framesets, just as there are nested tables, there are nested frames. Nested frames can help you organize your information better but also keep things loading faster. As long as you can keep track of specific targeting, you'll have no problems keeping track of the individual frames.

Here are the frame targeting attributes:

- TARGET="_self" (Default) Link loads in the frame from which it was clicked.
- TARGET="_parent" Link clears any previous framesets and loads in the full browser window.
- TARGET="_window" or "_blank" Link opens in a new browser window.
- TARGET="_top" Like parent, link clears framesets and loads in the full browser window.

With the Macromedia site, each frame has a purpose: corporate logo, ad banner, title bar, navigation, and main frame. These five frames work together to create a cohesive look so that each has its own purpose. In Figure 1.21, on the Macromedia corporate section home page, you can see the different frame elements in action.

Here's the code for the frameset. In order to create overlapping rows with columns, a nested <FRAMESET> tag is in order. First, the overall <FRAMESET> tag is divided into two columns. The next <FRAMESET> tag defines the first column (set to 150 pixels) of the overall frameset as having two rows.

```
<frameset frameborder=no border=0
framespacing=0 cols="150, *">
        <frameset frameborder=no border=0
framespacing=0 rows="80, *">
```

The Macromedia logo is the first row frame of the first column.

```
        <frame src="/00_mmlogo.html"
name="mm_logo" marginwidth=0 marginheight=0
scrolling="no" noresize>
```

Next, the navigation frame directly under it is the second row of the first column.

```
<frame src="00_machomenav.html" name="mm_nav"
marginwidth=0 marginheight=30
scrolling="auto" noresize>
        </frameset>
```

The second column is divided into three rows.

```
        <frameset frameborder=no border=0
framespacing=0 rows="80, 40, *">
```

The first row of the second column is the ad banner that is defined as being 80 pixels in height.

```
<frame src="http://ad.doubleclick.net/adf/
www.macromedia.com/macromedia/index.html"
" name="mm_ad" marginwidth=0 marginheight=0
scrolling="no" noresize>
```

The header that is 40 pixels in height is next.

```
        <frame src="00_machomehead.html"
name="mm_sectab" marginwidth=0 marginheight=0
scrolling="no" noresize>
```

Finally, the last row of the second column is the main area.

```
        <frame src="00_main.html"
name="mm_main" marginwidth=15 marginheight=10
scrolling="auto" noresize>
        </frameset>
</frameset>
```

1.21

1.21   Macromedia Web site.

CASE STUDY:

JOSH ULM, DESIGNER, EYE CANDY

One of the best things about the Eye Candy Web site (www.eyecandy.org) is its use of frames. Not one to use the typical frameset style, Josh Ulm, designer and creator of the Eye Candy site, designs a tight interface that's, well, great eye candy (see Figure 1.22).

The Eye Candy site serves many purposes. Functionally, it exists as a launching point to exceptional design on the Web. The site is periodically updated with a new set of links to Web sites around the world that show an honest attempt at solid design. But ironically, the Eye Candy site itself is a frames haven.

The complex framesets are actually not that hard to create. Ulm creates a kiosk-like interface by using the page "empty.html" that is completely black as a type of "frameborder" for the frame itself.

Here's the code:

```
<FRAMESET rows="5%,*,5%" MARGINWIDTH="0"
MARGINHEIGHT="0" FRAMESPACING="0" BORDER="0"
FRAMEBORDER=NO>
        <FRAME Name="top" SRC="empty.html"
Scrolling="No" MARGINWIDTH="0"
MARGINHEIGHT="0" FRAMESPACING="0" BORDER="0"
FRAMEBORDER=NO>
        <FRAMESET cols="*,620,*"
MARGINWIDTH="0" MARGINHEIGHT="0"
FRAMESPACING="0" BORDER="0" FRAMEBORDER=NO>
            <FRAME Name="left"
SRC="empty.html" Scrolling="No"
MARGINWIDTH="0" MARGINHEIGHT="0"
FRAMESPACING="0" BORDER="0" FRAMEBORDER=NO>
            <FRAME Name="master"
SRC="setCandy.html" Scrolling="Auto"
MARGINWIDTH="0" MARGINHEIGHT="0"
FRAMESPACING="0" BORDER="0" FRAMEBORDER=NO>
            <FRAME Name="right"
SRC="empty.html" Scrolling="No"
MARGINWIDTH="0" MARGINHEIGHT="0"
FRAMESPACING="0" BORDER="0" FRAMEBORDER=NO>
        </frameset>
        <FRAME Name="bottom" SRC="empty.html"
Scrolling="No" MARGINWIDTH="0"
MARGINHEIGHT="0" FRAMESPACING="0" BORDER="0"
FRAMEBORDER=NO>
</FRAMESET>
```

Ulm discusses his design behind the frames look:

"The black sea around the site serves the purpose of a buffer zone to take up the slack on resize. It also draws the focus into the center. The header and footer are the only rigid parts of the site, whereas the site's body also resizes to accommodate different browser sizes."

By using percentage values for the rows of the main frameset, the values allow for each individual browser to control the border space. So if a user visits the site with a large 20-inch monitor with the browser open to full capacity, the browser automatically adjusts the empty, black space according to the size of the user's window—thus fixing the "slack" on resize (see Figure 1.23).

"I really wanted to do a design of this character—a design that took full advantage of the screen space like most CD-ROMS do. In the initial draft of the design, I hadn't figured out a way to make it resize, and it was designed for 640×480, which left very little room for content after the header and footer took their bite of the real estate. The audience didn't care much for that, and let me know it. So I went back to the drawing board until I finally figured out a way to make the size dynamic." Ulm also adds that this technique helps the whole page seem more like a uniform element. "Web sites today aren't designed for computer monitors; they are designed for really long pieces of paper. Everything onscreen should work together, not rely on unseen and unconsidered elements. This full-screen design takes a crack at that belief." Figure 1.24 shows another page of the Eye Candy site that implements Ulm's frame design.

So what about frames in general? Ulm says that it's best to see everything together, not as individual frames. "The best uses of frames show no signs of frames at all. The technology should be transparent. The design should be cohesive from one corner to the other. And if you want some practical advice, get

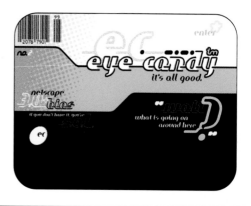

1.22

1.22   Eye Candy's main page.

a macro that types `MARGINWIDTH="0"` `MARGINHEIGHT="0"` `FRAMESPACING="0"` `BORDER="0"` `FRAMEBORDER="NO"` for you. In short, Ulm concludes that "frames are exceptionally stable and often times a surprisingly extensible layout technique." No doubt with Josh Ulm creating his innovative framesets we'll definitely see more than just eye candy on the horizon (see Figure 1.25).

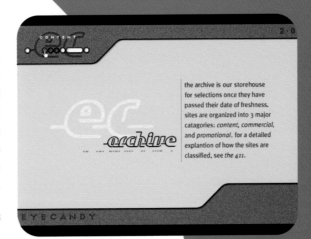

1.23

1.24

1.25

1.23　An example of the use of frames on the Eye Candy site.

1.24　Eye Candy Archive

1.25　Eye Candy freshies.

Summary

Whether you decide to use tables or frames, it's important to think of your layout as a whole and the needs of your audience. With so many available options, it's best to try a few techniques and see if they can work on your site. Tables are still probably the most widely used HTML for laying out content. Whether it's colored tables, graphics that are pieced together for different animation techniques, or more complex nested tables for full-page layout, tables are a staple in Web design. As for frames, they have become much easier to use, and creatively you can better utilize and organize the overall space of your browser window. The most important thing to keep track of is targeting the right links in frames. Nonetheless, both tables and frames can work together to help you build a great layout.

URLs in This Chapter

- Burner New Media http://www.brnr.com
- Eye Candy http://www.eyecandy.org
- Net Features http://www.netfeatures.com
- Macromedia http://www.macromedia.com
- Razorfish http://www.razorfish.com

Cross-Browser and Platform Comparison Guide

Property	Browser	Platform	Support
Tables	Netscape 3,4	Macintosh	Yes
Nested, Borderless,	Netscape 3,4	Windows	Yes
Colored Tables	IE 3, 4	Windows	Yes
	IE 3, 4	Macintosh	Yes
Frames	Netscape 3,4	Macintosh	Yes
Nested, Borderless	Netscape 3, 4	Windows	Yes
	IE 3,4	Windows	Yes
	IE 3,4	Macintosh	Yes

INSPIRATIONAL DESIGN MODEL:
Jeffrey Keyton and Tracy Boychuk, MTV

"I want my MTV" was the famous motto we first heard when the cable TV channel launched over a decade ago. Now in the '90s, we know that MTV is much more than just a music video channel. MTV has defined culture and youth and created a slick cutting edge style that has consistently been one step ahead of all the others. So how does MTV get its style? Look no further than Jeffrey Keyton, vice president of the Off-Air Creative Group and Art Director Tracy Boychuk.

Both Keyton's and Boychuck's work with the Off-Air Creative Group has garnered the team many design awards, especially their visionary Music Video Awards (MVA) books. With complete design freedom, the MVA books carry on themes such as Fluff (1995), Youth (1996), and Fetish & Fame (1997). What is meant to be programs to the awards ceremony have become pieces of art themselves. They aren't your average program even though they do list the nominees and award categories. Rather, the books take on their own personality because they center around certain themes, which, lately in the past two books, have both focused on people and their personal experiences.

This is especially seen in Youth, which featured interesting and personal email stories (gathered from the MTV Web site) with pictures of young viewers spread throughout the book. The colors of the page were bright neon, and the mylar cover gave the book a look to the future. It was known as "the shiny book." Similarly, Fetish & Fame centered around the theme where celebrities from all walks of life shared their special "fetish" (taken from the traditional meaning that fetish is "a sacred object that embodies a spirit").

1.1

1.1   *American Illustration Annual 16* Cover.

The layout of the book separated the fetishes from the stories, which allowed the reader to absorb the images before being touched by their personal significance (see Figure 1.3). "We weren't going to [include the stories], and then they started coming in with such great stories; somewhere, we had to include them. We wanted people to have the same experience we did and see the objects first and then take a little peek at the stories. They seemed almost religious or iconographic by the way that they were set up," remembers Boychuck. These touching stories, showing celebrities in their most basic human experiences and emotions, complemented the overall design of the book.

With all their busy work schedules at MTV, Keyton and Boychuck found time to team up off air, off MTV, for a project along with fellow MTV'er Stacy Drummond. The project was designing the *American Illustration Annual 16* book and the trio came up with the theme "sweet 16." Keyton, Boychuck, and Drummond solicited a group of 16 illustrators and had them create 16 illustrations of 16-year-olds. They broke all the rules on designing for a book and, not surprisingly, the end result was spectacular (see Figure 1.1).

With their trademark style of clean, classic type and bold-color combinations that can be seen throughout their work, Keyton and Boychuck make MTV fresh and classic at same time. We talked with them at MTV headquarters in the heart of New York's Time Square to share their thoughts on design and defining the culture we know as MTV.

What's the relationship between On Air and Off Air Creative Groups?

TB: Basically the on-air group does promotions, spots, and programming. The other thing that we do here that doesn't relate to what people see on the channels is a lot of trade print things: ad sales or people in the media buying departments and cable channels.

As far as on-air promos, they do the advertising that you see for different shows as well as some image spots. They oversee on-air graphics, which is the actual design of logos and show treatments and the openings for each identity. The way that we work with them is that we're sort of part of all that because a lot of the stuff that we do relates back to the TV shows. There are the print items that we conform to each franchise. Often, we'll be involved in some of the on-air graphics, and then we'll work as a team with them in order to create the identity for the show.

From a creative standpoint, a lot of what the designers at MTV create is so ahead of itself, so cutting-edge. How do you come up with new ideas? Where do you get your inspiration?

TB: I think a lot of it comes from Jeffrey as far as an overall creative vision. To his credit, he's been doing this for a long time. I'm not even quite sure why he's in touch with what he's in touch with. He's always interested in what's out there. For example, for the video music awards, he and Stacy Drummond came up with the fame and fetish theme, that was kind of risque´ for him to be interested in that. He's just a great creative thinker, quite frankly.

We try to come more from a conceptual standpoint. This might be a good point to make especially for Web design—because I think for me personally this is a problem with Web design—that it is very much sort of about tips and tricks and what the latest technology is. And the reality of it really comes down to a concept. Because if you have nothing to say, no matter what sort of decoration you put on something, it sort of falls flat. I think that's part of the strength of the things that come out of here. It is always designed around a concept; there's always an underlying idea or statement that it's making.

JK: I think inspiration for me is more about a spiritual thing as opposed to looking at someone's work or seeing something on the street. It's a little bit more about looking at nature. I think that what happens is that, through the years, part of the philosophy of myself and Stacy and Tracy is kind of like a scenario where we try not to do things that repeat ourselves. You set that as your goal and something will naturally happen. The thing that we'll do is that we'll get on each other when we see that "oh you've done that before" or "we've done that before."

1.2

1.3

1.3

1.2   Cover of the 1997 MVA Book *Fetish & Fame*

1.3   Inside the 1997 MVA Book, *Fetish & Fame*

What have been your favorite projects?

TB: MVA books. They're my favorite. I've only done three. They're commercial projects as far as having a client, but they're pretty open. I think that Jeffrey has built a reputation doing them; the company has allowed them the freedom and says, "Here. Here's your project." That's really rare (see Figures 1.4 and 1.5).

JK: And it's also one of the biggest budgets, so to have that kind of faith in me—I like that we can have that freedom because that's when I think it all just happens.

What are some of the projects you've done outside of MTV?

TB: A project that Jeffrey and Stacy and I did at the same time as the Fetish book, so we're all kind of a little crazed but surprisingly still here: This year's *American Illustration Annual* and its 16th one, so we came up with the "Sweet 16." We had 16 illustrators do 16 portraits of 16-year-olds in black and white. The idea was to sort of intersperse them throughout the book and the word "sweet." It helps to break up the book. The nice thing about it was that we were experimenting a little bit with color, but we wanted it to be really simply again.

What was the concept of the Web site for the MVA Youth book?

JK: What we originally thought with this book was coming up with a new idea; we wanted to turn it over to our audience and have our audience do the book. So we had this idea that we would create this Web site, which we did, and we would solicit artwork. It could be anything, basically tell us about your life, your stories, poetries. To make a long story short, we didn't really get any artwork or any photographs. The whole thing was kind of a disaster and we were trying to figure out what to do. We did get a good amount of stories. The stories were pretty good. But we needed some sort of visual stuff, so we went back and asked them to send us photos. I think what was interesting about that was that it was fun to finally see the faces.

TB: The design aspect of it basically was that the reflective material wasn't just about technology, but that it reflects the audience. This was sort of a play off of fax paper, it's kind of a lead-colored ink, so it's like the idea that it's still communication, the most basic communication of how people used to write. So we segregated it into sections. The photos all went on sort of crappy newsprint, the idea of almost being how bad can we make them until they look really bad? The snapshots from people are all crinkled [as if they had] been in their back pockets.

JK: We also wanted to do something that looked kind of like the stereotype of what the Internet was, a technology kind of thing. Everything is layed out so you have to surf the book. When you see the photos, it's not [in a] logical context. We thought it would be fun to read the things and to try to think about what the face might be. You go through it and read it; it kind of gives you a pretty good reflection of our audience.

What were your initial impressions of the Web after working on the Youth MVA book?

JK: I think really the great thing about it is that we're getting [in touch with] people from all over the world. We wanted to take something that was on the Web and take it off and [print it]. It won a lot of awards.

TB: I thought it was interesting to see who was on the Web. That was the biggest surprise for us. There's not a lot of ethnicity on the Web yet.

1.4

1.5

1.4   Cover of 1995 MVA Book, *Fluff*.

1.5   Inside the cover of 1995 MVA Book, *Fluff*.

CHAPTER 2

DESIGNING INTUITIVE NAVIGATION

Having a great home page and beautiful graphics on your Web site is just not enough to ensure a great Web site. If users to your site cannot find anything or don't know where to go, you can be sure that they probably won't come back. One of the most important (and hardest) aspects of designing a great Web site is having clear, concise navigation. How do you walk that fine line between design or functionality and your client's wish for links to everything on one page? As designers, we've all seen our sleek design work turn into a sea of turbulent links. Educate your clients and remind yourself about the intricacies and importance of clean navigation.

Navigation is not just a laundry list of links or cute buttons that decorate Web pages. Navigation should be thought of as the journey or path you want your users to take when they visit your site. Users need a sense of place—where they are—and direction—where to go from here. Books have an intuitive navigation because you know that you have to read it from front cover to end. With a Web site, it's different. Think of your Web site as a compact file cabinet. You have to organize your papers into categorical files and place them in a way so that you can quickly find specific topics. The key is in organization, presentation, and naming formats. Some sites lose grasp of this and create either a massive index of links or cute names to areas of their site that make no sense. This makes the user feel either overwhelmed or confused as to where to go.

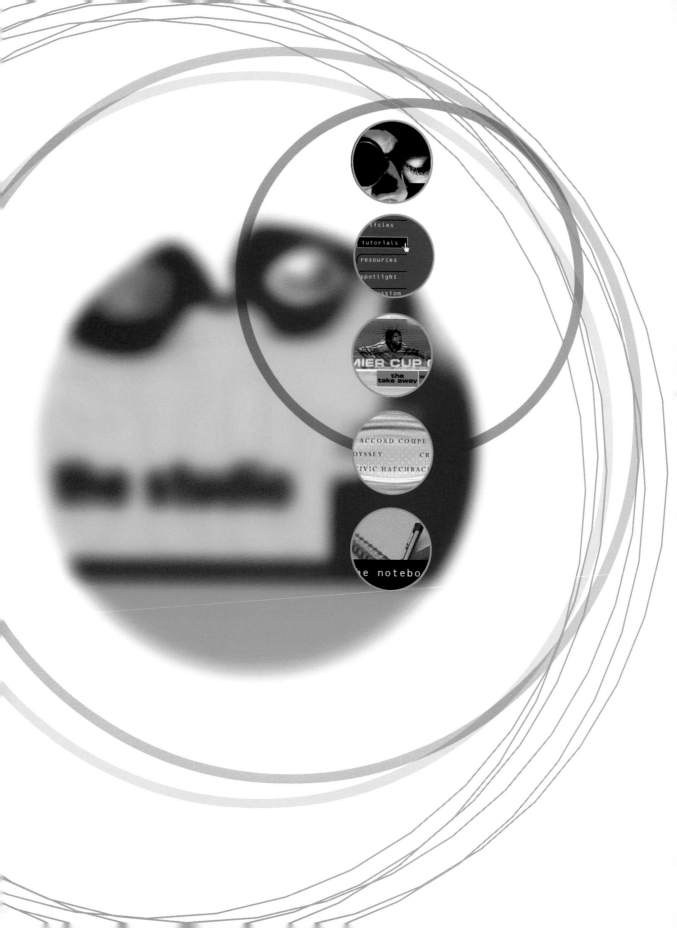

In this chapter, you see some of the best examples of what to do as you design intuitive navigation for a Web site. We'll not only refresh your memory with some navigation fundamentals, we'll show you how with HTML and JavaScript. You'll find the code to create virtual headers and footers, client-side imagemaps, text rollovers, image rollovers, and more.

Good Navigational Elements

To begin, there are some fundamental things to think about as you start to design navigation for your site. Here are just a few of them:

- **Organization/Presentation:** Include a clean, clear direction and structure; limit the number of links.
- **Naming Convention:** Use intuitive names for areas on your site.
- **Hierarchy:** Place the important information first or on top.

Organizing Your Links

One of the keys to designing navigation is organization. By organizing your site well, you can focus on the areas you want to promote on your site. Cluttered pages with millions of links only confuse your users and leave you with a big mess! Instead, choose to have a limited number of links from the beginning and have more links within each subsection. The best designed sites offer only a handful of links off of the main home page. In turn, the rest of the links lie within specific category pages. This allows you to better control the direction of where you want your users to go.

Figures 2.1 and 2.2 illustrate how clean navigation and a limited number of links help steer a direction for your users. Phoenix-Pop Productions (www.phoenix-pop.com) wanted to keep the initial page to a minimum number of links. The navigation

appears as more of a toggle between layers of information in a single space. The link taps on the top left again allude to the metaphor of the filing cabinet discussed earlier.

Naming Your Links

If you have an area on your site for feedback, call it "feedback." Just say what you mean and users can easily find where they want to go. This is especially important as the Web is also an international communications medium, and visitors from other countries may not understand cute terms for areas of a site. Pick a simple word or two that justly describes the area of your site without getting too verbose.

NY Style's Web site (http://www.nystyle.com) uses simple words to describe areas on its site (see Figure 2.3). Sections named "magazine," "shopping," and "email" make enough sense giving you a general idea of what type of content lies behind those links.

Click Here First

As a general rule, most people read things in order either top to bottom or left to right (or right to left, depending on which country you are from). When designing your navigation, have the most important links appear first because more often than not, those will be the first things people choose to click. That's why you usually see contact us, email, or search links at the end of most navigation bars. Think of it like movie credits—yes, but your navigation should never be that long. Most of the actors and actresses listed are in descending order. That is, the main characters are listed first, supporting characters next, and so on.

Honda's Web site (www.honda.com) better illustrates this point (see Figure 2.4). The models section of the site, as shown in Figure 2.5, is the link to all the different models of cars for the season. Honda uses its site to showcase the cars, and their importance in the navigation hierarchy tells us that.

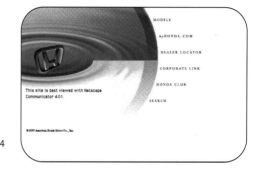

2.3

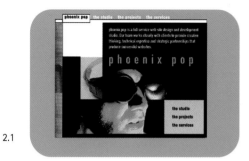

2.1

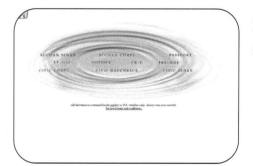

2.4

2.2

2.5

2.1 Phoenix-Pop Production's home page gives you three choices when you enter the site.

2.2 A second level page, the studio, shows more choices.

2.3 NY Style's Web site has simple words for navigation.

2.4 Honda's main page navigation has the links orgainized in a hierarchy.

2.5 The model's area of the Honda Web site.

CASE STUDY:
SIMON SMITH, CREATIVE DIRECTOR & PARTNER, PHOENIX-POP PRODUCTIONS

With a background in architecture, Simon Smith of Phoenix-Pop Productions (www.phoenix-pop.com) abandoned his straight-edge ruler and drafting table for a new and different design world—the Web. Since forming his company with partner Bruce Falck in 1995, Smith has overseen creative Web projects for clients such as Nike, Levis', Dockers, Hewlett-Packard, and NCI. When talking about issues in Web design, in this particular case, navigation, Smith candidly gives us his take on this difficult subject showcasing Phoenix-Pop's work on the Nike Soccer site created in July, 1997.

"Because it's not like a book that opens from cover to cover or a movie where you lay out the sequence, the user has complete control over his/her direction on the Web," explains Smith. "The Web is moving beyond the cheap tricks era where everyone feels a little dizzy from too much zooming in and out; audiences are beginning to appreciate appropriate and useful applications of information."

In order to design intuitive navigation, Simon believes there must be some sort of communication between him and the client. "I need to know where they want people to go—what's the main focus/audience?"

The Nike International Premier Global Cup site (Figure 2.6) was a success on many levels. The goal was to produce a 60-page site for a boy's soccer tournament held in South Africa—on a two-week production schedule. Clearly the limited time frame presented several challenges. But Smith and his team found effective solutions, combining good process with an intense week of production. In collaboration with Twenty2 Product's Terry Green for the design and video components of the site, they created an interface that spoke of movement with the main page and its two sets of navigation.

The main navigation (Figure 2.7) on the opening page consisted of animated gifs cropped from the Nike film crew video footage. Small and fast, this different approach to navigation was reflective of who the site was for.

"We sought the expertise from the site's audience—teenage boys—for feedback and found the moving images and infobytes were on the right track," Smith recalls.

2.6

2.7

2.6   Nike International Premier Global Cup main page.

2.7   Animated gifs make up the main navigation bar.

Similarly, the second lower navigation bar (Figure 2.8) consisted of a row of small flags each representing a particular team and their country (Figure 2.9). With descriptive rollovers to boot, the combination of the two navigations worked well to convey movement, action, color, and, of course, soccer. The simplicity and visual nature of the navigation reinforced the site design to create a unified and distinctive site that was one of Nike's many 1997 "Thematic Sites."

The rollovers use JavaScript code in conjunction with the HTML to create each rollover instance with the flags. Each flag is numbered 1 through 12 with the

image representing the rollover state of the flag that includes the corresponding team and country name.

```
firstImage = new Array()
firstImage[1] = new Image()
firstImage[1].src =
"./assets/images/holder.gif"

secondImage = new Array()
secondImage[1] = new Image()
secondImage[1].src =
"./assets/images/us_txt.gif"
secondImage[2] = new Image()
secondImage[2].src = "./assets/images/
portugal_txt.gif"
secondImage[3] = new Image()
secondImage[3].src =
"./assets/images/s_korea_txt.gif"
secondImage[4] = new Image()
secondImage[4].src =
"./assets/images/s_africa_txt.gif"
secondImage[5] = new Image()
secondImage[5].src =
```

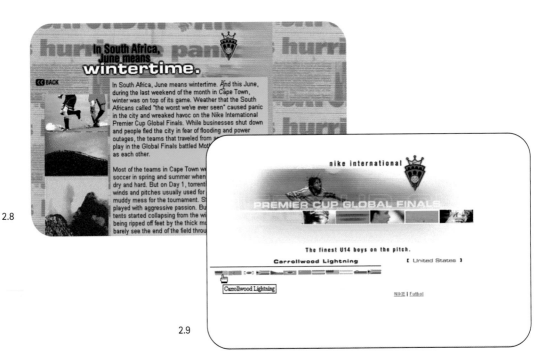

2.8

2.9

2.8   A second level screen from the main navigation bar.

2.9   Flags make up the rollover navigation for the teams. Rolling over the flags triggers team names and representing country.

```
"./assets/images/czech_txt.gif"
secondImage[6] = new Image()
secondImage[6].src =
"./assets/images/brazil_txt.gif"
secondImage[7] = new Image()
secondImage[7].src =
"./assets/images/china_txt.gif"
secondImage[8] = new Image()
secondImage[8].src =
"./assets/images/spain_txt.gif"
secondImage[9] = new Image()
secondImage[9].src =
"./assets/images/us2_txt.gif"
secondImage[10] = new Image()
secondImage[10].src =
"./assets/images/argentina_txt.gif"
secondImage[11] = new Image()
secondImage[11].src = "./assets/images/
slovenia_txt.gif"
secondImage[12] = new Image()
secondImage[12].src =
"./assets/images/s_africa2_txt.gif"

function refresh_holder() {
document.holder.src = firstImage[1].src;
}
function update_desc(image) {
   document.holder.src =
secondImage[image].src;
}
```

Each number in the JavaScript is later referenced in the HTML code to trigger the onMouseOver rollover. The <IMG SRC> contains the static state of the rollover.

Here's an example for image 8, which is the flag for Spain.

```
<a href="bin/nike.cgi?../html/spain_js.html"
onMouseOver ="update_desc(8)"; onMouseOut
="refresh_holder()";><IMG HEIGHT=10 WIDTH=29
SRC="./assets/images/spain.gif"  BORDER=0
ALT="Sevilla FC" ></a>
```

Smith believes there are three things that create good navigation.

- **Ease of Use:** What are the barriers to click?
- **Intuitive:** What is the learning curve?
- **Engaging:** The difference between passive and active navigation.

When Smith works with his clients on a design strategy, he focuses "on defining the flow of information, then designing the physical structure that provides the spaces, paths, and mechanisms that house the information." And so it is that creative flow that keeps Simon Smith and the team at Phoenix-Pop Productions busy as they create more intuitive and interactive Web sites for us to enjoy.

Graphics Versus Text Links

Up to now you've seen different examples of navigation, but most of them have been graphics rather than HTML text links. An alternative to graphics, the text link enables you to quickly edit and update your links rather than having to go through the tedious task of redoing all your graphics. You've seen them all over sites such as c|net in Figure 2.10 (www.cnet.com). However, you can take your links one step further in different ways. From text status messages to rollovers, you can find the best navigational enhancement for your site.

It can be easy to update text links rather than having to make new graphics each time you add a section to your site but having only text can be a bit drabby for your Web pages.

You can combine both the use of a graphical navigation bar with an alternative text link for a more balanced look. Most sites now have text footers on their pages with links to the top areas of their sites in case visitors have their images turned off or if the images in the navigation bar had trouble loading. Macromedia provides a bottom navigation bar that mirrors its graphical site navigation on each page (see Figure 2.11).

2.10

2.11   [home] [shockwave] [software] [support] [macromedia] [shockzone] [help]
        Copyright ©1997 Macromedia® Inc. All rights reserved. Disclaimer.
        Mirror Sites: [Asia] [USA]

2.10   c/net's text navigation bar.

2.11   Macromedia's text link navigation footer.

Text footers provide the user optimum methods from which to navigate around your site. Whether people are more comfortable with text links or graphics, you'll know that they can get around no matter which method of navigation they prefer. Also, in instances when the user has images turned off or if some of the graphics do not fully load, he always has an alternative to move around the site.

Using Client-Side Imagemaps

When creating navigation graphics, most designers use imagemapping software to create links for the hot areas in the graphic. These are actually server-side imagemaps. Server side maps have the coordinates of the graphic and their corresponding URL recorded on a text file somewhere on the server. By referencing that .map file in the HTML, the browser calls upon that file to find out where to go. This is why when you rollover server-side imagemaps, the graphic coordinates show up instead of URLs in the bottom-left-area of your browser window. This process can slow things down on your site.

A faster and more HTML-friendly alternative is having client-side imagemaps (see Figures 2.12 and 2.13). Client- side imagemaps have both the coordinates and their respective location recorded right on the HTML page. This saves valuable surfing time because users don't have to wait for the server to retrieve the URL; it's all on the page. Another plus is that the bottom browser status bar displays the actual location you'll be going to instead of numbered coordinates. Combine that with the text status rollovers that are discussed later in this chapter and you can have an effective combination of graphic navigation and textual browser status messages.

A variety of imagemap making tools are available for the Mac and Windows. "Mapper utility" Mapper (www.calles.pp.se) is one of the great imagemapping utilities for the Mac, and Mapedit (www.boutell.com/mapedit/) is excellent for Windows. Both are shareware programs where you can create client-side imagemaps. Check out the Web site companion for this book, www.htmlartistry.com, for links to these and other valuable Web resources.

2.12

2.13

2.12 CNN's site utilizes client-side imagemaps for its side bar navigation.

2.13 Creating a client-side imagemap in Mapper.

Macintosh Client-Side Map

You can easily create client-side imagemaps on the Macintosh with the help of Mapper, as shown in Figure 2.14. Launch Mapper and a dialog box appear to open a graphic. Find the graphic you created and select Open. Another box appears asking you to open a map; select new. A Map Settings box appears. In Format, select Client-side. Enter in a name for the map (here it's navbar) and frame reference for the Target field if necessary.

Mapper then proceeds to work just like any other imagemapping software. Use the square, circle, or polygon shapes to select the shape of the area you want to be a link. Enter in the respective URL for that selection as in Figure 2.15. Continue this for each area you want to be a link. When you finish creating hot areas, you're ready to output the code for this process. Go to the menu and select File, Save As. The selection gives you a document with an .html extension. In this case, it is navbar.html. This is your client-side imagemap file. The contents of the client-side map file will be cut and pasted into the HTML document where your graphic is referenced. Here we will call that HTML document main.html.

Here's what the navbar.html output looks like:

```
<MAP NAME="navbar"><!-- Created with Mapper
1.0, http://www.calles.pp.se -->
<AREA SHAPE="rect" COORDS="201,1,252,14"
HREF="ads/">
<AREA SHAPE="rect" COORDS="138,1,198,16"
HREF="web/">
<AREA SHAPE="rect" COORDS="68,1,138,15"
HREF="contact.html">
<AREA SHAPE="rect" COORDS="33,0,66,15"
HREF="info/">
<AREA SHAPE="rect" COORDS="0,1,32,15"
HREF="index.html">
</MAP>
```

Now you need to transfer the client-side map code to the HTML document where your graphic is referenced, main.html. After you have done that, find the `<IMG SRC>` reference for the graphic. Because the map name is "navbar", in the `<IMG SRC>` code, add USEMAP="#navbar" like this:

```
<img src="images/nav.gif" width="250"
height="14" USEMAP="#navbar" alt="site
navigation">
```

But you aren't done yet. Yes, client-side maps are good, but you should always have a backup with a server-side map reference as well. Return to the top menu bar and select Object, Map Settings. Choose NCSA or CERN (most sites use NCSA) from the pop-up menu as your format and enter in the name of your HTML document (the one where the graphic reference is) in the Default box as shown in Figure 2.15.

2.14

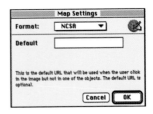

2.15

2.14   Attributing URLs to the graphic.

2.15   Creating an additional server-side imagemap.

This will ensure that if a user clicks outside a hot area, it will not go to an error 404 page, rather it will only refresh the page. Now go to File, Save As and you see a filename with a .map extension. Rename it if you want, but make sure you keep the .map extension. Upload the map file to your site somewhere and keep note of the location because you will reference it in the HTML. Link the map to the graphic with `<A HREF="navbar.map">`.

In the `<IMG SRC>` code, add `ISMAP` that designates a server-side imagemap and add `BORDER="0"` so that the whole graphic isn't highlighted.

Here's what the final code looks like:

```
<MAP NAME="navbar"><!-- Created with Mapper
1.0, http://www.calles.pp.se -->
<AREA SHAPE="rect" COORDS="201,1,252,14"
HREF="ads/">
<AREA SHAPE="rect" COORDS="138,1,198,16"
HREF="web/">
<AREA SHAPE="rect" COORDS="68,1,138,15"
HREF="contact.html">
<AREA SHAPE="rect" COORDS="33,0,66,15"
HREF="info/">
<AREA SHAPE="rect" COORDS="0,1,32,15"
HREF="index.html">
</MAP>
<a href="navbar.map"><img
src="images/nav.gif" width="250" height="14"
USEMAP="#navbar" ISMAP border="0" alt="site
navigation"></a>
```

That's all there is to it! There's no excuse and no reason not to use client-side maps for all your imagemaps.

Windows Client-Side Imagemaps

Creating client-side imagemaps is just as easy in Windows, and you use pretty much the same process as for the Macintosh. (The software is different—for Windows; use Mapedit.) First, launch the application and find the HTML document where the graphic you want imagemapped is. Mapedit automatically outputs the map attributes onto the HTML document and modifies the img src for you.

In Figure 2.16, you can see the Mapedit interface is simple to use. Choose the shape of your hot area and the corresponding URL link. There are even more complex dialog entries you can use, such as which

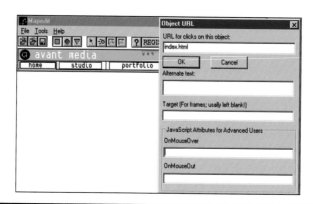

2.16

2.16   Making imagemaps in Mapedit.

frame to target, special tool tips text, or JavaScript onMouseOver rollover text. The output code is automatic, and it will name your map and enter the name for you in <IMG SRC> usemap. After you have gone through and selected each of the hot areas, you can save the HTML document from the file menu.

Here's the output code:

```
<map name="banner">
<area shape="rect" coords="2,24,72,38"
href="index.html">
<area shape="rect" coords="88,24,162,37"
href="studio.html">
<area shape="rect" coords="182,23,295,37"
href="portfolio.html">
<area shape="rect" coords="309,23,399,37"
href="books.html">
<area shape="rect" coords="406,24,494,38"
href="contact.html">
<area shape="default" href="index.html">
</map>

<img src="../images/banner.gif" width="500"
height="40" border="0" alt="avant media
contents" usemap="#banner">
```

Figure 2.17 shows the results.

Customized Status Bar Rollover Messages

Most people rely on the bottom status bar to let them know where the link will take them. Why not take it a step further and tell them where they are going rather than show the URL? With simple JavaScript added to your HTML, you can show customized messages when users rollover a link or a graphic.

In Figure 2.18, you can see how different and more descriptive your links can be by adding your own

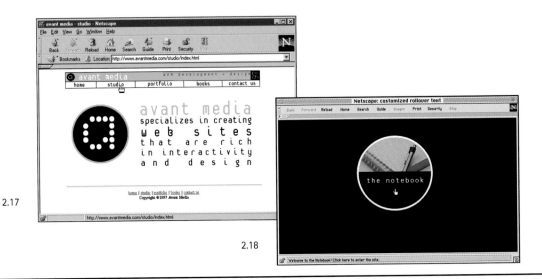

2.17

2.18

2.17   The final imagemap on the Web page.

2.18   A customized rollover status bar text.

text. Now you can actually name areas and tell your users where they are going.

The code for this is quite simple. All that is added to the HTML is a simple JavaScript `onMouseOver` command:

```
<a href="main.html"
onMouseOver="window.status='Welcome to the
Notebook! Click here to enter the site.';
return true">
<img src="notebook.gif" width="203"
height="191" border="0" alt="Click here to
enter the Notebook"></a>
```

As you can see, we also added a brief version of the rollover text to the `<ALT>` tag of the `<IMG SRC>`. It shows what the graphic is as it loads and also shows up in the Tool Tips mouseovers in the 4.0 browsers on Windows machines (see Figure 2.19).

But you don't have to limit this to graphics. You can also transform your text links the same way.

Here's the code:

```
<a href="../index.html"
onMouseOver="window.status='Avant Media
Home'; return true">home</a> ¦
<a href="index.html" onMouseOver=
"window.status='Explore the Studio'; return
true">studio</a> ¦
<a href="portfolio.html" onMouseOver=
"window.status='See Examples'; return
true">portfolio</a> ¦
<a href="../books/index.html"
onMouseOver="window.status='Check out the
Books'; return true">books</a> ¦
<a href="mailto:info@avantmedia.com"
onMouseOver="window.status='Contact Us';
return true">contact us</a>
```

Creating Impressive Image Rollovers

With JavaScript, you can create image rollovers for your navigation. When users roll over a certain graphic, it automatically switches to another graphic of your choice. Rollovers can enhance your navigation, taking your site to the next level of interactivity.

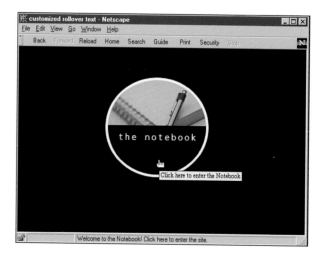

2.19

2.19   Tool Tips appear from the alt text in 4.0 browsers.

Created for the Dynamic HTML Zone Web site (www.dhtmlzone.com), the rollovers are an integral part of the side frame navigation of the whole site. Because the links target the main frame window, the side navigation frame is always present. This makes the navigation accessible at all times. The rollover effects of switch graphics give the site an extra piz-zazz because the site deals with the cutting-edge technology of Dynamic HTML. The rollovers not only work in the 4.0 browsers; they also work on version 3.0 of the browsers as well. This is because the code is all JavaScript. (For more on Dynamic HTML, see Part 2 of this book.) The look is simple but the effect of the rollovers really add to the interactivity that defines the site.

Creating the Rollover Graphics

Before you start scripting, you need to create graph-ics to use that are small in file size, about 2–4K. You can achieve this by using a limited amount of colors—2 to 3 is sufficient—you don't want your graphics to be too heavy. In a sense, you are creating two navigational looks: one for the main static look and one rollover look. Each link is a separate graphic stacked on top of each other, which you can lay out using an HTML table. However, here we just separated the graphics with
s.

Find an appropriate size for a link in your navigation. Because there is a limited amount of vertical space in the frame before you get that ugly scrollbar, the link graphics are 100×26 pixels. When you are in Photoshop 4, it is helpful to use the guides to align text and objects properly. To drag a vertical or hori-zontal guide, take your mouse to either the top or left side of your image and drag to your desired location. By using these guides, you can type each word and perfectly align them in their own Photoshop layer, one on top of each other. Save this file with all the Photoshop layers as navigation.psd.

Begin by creating one simple graphic as shown in Figure 2.20. The curved line is the main navigation state, not the rollover effect. Turn on the text layer to create one link graphic. We'll start with articles.

Here are the steps to create one graphic:

1. Make sure the articles layer is selected and all the other text layers are deselected.

2. Have the black curved line turned on as a layer.

After you have all the correct layers on, create a GIF by indexing the image to the lowest possible colors. This keeps the file size down to its absolute minimum.

3. Begin by indexing the graphic first to the 216 browser-safe colors by selecting from the File menu Image, Mode, Indexed Color.

4. Select the Web palette in the dialog box and press OK (Figure 2.21). Now the graphic is saved to the Web palette.

5. To make it exact, go back to the File menu and select Image, Mode, RGB, and repeat the steps to index. This time select Exact in the dialog box and choose OK (Figure 2.22).

You'll find that the dialog box has a smaller number of colors. Having the whole browser palette is unnecessary and takes up valuable file size!

Another option is using Photoshop plug-ins such as PhotoGif that indexes and compresses gifs nicely (Figure 2.23).

Note:

PhotoGif is a cool Photoshop plug-in created by Box Top Software (www.boxtopsoft.com). There are demo versions for you to download off its Web site available now for both Macintosh and Windows.

Now you are done with the articles graphic; you are ready to finish the rest of the main navigation graphics. Repeat steps 1 through 5 for the rest of the static state.

For the rollover graphics, repeat steps 1 through 5, but instead, replace step 2 with the following:

2. A simple black box is the rollover background state. Deselect the black curve layer and select the black box layer in your Photoshop Layers menu (Figure 2.24).

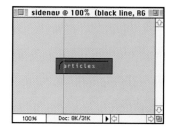

2.20

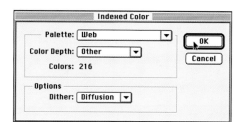

2.21

2.22

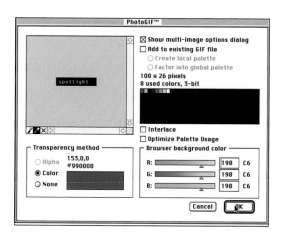

2.23

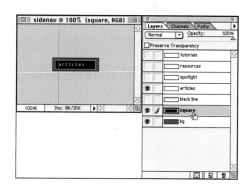

2.24

2.20   The articles graphic.

2.21   Indexing to the Web palette.

2.22   Indexing to the exact palette.

2.23   Using PhotoGif.

2.24   The articles rollover graphic.

The Rollover Code

After you create all your gifs, lay out what the basic frame will look like without the rollovers so that you can easily add the scripting. For the `<IMG SRC>` code, add a name attribute for each graphic such as `NAME='articles'`. This name also goes into the JavaScript code designating each rollover effect. The code looks like this:

```
<html>
<head>
<title></title>
</head>
<body bgcolor="#990000" text="#00000"
vlink="#ffffff" link="#333399">

<A HREF="index.html" target="_top">
<img src="images/dhtmlzone_small.gif"
width="97" height="47" border=0 name=
"dhtmlhome" alt="DHTML"></a>
<BR>
<A HREF="articles/main.html" target="main">
<img src="images/sidenav_articles.gif"
width="100" height="26" border=0 name=
"articles" alt="Articles"></a>
<BR>
<A HREF="tutorials/main.html" target="main">
<img src="images/sidenav_tutorials.gif"
width="100" height="26" border=0 name=
"tutorials" alt="Tutorials"></a>
<BR>
<A HREF="resources/main.html" target="main">
<img src="images/sidenav_resources.gif"
width="100" height="26" border=0
name="resources" alt="Resources"></a>
<BR>
<A HREF="spotlight/main.html" target="main">
<img src="images/sidenav_spotlight.gif"
width="100" height="26" border=0 name=
"spotlight" alt="Spotlight"></a>
<BR>
<A HREF="discussion/main.html" target="main">
<img src="images/sidenav_discussion.gif"
width="100" height="33" border=0 name=
"discussion" alt="Discussion Group"></a>
<BR>
<A HREF="swdhtml/main.html" target="main">
<img src="images/sidenav_swdhtml.gif"
width="100" height="33" border=0 name=
"swdhtml" alt="Shockwave"></a>
<BR>
<A HREF="http://www.macromedia.com/
"target="mm_window">
<img src="images/mmlogo_small.gif"
width="100" height="39" name="macromedia"
border=0 alt="Macromedia"></a>
</body>
</html>
```

If the layout looks fine, begin scripting the rollover process. Copy and paste the JavaScript code below. First, after the `<BODY>` tag, specify the JavaScript code by inserting the line:

```
<SCRIPT LANGUAGE="JavaScript">
```

The only other thing you have to modify is the HTML for each rollover instance. That HTML is defined by the `A HREF` code for each link of the graphic. The `onMouseOver` code is the rollover instance. The additions you need to make are between the apostrophe quotes of `MM_hiliteImg`. The first apostrophe quotes will contain the exact name of the image as specified in the `<IMAGE ALT>` tag. Here it will be `'articles'`. The second quotes are for the location of the rollover graphic that is `'images/sidenav_articles2.gif'`.

```
<A HREF="articles/main.html" target="main"
onMouseOver="MM_hiliteImg('articles','images/
sidenav_articles2.gif')"
onMouseOut="MM_hiliteImgRestore()">
```

To further explain this technique, there are two commands: `onMouseOver` and `onMouseOut`. It is sort of like the customized text messages for the `onMouseOver`, only here you use a graphic and add an `onMouseOut` command to restore the original graphic.

Here's the full code for the whole side navigation:

```
<html>
<head>
<title></title>
</head>
<body bgcolor="#990000" text="#00000"
vlink="#ffffff" link="#333399">
<SCRIPT LANGUAGE="JavaScript">
<!-- //Hide from old browsers - Courtesy of
www.coolnote.com
function MM_hiliteImg()  {
   srcImgArray = new Array;   //used for reset
   for (var i=0; i < (MM_hiliteImg.
arguments.length-1); i+=2) {
     theObj = MM_hiliteImg.arguments[i];
     srcImgArray[i] = theObj;
     newImgFile =
MM_hiliteImg.arguments[i+1];
     srcImgArray[i+1] =
eval('document.'+theObj+'.src');
     eval('document.'+theObj+'.src =
"'+newImgFile+'"');
   }
   document.MM_hiliteImgSrcs = srcImgArray;
//used for reset
}
function MM_hiliteImgRestore()  {
   if (document.MM_hiliteImgSrcs != null) {
     scrImgArray = document.MM_hiliteImgSrcs;
     for (var i=0; i < (scrImgArray.
length-1); i+=2) {
       theObj = scrImgArray[i];
       srcImgFile = scrImgArray[i+1];
       eval('document.'+theObj+'.src =
"'+srcImgFile+'"');
     }
   }
}
//stop hiding   -->
</SCRIPT>
```

```
<A HREF="index.html" target="_top"
onMouseOver="MM_hiliteImg('dhtmlhome','images
/dhtmlzone_small2.gif')"
onMouseOut="MM_hiliteImgRestore()">
<img src="images/dhtmlzone_small.gif"
width="97" height="47" border=0 name=
"dhtmlhome" alt="DHTML"></a>
<BR>
<A HREF="articles/main.html" target="main"
onMouseOver="MM_hiliteImg('articles','images/
sidenav_articles2.gif')"
onMouseOut="MM_hiliteImgRestore()">
<img src="images/sidenav_articles.gif"
width="100" height="26" border=0 name=
"articles" alt="Articles"></a>
<BR>
<A HREF="tutorials/main.html" target="main"
onMouseOver="MM_hiliteImg('tutorials','images
/sidenav_tutorials2.gif')"
onMouseOut="MM_hiliteImgRestore()">
<img src="images/sidenav_tutorials.gif"
width="100" height="26" border=0 name=
"tutorials" alt="Tutorials"></a>
<BR>
<A HREF="resources/main.html" target="main"
onMouseOver="MM_hiliteImg('resources','images
/sidenav_resources2.gif')"
onMouseOut="MM_hiliteImgRestore()">
<img src="images/sidenav_resources.gif"
width="100" height="26" border=0
name="resources" alt="Resources"></a>
<BR>
<A HREF="spotlight/main.html" target="main"
onMouseOver="MM_hiliteImg('spotlight','images
/sidenav_spotlight2.gif')"
onMouseOut="MM_hiliteImgRestore()">
<img src="images/sidenav_spotlight.gif"
width="100" height="26" border=0 name=
"spotlight" alt="Spotlight"></a>
<BR>
<A HREF="discussion/main.html" target="main"
onMouseOver="MM_hiliteImg('discussion',
'images/sidenav_discussion2.gif')"
onMouseOut="MM_hiliteImgRestore()">
<img src="images/sidenav_discussion.gif"
width="100" height="33" border=0 name="dis-
cussion" alt="Discussion Group"></a>
<BR>
<A HREF="swdhtml/main.html" target="main"
onMouseOver="MM_hiliteImg('swdhtml',
'images/sidenav_swdhtml2.gif')"
onMouseOut="MM_hiliteImgRestore()">
<img src="images/sidenav_swdhtml.gif"
width="100" height="33" border=0 name=
"swdhtml" alt="Shockwave"></a>
<BR>
<A HREF="http://www.macromedia.com/" tar-
get="mm_window"
onMouseOver="MM_hiliteImg('macromedia',
'images/mmlogo_small2.gif')"
onMouseOut="MM_hiliteImgRestore()">
<img src="images/mmlogo_small.gif"
width="100" height="39" name="macromedia"
border=0 alt="Macromedia"></a>
</body>
</html>
```

In Figures 2.25 and 2.26, you see the full layout and effect of the rollovers. It's really simple and can transform a static site into an interactive interface instantly. Dynamic HTML is even better; you can also create rollovers for HTML text links by attributing a color change. See Part 2 of this book on Dynamic HTML for more.

2.26

2.25

2.25   The navigation for the Dynamic HTML Zone.

2.26   The rollover effect.

Targeting New Browser Windows

You often have links that go off your site, and although you want your visitors to go off and explore, you also want them to find their way back. Your best option is to target a new browser window each time you have a link off of your site. The new browser window opens with the new link while the other browser window stays in the back. Large sites such as Macromedia use this when linking to their extensive database of Shockwave sites so that although people have fun and explore different Shockwave games, they can always go back to Macromedia (see Figure 2.27 and Figure 2.28).

2.27

2.28

2.27   Macromedia's Shocked Site of the Day...

2.28   ...target's a new browser window.

To target a new browser window for any given link, all you have to do is add the target property to that link.

```
<a href="http://www.macromedia.com"
target="window">
```

OR

```
<a target="window" href="http://www.
macromedia.com">
```

It doesn't matter where you put the target attribute, just as long as it's in the <A HREF> tag somehow. You must also make sure the target is set to "window" so that a new browser window will open.

Implementing Virtual Headers and Footers

For managing large Web sites, an easy way to keep your navigation updated is to use virtual headers and footers. These are the standard interface elements that are always on most pages such as ad banners, header graphics, text link navigation, and so on. Making virtual headers and footers means that instead of having the full HTML code on all the pages, you have it on just one. That way, all you have to do is update one file for the rest of the site. It doesn't even have to be a header or footer. If you need information duplicated in multiple areas, having to update just one text file makes it fast and easy. Most virtual headers and footers involve cgi scripts because they are server-side includes. But if you want to avoid the complications that come with cgi scripting, JavaScript can now be used to create virtual files for your site.

First, you need to create an external JavaScript file to live on your site.

```
//JavaScript File for virtual footer
//Update this document only to change footer
on site
    function printVirtualFooter(){
document.write('<hr width="500">');
document.write('<font size="1"><a
href="../index.html">studio</a> ¦ <a
href="portfolio.html">portfolio</a> ¦ <a
```

```
href="../books/index.html">books</a> ¦ <a
href="mailto:info@avantmedia.com">contact
us</a><br>');
document.write('Copyright 1998</font>');
}
```

Note:

Each document.write has to be on its own separate line. Don't word wrap the code as it will mess it up.

Save this file as footer.js. (You can name the file whatever you want, but it must have the .js suffix). Now when you need to update the content of your footer, you just have to modify your .js document. You can add as many lines as you want and updating it is a breeze.

For your HTML pages, you need to use <SCRIPT> to reference the .js file at the top of any HTML document in which the footer should appear, like this:

```
<html>
<head>
<title>avant media - studio</title>
<SCRIPT Language="JavaScript"
SRC="footer.js">
</SCRIPT>
</head>
```

Then for the exact area in which you want the footer to appear, add this code:

```
<script language="JavaScript">
        printVirtualFooter();
</script>
```

The final result, as seen in Figure 2.29, is a virtual footer that can be made once and used throughout your site.

To create a virtual anything, just follow the same previous steps for the virtual footer. If you use multiple virtual files, make sure you go through the code and change the names for each of the commands such as printVirtualHeader Or printVirtualText.

Note:

Cascading Style Sheets are also another alternative to the virtual header and footer. See Chapter 9, "Creating the Animations of Your Dreams," for more.

Summary

Navigation is one of the most important aspects in Web design and hopefully this chapter has helped you think more about designing good navigation. By having good organization and also by presenting your links in a clean, clear manner, you'll have no trouble with user difficulty on your site. The techniques, HTML, and JavaScript code can help enhance the navigational structure of your site. From basic HTML text links, graphical client-side imagemaps, and the interactivity of rollover navigation, there are many different options on how you can present your site navigation. Now it's time for you to decide which options you want to use!

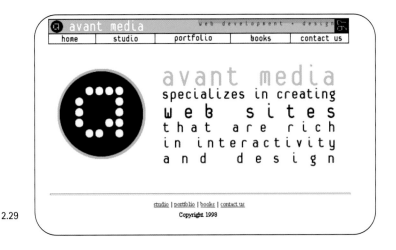

2.29

2.29   A virtual footer on Avant Media.

Cross-Browser and Platform Comparison Guide

This is a comprehensive list of the techniques used in this chapter and their support on the top two browsers: Netscape and Internet Explorer on both Macintosh and Windows.

URLs in This Chapter

- Avant Media: www.avantmedia.com
- c|net: www.cnet.com
- CNN Style: www.cnn.com/STYLE/
- Dynamic HTML Zone: www.dhtmlzone.com
- E!Online: www.eonline.com
- Honda: www.honda.com
- Macromedia: www.macromedia.com
- Macromedia Shocked Site of the Day: www.macromedia.com/shockzone/ssod
- New York Style: www.nystyle.com
- Nike International Premier Global Cup: www.phoenix-pop.com/nike/
- Phoenix Pop Productions: www.phoenix-pop.com

Property	Browser	Platform	Support
Client-side Imagemaps	Netscape 3,4	Macintosh	Yes
	Netscape 3,4	Windows	Yes
	IE 3, 4	Windows	Yes
	IE 3, 4	Macintosh	Yes
Alt Tag Tool Tip	Netscape 3,4	Macintosh	No
	Netscape 3	Windows	No
	Netscape 4	Windows	Yes
	IE 3, 4	Windows	Yes
	IE 3, 4	Macintosh	Yes
Image Rollovers	Netscape 3, 4	Macintosh	Yes
	Netscape 3, 4	Windows	Yes
	IE 3, 4	Windows	Yes
	IE 4	Macintosh	Yes
Targeting New Windows	Netscape 3, 4	Macintosh	Yes
	Netscape 3, 4	Windows	Yes
	IE 3, 4	Windows	Yes
	IE 3, 4	Macintosh	Yes
Virtual Headers/Footers	Netscape 3, 4	Macintosh	Yes
	Netscape 3, 4	Windows	Yes
	IE 3, 4	Windows	Yes
	IE 4	Macintosh	Yes

INSPIRATIONAL DESIGN MODEL:

Carol Chen, Sony Music

Sitting in her New York Madison Avenue office with her walls filled with poster art of Cyndi Lauper to the Indigo Girls, Carol Chen, design director at Sony Music humbly discusses her experience working in the high-impact job of designing and creating packaging for various Sony Music recording artists—jobs that range from overseeing 13 to 17 art directors to approving and guiding the design of CD covers, posters, and more. Chen is not only at the top of her game, she has also shown through her years of experience in the design business that she has definitely worked hard to get where she is today.

We first met Chen at the New Orleans AIGA Design Conference in late fall of 1997. She was giving an impressive talk on "The Music Industry Now." She showed some beautiful slides of CD covers and posters, but then she did something different. Chen was the only one who recognized her staff by showing slides of all of them. That's the kind of person she is.

A self-taught designer, her story is likely to make anyone follow their heart to do what they really want in life. She has the singular ability to balance being both a designer (once a designer, always a designer) and holding an administrative position while guiding so many different design projects from pop, hip-hop, dance, rock, alternative, and even classical music at the same time.

No one can deny the impact of how music affects design. What we love is how Chen and her staff take music to create things that become the final harmonizing package of what we hear and what we see.

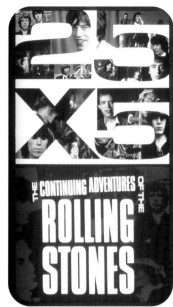

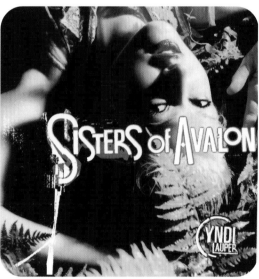

2.1

2.2

2.3

2.4

2.1	Living Colour CD cover	2.3	Cyndi Lauper CD cover
2.2	Rolling Stones Video Box	2.4	Carol Chen

It's an interesting balance and we got the chance to find out more about Chen and how design works in the music biz.

Please describe your background for us.

I was interested in graphic design when I was a teenager. But it wasn't a very socially acceptable thing in my family to do art. So I studied something else that was practical. By the time I finished in that degree, which was in the sciences, I decided that I needed to go back to where my heart was, which was design. I did it by working and observing. When I was in college, I designed posters and programs for concerts, dance, music, and theater on campus and for speakers. [After college] I worked for an artist bookmaker who had a letterpress studio in Santa Monica and I hand-set type there. I printed things the old-fashioned way, very slowly. I worked with Cindy Marsh, who was an illustrator in the entertainment industry, and her illustrations were done with silk-screen techniques and also offset printing. So I was helping her shoot negatives and strip them together, and so on. Fun stuff.

How did you get your start in the music industry?

Cindy actually told me about a job opening at a record company. Music and me—that was a big thing. It was really a natural combination. I was already inclined toward music, and I was listening to a lot of it anyway while I worked. It was my inspiration. Working in the music industry was a dream match though I didn't consciously pursue it.

Out of curiosity, in terms of the music that your group designs for, is it music that you listen to, or does it happen to be that way?

What kind of personal attachment do I have to the music? I'm very fond of a lot of the music. That's a happy coincidence because I have to listen to the music—to all of it— in order to assign the right people to it, and also in meetings to have something constructive to say about it. Because if I haven't heard the music, and I don't know anything about it, my opinion's not very valid.

What are the variety of the projects you handle?

It's everything for Epic Records. It ranges from Rage Against the Machine to Gloria Estefan. Posters, CD covers, advertising....

How demanding is it? Turnaround time?

Well, the record business is a very interesting one. It's predicated on getting records into the store by a certain date, and sometimes that date is set because "it's time" for that artist to release a record. But an average time is two months to learn about a project, meet the band, and determine a direction. We either commission illustration or set up a photo shoot, select the photographs, retouch them if necessary, show comps of covers, do revisions, design the inside, get them approved. Then we do all the collateral, the advertising, and the other configurations—cassettes and minidiscs. Also, design a Web site and possibly a CD-plus.

What else? With music, it has to be so of the moment...how do you find ideas?

Actually, through a lot of other media. Magazines. A lot of international magazines, movies. International *Vogue*s for shoots, for style. A lot of design magazines, too, *Eye, ID, Graphis*. Many times, we see something in there that we really can't apply to what we're doing, but some piece of it might work.

How far are you from the actual production?

Well, I still art direct some photo sessions, and I work with designers and art directors here to complete the project, to lay it out and to do revisions and see it through. But most of the time, I learn about a project and decide which art director would be appropriate. Then I take meetings with the artist and their manager and the art director.

Is there anything else that you do? Do you keep a sketchbook? Do you go off and do your own personal designs?

I used to. Especially when I was out in Los Angeles. I was very much used to working in a studio and creating things, so that's what I would do in my spare time and overnight usually. Stay up all night and make something and print it for myself. Frankly, that's how I got the job—the first record company job. I had some real pieces in my portfolio, but I hadn't gone to design school. Because I knew how to print, I printed the things that I liked and they looked like real jobs! You know, that's the toughest thing, to get a client to agree to something you've done the way you've done it and have it realized in print. I had complete control over that and I enjoyed it. And I do some photography. But I have to say that I don't have a lot of spare time now.

In the Web, stuff is changing all the time in terms of what you can do. Is that the same for print?

I don't want to sound really dire about this, but I think new media and some computer games and Internet surfing, plus movies and music videos, have all taken away a little bit of the specialness of pack-aging. Plus, packages have become a lot smaller, so there's a lot less to look at. Where I work, we do fewer special packages. There's a lot of standard packaging, so right now, it's not so much like trying to figure out a new technique. We're creating, in many cases, eye candy—something that will grab people's attention in stores, something bright and flashy and actually, simple because it's small. But printwise, it's what can be done in Photoshop, what can be done in Illustrator. A lot of photographers that we hire use different processing techniques in printing that we then incorporate. But it's not as though a lot of the print itself is changing. The papers are roughly the same. Frankly, I don't know if it's really new or if it's old. Sometimes, we've been doing something in a certain way for so long that what seems new is actually an old technique, like letterpress.

What kind of direction do you provide the art directors?

Sometimes I know how important a project is to the label or I know how they plan to market it or what opportunities there are to tour, be on TV, or if it's in connection with a movie. So naturally, I'll give the art directors as many hints as I can without telling them what to do. I never want to tie their hands that much. I'll tell them what I know will fly with the label, but they don't have to do that. And, frankly, I really enjoy seeing the solutions that they come up with that are completely off the spectrum, off the page.

"Study Hard" advised Chinese parents to their "Jook-Sing" (Bamboo Heart—Culturally empty) American-born Children

2.5   "Study Hard" a personal design piece by Carol Chen commemorating her father.

If an art director is all about detail, how did you work with designers?

Actually, here, art directors do it all. We have graphic artists, some of whom were formerly mechanical artists. Sometimes, they'll take a CD and do a comparable version of a cassette, or let's say there's an ad ordered in 12 different sizes. Graphic artists will resize it and do all the typographical tweaks, but an art director here will actually do the design. When I referred to designers earlier, we have a few junior people who in a very short time will become art directors. We're not that hierarchical around here. Talented designers end up art directing before you know it.

Have you seen anything on the Web that you like? What are your thoughts about where that's going? Is it a threat to what you're doing?

I don't think it's a threat to what we're doing because perhaps what we're doing is going to disappear. Resources are being reallocated these days away from print, and away from special packaging to videos and to new media, touring, and other aspects of an artist's career. Then there's liquid audio for downloading music. In the future, I'm sure you'll be able to download some files that detail the credits, songwriters, photos, and stuff like that. I don't think print as we know it is a necessary part of our future. So I don't see it as a threat. It's evolution. I think we're headed in a more paperless direction. If I were to say that that's the enemy, I would be shortening my usefulness. So instead I embrace it. I say, "Everybody, check this out!" Because if you don't, you'll become a dinosaur.

CHAPTER 3
TYPE EFFECTS: ENHANCING YOUR INTERFACE WITH STUNNING TYPOGRAPHY

Graphic design has always been a mixture of pop culture, experimentation, and creative typography—the latter being one of the most exciting and difficult to achieve. How can you create something out of letters that can be both different, beautiful, and legible at the same time? With hip font foundries such as Emigre that create typefaces that can literally inspire a designer to create works of art around type, designers can no longer ignore the importance of the forms, shapes, and intricacies of letters. (Emigre fonts can also seem to invoke drooling among most designers who patiently crave the next issue of the Emigre quarterly magazine.)

Unfortunately, it has been difficult to translate some of the same excitement for type on the Web. Web designers today are often working with limited resources, having to worry more about download speed and browsers than being able to freely express themselves with type. Although this chapter talks about some of the standard and most common usage of HTML for achieving various type effects, we also cover some new and exciting techniques such as text color rollovers and dynamic/embedded fonts. We also cover how to create effective type in your graphics by using the most popular vector graphics tools, Macromedia FreeHand and Adobe Illustrator. Discover just how much more you can do with your type on the Web.

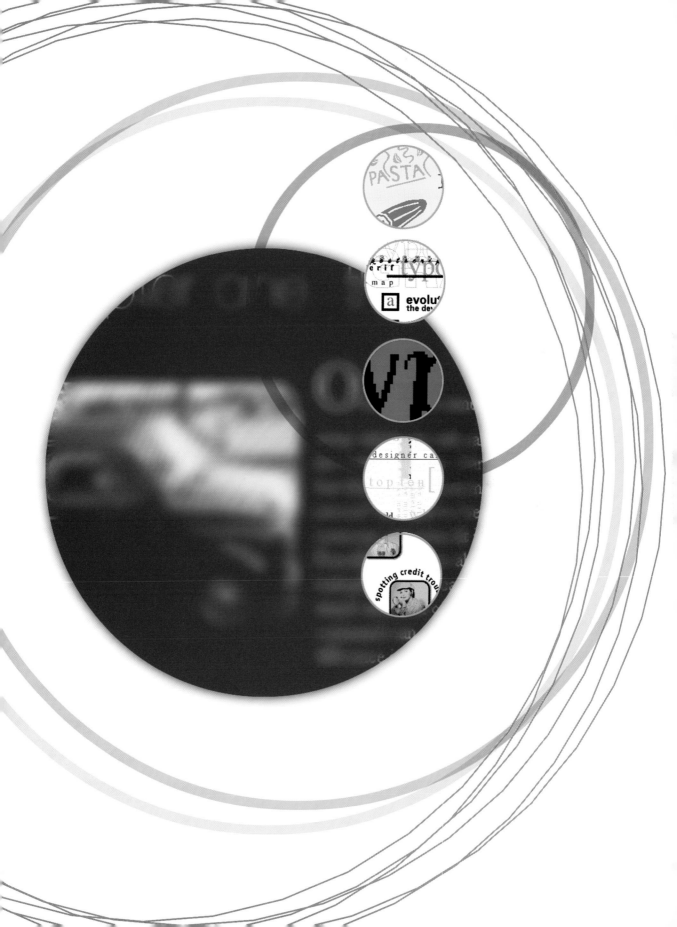

Type and the Web

The fundamental basis of design is typography and the ability to use type in both a communicative and beautiful manner. With the Web, there have been many problems in trying to achieve the caliber of design predicated by print and motion graphics. HTML type served a clear purpose in the beginning because it was used more for communicating rather than being beautiful. With the rise of the Web, there was a clear indication that the aesthetics of type needed to be there also.

To gain a better grasp of typography, there are two great sites that can introduce you to the intricacies and history of the evolution of type. One site, called typoGRAPHIC (Figure 3.1), is created by Razorfish and contains valuable information on the history of type, a full glossary, and recommended readings. Another great site, simply called The FontSite (Figure 3.2), is a monthly type 'zine that contains full-length meaty articles on different type-related topics.

With the progression of typography leading us now on to the Web, the 4.0 browsers are finally introducing us to the great possibilities of what lies on the horizon.

Font Attributes: The Basics

The basics of HTML typography is to understand all the attributes so that you can later mix them together for a look that can be cool, classic, or whatever you want. Font sizes, colors, HTML, and system typefaces all come into play when dealing with type for the Web. You can build upon these basics to create the special effects later in this chapter.

Here are the common tags used for HTML fonts:

- Font Sizing   `<FONT SIZE>`
- Coloring Fonts   `<FONT COLOR>`
- Naming Fonts   `<FONT FACE>`

It can be difficult to think of creative ways in which to use HTML text. But it can be done. Just look at the Design Mind Web site in Figure 3.3. Using the Netscape space tag, ` `, the site combines HTML text in different sizes in a subtle gray color that compliments well with the link text. The mixture and combination with the background image work well to create a seamless integration.

In Figure 3.4, we highlighted the HTML text in order to better differentiate it from the graphical background.

> ## Note:
> When choosing colors for your text and links, make sure that the colors don't clash in a way that would be hard for the user to read. Legibility is also a part of the overall design aesthetic.

There is a limited range of font size as dictated by HTML; they usually go from size 1 to 6, with 1 being the smallest and 6 being the largest. The standard base font is a size 3. The code for specifying fonts is quite simp

```
<font siz
<font siz
<font siz
<font siz
<font siz
<font siz
```

You can se
in Figure
(460×60) f

Take also ir
specify fon
browser siz
can be a g
changed his

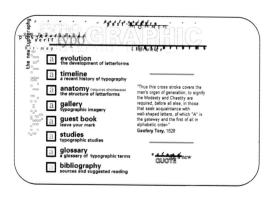

3.1

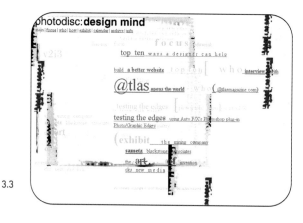

3.3

3.2

3.4

3.1   The typoGRAPHIC Web site.

3.2   The FontSite.

3.3   The Design Mind site combines different elements of HTML typography.

3.4   Highlighting the HTML text.

HTML Default Fonts Versus Computer System Fonts

Tired of the default font Times New Roman? Most designers are. That's why you often see pages displayed with HTML type such as teletype, code, or preformatted text. Teletype (`<tt></tt>`), code (`<code></code>`), and preformatted text (`<pre></pre>`) look very much the same, using Courier as the display text (see Figure 3.6). Depending on the monitor and platform, code is supposed to appear as a fixed-width font and teletype is supposed to create a keyboard typeface. Preformatted text can be an alternative usage for layout because it aligns the items within the `<pre>` tags in the exact same place on the Web page as it appears on the HTML document.

But most designers have found that for even more type options, they choose to specify system typefaces with the `<FONT FACE>` tag to have a customized look. Because there are a few base fonts that come with every Macintosh and Windows machine, you won't have to worry about whether or not these fonts are installed on a user's machine. Figures 3.7 and 3.8 show the system fonts for Macintosh and Windows machine.

Arial on Windows and Helvetica on Macintosh are very similar, therefore most designers use them both so that the overall look will be the same cross-platform. The only other common font between the two platforms is Courier. So this limits usage of system fonts to just about three typefaces.

The best rule of thumb for naming fonts is to name them according to how your system lists them and don't worry about upper- or lowercase—both seem to work fine. Naming fonts is easy on Windows, but for Macs you should test it out. If nothing works, try putting the font name together as one word such as "metacondensedbold."

The Dynamic HTML Zone (www.dhtmlzone.com) uses the combination of Arial and Helvetica for the Windows and Macintosh system fonts respectively because of their similar typeface look (see Figures 3.9 and 3.10).

Mac Type Versus PC Type

You've seen the differences in system fonts on the Mac and PC, but as a designer, I'm sure you're also aware of the many other differences that go on between these two platforms.

For instance, there are visible font size differences on Macs and PCs. Fonts on PCs tend to be larger. See Figures 3.11 and 3.12 for a side-by-side comparison. Yes, it can be frustrating because sometimes this can affect the design. From text in tables to text in frames, you have to keep in mind the slight differences as you design.

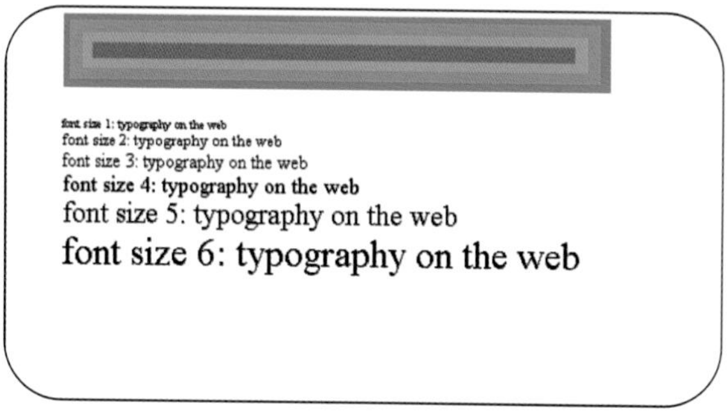

font size 1: typography on the web
font size 2: typography on the web
font size 3: typography on the web
font size 4: typography on the web
font size 5: typography on the web
font size 6: typography on the web

3.5

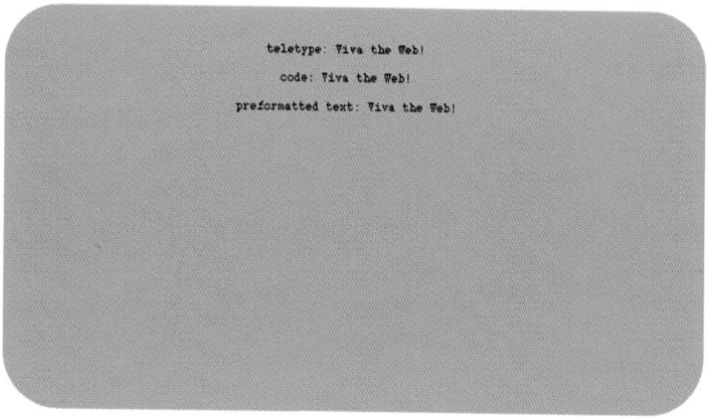

teletype: Viva the Web!
code: Viva the Web!
preformatted text: Viva the Web!

3.6

Chicago
Courier
Geneva
Helvetica
Monaco
New York
Times New Roman

3.7

Arial
Comic Sans
Courier
Courier New
Impact
Times New Roman
Verdana

3.8

3.5 Font size measurements.

3.6 HTML typefaces.

3.7 Macintosh system fonts.

3.8 Windows system fonts.

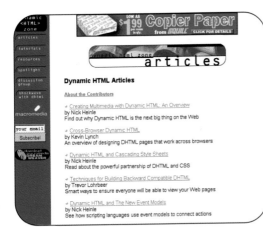

3.9

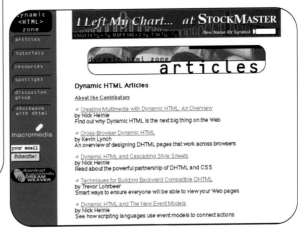

3.10

3.11

font size 1: type on a mac
font size 2: type on a mac
font size 3: type on a mac
font size 4: type on a mac
font size 5: type on a mac
font size 6: type on a mac

3.12

font size 1: type on a pc
font size 2: type on a pc
font size 3: type on a pc
font size 4: type on a pc
font size 5: type on a pc
font size 6: type on a pc

3.9   Windows displays Arial.

3.11   Macintosh font sizes.

3.10   Macintosh displays Helvetica.

3.12   Windows font Sizes.

Special Type Effects

There are a few quick and simple HTML type effects you can do to enhance the design of your site. Special looks such as creating drop caps and creative text alignment can give some style to your site without leaving you bandwidth heavy.

Another great effect is the text color change rollover that gives some simple link color changing to your HTML links, thanks to the new 4.0 browsers. If you find yourself out of ideas for HTML type, this section shows you how to achieve the right effect you want.

Drop Caps

Creating the drop cap look is a simple combination of FONT SIZE and even FONT COLOR. To create this look that is often used in books and magazines, see Figure 3.13.

Here's what the code would look like:

```
<FONT SIZE="6"COLOR="#FFFF66">O</FONT>nce
upon a time
```

But what about when you want more size options? This is when simple style sheet commands such as inline HTML styles come into play (more on style sheets in Chapter 7). Without coding a whole document in style sheets, you can insert styles directly within your HTML.

Within your HTML, instead of FONT SIZE, use FONT STYLE and the accompanying font-size attribute and pick a font size you like.

```
<FONT STYLE="font-size: 40pt"
COLOR="#FFFF66">O</FONT>nce upon a time
```

The final result (Figure 3.14) is a font displayed in 40 points. Quite a difference from a simple FONT SIZE=6!

Text Color Change Rollovers

Another 4.0 browser enhancement is creating simple rollovers that change the link color of the HTML text. It's more of a special effect than navigational necessity and can be any simple way to call attention to your links. Figure 3.15 looks like a normal page of links on the Dynamic HTML zone.

For Internet Explorer 4, you can change the color by adding ONMOUSEOVER="javascript:this.style. color='colorname'" to set the color for the rollover

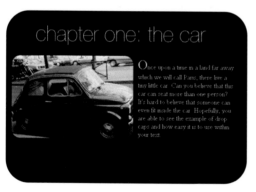

3.13

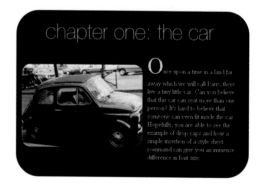

3.14

3.13   Drop Caps with FONT SIZE=6

3.14   Drop caps with inline styles.

state. You can do the same for ONMOUSEOUT command if you want, but by leaving it blank it defaults to the HTML link color that you specified in the BODY of your HTML.

The code here shows that the link color changes to blue when the mouse is rolled over (Figure 3.16). You can use color names or the equivalent hex codes to name colors.

```
<A HREF="page.html"
OnMouseOver="javascript:this.style.color=
'blue'" OnMouseOut="javascript:this.style.color=
''">Link Here</A>
```

For Netscape, the JavaScript is a bit different and takes a little more effort. The JavaScript needs to live in the HEAD of your HTML document. Each link has to be named a layer; here "text" is specified as a layer. The first part indicates the rollover state of the link color (blue) and the second part indicates the static link color (red).

```
<head>

<script language="JavaScript1.2">

function changeto(){
setTimeout(changeto1, "1");
}

function changeto1() {
document.layers["text"].document.write("<font
color=blue><a href=http://www.urlhere.com>Link
Here</a></font>");
document.layers["text"].document.close();
}
```

```
function changefrom(){
setTimeout(changefrom1, "1");
}

function changefrom1() {
document.layers["text"].document.write("<font
color=red>Link Here</font>");
document.layers["text"].document.close();
}

function link(){
}
</script>
```

Then in the BODY of your HTML document, you need to specify the link with the LAYER tag.

```
<LAYER NAME="text" OnMouseOver=changeto()
OnMouseOut=changefrom() OnMouseDown=link()><FONT
COLOR="Red">Link Here </FONT>
</LAYER>
```

You get the same results as Internet Explorer but make sure when you have more links you organize and separate the code well.

3.16

3.15

3.17

3.15   Links on the Dynamic HTML zone.

3.16   Rollover the text links and the color changes to red.

3.17   Using the <PRE> tag to create different text alignments.

Text Alignment

With some creative text alignment, you can allow your text to jump out and blend within your pages in creative ways. Use tables or <PRE> tags to get the effect you want.

Here's the code for a simple text alignment example in Figure 3.17:

```
<img src="images/circle.jpg" align="left">

<CENTER>
<PRE>
there are ways you can align your text so
that
there are different curved lines.  there
are ways you can align your text
so that there are different
curved lines. there
are ways you
can align
your
text
</PRE>
</CENTER>
```

By using <PRE></PRE> tags, you can format your pages based on how you format the text within the tags. That means any line breaks, spaces, and so on will appear! It's not meant for general formatting of HTML pages, but you can use them for special creative text instances.

Antialiasing Type

So you're in Photoshop and you see that Antialias button in the type box. What does that mean? By simply checking the antialias box, your text will appear more blended. Antialiasing removes all the *jaggies*—those pixels that line around the edge of the graphic text—and blends them to the background.

For example, in Figure 3.18, the bottom graphic is antialiased to a red background and the top is not. Notice the difference that antialiasing can do. In Figure 3.19, in 500% zoom, you can see how when

text is aliased the pixels of the text to the background are defined by harsh lines that are in turn blended in the aliased version on the bottom.

So, is it a good idea to always antialias your graphics? Well, sometimes when working with transparent graphics, you can get better results by leaving your text aliased. This is especially so when you work with patterned backgrounds or when you create pixel-like text on purpose for the sake of design.

Using Vector Graphics Tools to Achieve Maximum Type

You might be asking when should you use HTML text and when should you use graphics? The answer is simple. Use HTML text for the main body of text and

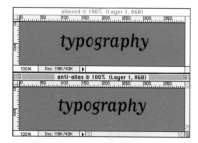

3.18

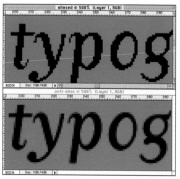

3.19

3.18   Antialiased and aliased text.

3.19   A close-up view of the text.

for things that need to be updated quickly and easily. Use graphics for when you want to use special text effects, blend text and images, or use color combinations for enhancement to pages through graphic headers, buttons, and navigation.

Most designers use Photoshop when creating their graphics for the Web. What some designers don't know is that vector graphics tools such as Macromedia FreeHand or Adobe Illustrator can give you more precise text leading, kerning, and more.

FreeHand has the most text power over Illustrator, and the intricacies of how you can create layouts and automatically export them to GIFs or JPEGs gives it a definite one up. Nonetheless, Illustrator and Photoshop are virtually seamless, and Photoshop users will find the same interface a breeze to use. We aren't going to be biased here, so whichever product you have, here are some techniques on how to create some type that will look good on the Web.

Laying Out Your Type

For best text results, you can lay out all your type in FreeHand or Illustrator and save it as an EPS file. This ensures that you can keep all the kerning and leading information that doesn't work well in Photoshop. The result is that you'll have more control over your text, and smaller point sizes will be more legible.

First, create all your type in FreeHand/Illustrator (Figure 3.20). For words that are going to live ultimately on the same line, make sure you have them aligned all together on one line in Illustrator/FreeHand so that they antialias the same.

Then as you import the file into Photoshop (Figure 3.21), you can cut and paste each word as you need them in your graphic. Notice that even the small 10-point text looks nice and legible.

Curved Text

For even more text effects, you can create curved text such as those created in FreeHand for the Visa Inform site (Figure 3.22).

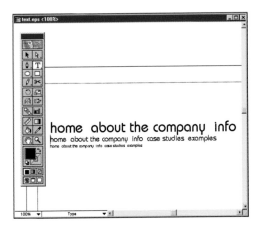

3.20

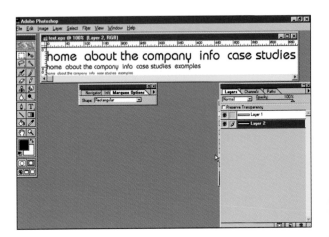

3.21

3.20   Text layed out in Illustrator.

3.21   Importing the eps into Photoshop.

First, type in your desired text. Then create the path shape from which you want the text to follow (Figure 3.23).

Then select the text and the circle with the Arrow tool. From the File menu, choose Text/Attach to Path. Your text will now curve along the circle path (Figure 3.24).

Finally, export the document as Photoshop 4 eps and import the text in Photoshop you want included with your graphic (Figure 3.25).

That's it! Now you created some curved text for a graphic. You'll find that when you start using vector graphics tools, you'll start to rely on them for more creative approaches and better control for text in your graphics.

3.22

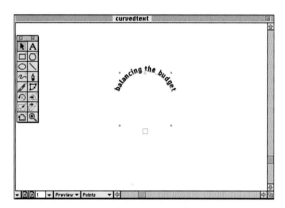

3.24

3.25

3.23

3.22 The curved text on Inform.

3.23 Creating the text in FreeHand.

3.24 Attaching the text to the path.

3.25 Importing the text into Photoshop.

CASE STUDY:

GEORGE ARRIOLA, MACROMEDIA

With an extensive design and film background both in the United States and Japan combined with his singular ability for creating great type, George Arriola and the Macromedia Web team were awarded the 1997 Communication Arts Award for "Best Business Web Site." Arriola is currently an executive producer at MetaDesign San Francisco, but his many years at Macromedia allowed him to experiment with his most innovative design concepts for the Web.

While at Macromedia, Arriola did dual duties as the Japanese Web development manager as well as senior designer/information architect. His concept for the site navigation (Figure 3.26) was intricate in its inception. The modular navigation was created entirely in Macromedia FreeHand for accurate and crisp text. "I wanted the navigation to be easily scalable and at the same time aesthetically pleasing," Arriola remembers. "I chose 'plug-ins' as a metaphor for my concept which would allow each part/section/word to be an interlocking object with one another. I initially found myself drawing my inspiration from many of Neville Brody's previous works." (Neville Brody designed Macromedia's new corporate identity.)

So why did Arriola use FreeHand? "I choose to work within a vector graphics tool because of typography. I have more precise control over the way I want my text to look and feel," admits Arriola. "When you use a tool like FreeHand to lay your type, outline it, and then bring it into Photoshop, you can achieve better legibility." When comparing FreeHand with Photoshop text side by side (Figure 3.27), you can see the visual difference Arriola is talking about.

Here are some of the steps Arriola used to create the navigation graphic. Using a template for each different navigation piece, he first entered each navigation line and adjusted the pill to fit the newly entered text (see Figure 3.28). Next he adjusted the kerning that varied from word to word. The words were set up so that they aligned within the navigation pill. The font size is set to 12, but in some cases, he took it down to 8. Text-leading also varied depending upon word length (see Figure 3.29).

After all the navigation text was layed out in FreeHand, Arriola then outlined the text and pasted it into Photoshop as a paths layer (see Figure 3.30). By selecting the paths layer, he double-clicked the layer to turn it into a savable Work Path layer. Then

by using the Direct Selection tool, the paths of the text just brought into Photoshop were selected. Arriola then changed the foreground color to what the text color should be. He then applied the color to the selected paths using the Paths/Fills Path with Foreground Color button.

Next by choosing to view rulers, he dragged guides out to align under the text. These guides were eventually used with the Pen tool to add section color hyperlink lines (see Figure 3.31).

With the curved lines, pill shape, and superb text, George Arriola has created not only a textual work of art but a navigational one as well.

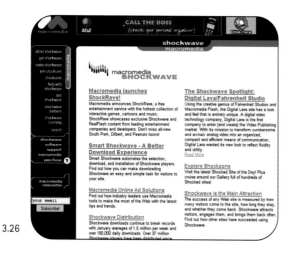

3.26

3.27

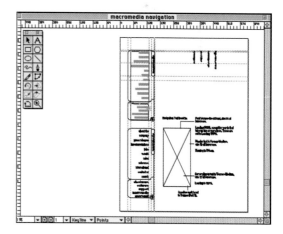

3.28

3.26 The modular navigation on macromedia.com.

3.27 A comparison: type differences in Photoshop and FreeHand.

3.28 The FreeHand template includes everything for creating the navigation for the four main areas of the site.

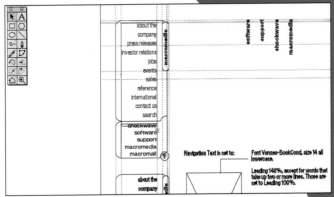

3.29

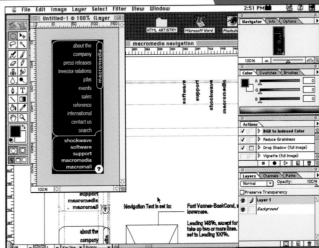

3.30

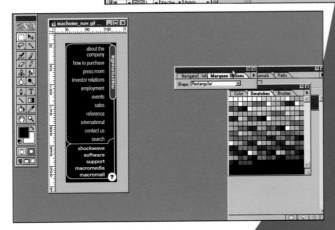

3.31

3.29 Modifying the text in FreeHand.

3.30 Copying paths to Photoshop.

3.31 The final navigation graphic.

Creating Embedded Fonts

How great would it be to have your HTML text displayed in whatever font you want regardless of whether your users have it? Well, the time is here for embedded fonts!

Although it's still relatively new and not yet widely used due to the two different standards proposed by Netscape and Microsoft, designers will soon find that embedded fonts will solve one of the major type problems on the Web: font variety.

This section focuses on introducing the two methods for embedding fonts as proposed by Netscape and Microsoft. We'll show you how to create the fonts and include them in your HTML pages. For more on designing with embedded fonts, see Chapter 7, " Cascading Style Sheets: Typography Made Simple."

Microsoft's Embedded Fonts

Microsoft has some of the most detailed instructions on how to create embedded fonts on its typography site (www.microsoft.com/typography). By downloading the free *Web Embedding Fonts Tool* (WEFT) from its site, you can include any font you want on your Web site.

WEFT is easy to use with a built-in wizard that helps guide you through the embedding process. Before you begin to embed your font, first design and create your HTML page. Then specify which fonts you want to use with the familiar <FONT FACE> tag or specify them within a style sheet rule.

We'll work with something simple first in this section, such as this HTML text header (Figure 3.32).

We'd like to display it with the Platelet fonts so add the FONT FACE name in the HTML.

```
<FONT SIZE="6" FACE="Platelet">HTML Artistry:
More Than Code</FONT>
```

Upload your HTML document to your site and start up the WEFT application to begin the embedding. You'll be prompted to enter the URL of the HTML document containing the font you want to embed.

After you finish, proceed to the next screen to "Analyze Pages." Click this button and you receive a list of the fonts of your Web page. This list lets you know whether your font is okay to embed. Highlight and choose not to embed Times New Roman.

Next chose the ftp path to where the embedded font will live (Figure 3.35). You must display the full path including the closing forward slash, /.

```
file:///c:/website/avantmedia/fonts/
ftp://ftp.avantmedia.com/fonts/
```

After you chose the path, click Create to start the embedding process. You'll be notified during the process if there is an error and when the process is complete. Figure 3.36 shows the final embedded font example as displayed in Platelet.

You can create more advanced techniques, such as the "Healthy Eating Recipes" (Figure 3.37) that's included on the Microsoft Embedded Fonts Gallery.

Netscape's Dynamic Fonts

Netscape also has a lot of information on its embedded font technique called "dynamic fonts." Using a new technology called TrueDoc, the font embedding is supposed to provide a secure way to transfer font data information (www.bitstream.com/world/dynamic.htm). You'll find that the fonts displayed with dynamic fonts (Figure 3.38) are much like Microsoft's embedded fonts, and you can include them in your HTML in the same manner with the <FONT FACE> tag and within style sheet rules.

The tool used to create dynamic fonts is called HexWeb Typograph, now on version 2.0 (Figure 3.39). It's available from the HexMac Web site (www.hexmac.com) for both Mac and Windows. The only difference from the Microsoft tool is that this one isn't free and costs approximately $129–145.

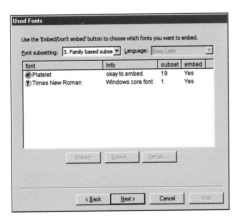

3.32

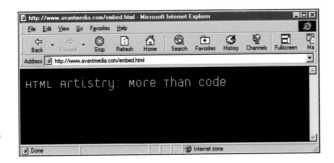

3.33

3.34

3.35

3.36

3.32   A simple HTML text header.

3.33   Entering in the URL.

3.34   The font list display.

3.35   Entering your ftp path.

3.36   HTML text displayed in the embedded font Platelet.

The results you find allow you to create stunning Web pages where you can included any font you want, such as the Stockwatch demo (Figure 3.40) on the Netscape site (`home.netscape.com/comprod/products/communicator/fonts/index.html`).

Chapter Summary

Although typography on the Web is still in its infancy, it is finally gaining some momentum. We aren't quite there yet, but from what's brewing now, there's plenty of hope for the future. Netscape and Internet Explorer both have their own embedded font standards, but hopefully there should be a resolution for one standard on the horizon.

No matter what text treatment you choose to use, don't think that you are limited by the options provided by HTML. With combinations of font color, size, type, and working with lists, you can successfully achieve some different techniques that definitely enhance your Web pages. If you do feel a bit limited in terms of design, go on to Chapter 7 where we'll discuss style sheets and show more examples of typography for the 4.0 browsers.

3.37

3.38

Bitstream Chianti Extra Bold in a Headline *
*Bitstream Cataneo in a Headline ***
Typical Typeface in an H2 Head

3.37 Healthy Eating Recipes created with embedded fonts.

3.38 Dynamic font displays.

Cross-Browser and Platform Comparison Guide

Property	Browser	Platform	Support
Font Size, Color, HTML Type	Netscape 3,4	Macintosh	Yes
	Netscape 3,4	Windows	Yes
	Internet Explorer 4	Windows	Yes
	Internet Explorer 4	Macintosh	Yes
System Typefaces (according to platform)	Netscape 3,4	Macintosh	Yes
	Netscape 3	Windows	Yes
	Netscape 4	Windows	Yes
	Internet Explorer 4	Windows	Yes
	Internet Explorer 4	Macintosh	Yes
Inline Font Styles	Netscape 3	Macintosh	No
	Netscape 3,	Windows	No
	Netscape 4	Macintosh	Yes
	Netscape 4	Windows	Yes
	Internet Explorer 3,4	Windows	Yes
	Internet Explorer 3,4	Macintosh	Yes
Text Color Change Rollovers	Netscape 3	Macintosh	No
	Netscape 3	Windows	No
	Netscape 4	Macintosh	Yes
	Netscape 4	Windows	Yes
	Internet Explorer 3	Windows	No
	Internet Explorer 3	Macintosh	No
	Internet Explorer 4	Windows	Yes
	Internet Explorer 4	Macintosh	Yes
Embedded/Dynamic Fonts (for IE and Netscape respectively)	Netscape 3	Macintosh	No
	Netscape 3	Windows	No
	Netscape 4	Macintosh	Yes
	Netscape 4	Windows	Yes
	Internet Explorer 3	Windows	No
	Internet Explorer 3	Macintosh	No
	Internet Explorer 4	Windows	Yes
	Internet Explorer 4	Macintosh	Yes

URLs in This Chapter

- Dynamic HTML Zone: http://www.dhtmlzone.com
- HexWeb: http://www.hexmac.com
- Inform: http://www.rankit.com/cgi-bin/bestguml/Inform/main.html
- Macromedia: http://www.macromedia.com
- Microsoft Embedded Fonts Gallery: http://www.microsoft.com/typography/web/embedding/default.htm
- Microsoft Typography: http://www.microsoft.com/typography
- Netscape Dynamic Fonts Resources: http://developer.netscape.com/library/documentation/htmlguid/dynamic_resources.html#fonts
- stock watch demo: http://home.netscape.com/comprod/products/communicator/fonts/index.html
- True Doc Info: http://www.bitstream.com/world/dynamic.htm
- True Type Typography: http://www.truetype.demon.co.uk/
- Typographic: http://www.rsub.com/typo/index0.cgi

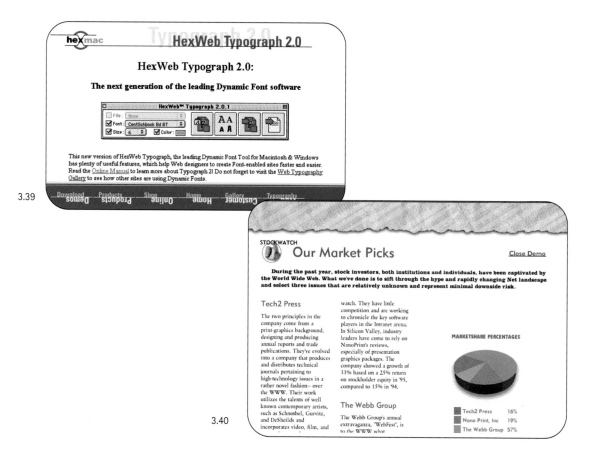

3.39

3.40

3.39   HexWeb Typograph 2.0.

3.40   Netscape's Stockwatch demo used dynamic fonts.

INSPIRATIONAL DESIGN MODEL:
Terry Green and Nori-Zso Tolson, twenty2product

For some of the most insightful and intricate ways to look at type, Terry Green at twenty2product (www.twenty2.com) is your man. Green and partner Nori-Zso Tolson design not only some of the slickest motion graphics for clients such as Nike, Hewlett-Packard, and NEC but also some of the coolest Web interfaces. With ten years of experience under their belts, Green and Tolson combine their traditional design school backgrounds with the fast, technologically advanced world of motion graphics and Web design.

Details mean a lot to Green. He works on building elements for his projects—things such as shapes, forms, or letters that will inspire the project as a whole. But instead of getting lost in a sea of elements, Green has the ability to bridge them and take them to the next level. From the hexagon shape element of the NEC Web site to the cool moving type in a Nike demo video, Green's design eye is always on the lookout for creative and innovative techniques.

But the most interesting thing about Green is his attention to perfection in creating type. Never before had we seen or heard anything like what Green does. He sees things that other designers in his situation would dismiss and say, "Well, you can't do that." But Green knows he can and he has found ways of doing it. It's no surprise that Green has built a reputation as the man to talk to about typography.

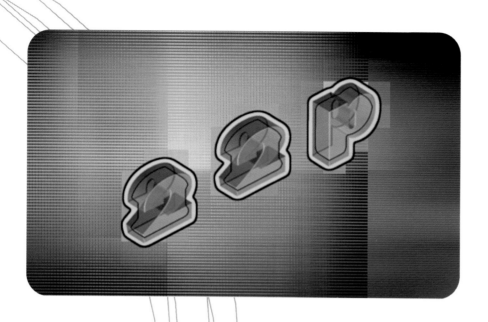

4.3

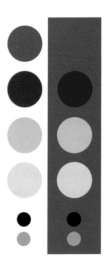

4.3   A warm color palette shared throughout the Qpid
        site in honor of Valentine's Day.

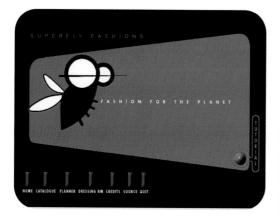

4.4

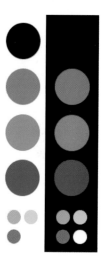

4.4   Using bold and bright colors to support the fun
and somewhat crazy content of the SuperFly
Fashions Web site.

Hence, the object's color behaves a certain way depending upon its surrounding color. What appears to be bright and bold on a black background might conversely appear dull and muted on a white background. Remember, that white added to a color diminishes its saturation.

Painters use this juxtaposition of color not just to create other colors but on a larger scale to create dimension and depth of field in their works. If they want something to appear in the foreground of a painting, they apply specific colors to create that effect (see Figure 4.6). In this still life piece, the white spoon appears closest to the viewer against the dark backdrop of the table, metal pot, and wall. Notice how the second spoon recedes from the foreground because of how similar its hue and value are similar to the background. A photographer might illustrate dimension by working with light and shadows—chiaroscuro (see Figure 4.7). Makeup artists use these notions of color to emphasize or de-emphasize a person's facial features, and so on. How does this apply to you, the Web designer, other than the realm of creating graphics? Through color, you can emphasize or accentuate certain parts of a Web page. Read on.

How Color Applies to a Web Interface

Color plays a significant role in the Web sites that you create. It possesses the power to bring out the images or perhaps words that need emphasis while unifying the entire aesthetic of the page. What are the different elements of a Web site and how do they relate to color? Let's break it down by looking at an individual page:

- **Background**: The backdrop or canvas against which all content and information appears.
- **Textual content**: The written words that relay information, news, stories, and so on.
- **Graphical content**: The images that either support the main content of the site or serve as the purpose of the site.
- **Navigation**: The hypertext links or buttons that take the user from one page to another.

Coloring these distinct elements with the exact same color renders them invisible! (Not very practical or interesting from a design standpoint. Perhaps from a philosophical one?) Each element must bear a different color specific to its function; together, they must belong to a cohesive family of colors, otherwise known as a color palette. We recommend using a limited number of colors—five to seven main colors—to best achieve a visual balance between them. Remember that color is its own noticeable design element on a page. The more colors you add, the more chaotic and confusing the information appears. (It's another story if that's your intention.) And remember, that just as in paintings or photographs, colors juxtaposed against each other on a Web page might create unexpected and unintended effects.

How do you pick colors for your Web sites? Start with a list of adjectives describing emotions and styles related to the content of the site. As discussed earlier in this chapter, emotions or ideas are clearly associated with color. Consider for a moment the two watercolors of the exact same crab. Although the one in Figure 4.8 seems to be a bright and cheerful illustration, the other in Figure 4.9, presents the crab as a dark, grubby, scum-sucking crustacean from the bottom of the sea. Same drawing. Different colors. Different emotions. The same concept holds true for a Web site.

4.5

4.6

4.7

4.5 Which appears closer? The red sphere or the blue one?

4.6 Light objects seem to immerge from a dark canvas.

4.7 Creating dimension and depth with light and dark values.

4.21

4.22

4.23

4.21 An adaption of the same spotlight element in a different section.

4.22 To accentuate the dark look of the site, Akimbo downplayed the contrast between the drawings and the background by creating simple, red line art set over a deep red background.

4.23 The navigation always looks the same, except for the active link color when the text link is clicked.

Besides, by using a limited number of colors, we can push ourselves and teach ourselves to focus on design and avoid superfluous decorations of color and applications of technology for the sake of technology.

This brings us to this chapter's case study about color treatments that are so simple and effective that you only need to know how to apply hexadecimal values to their HTML code. The magic of these designs lies simply in the background colors.

Note:

Some technical information is available concerning such topics as adjusting the gamma level of your monitor to achieve the optimal color results in designing Web graphics. We encourage you to check out a well-written article, "It's the Difference That Makes the Difference!" by Joe Gillespie, located at http://www.highfive.com/feature/past/feature_07.97.html and of course, our companion Web site at http://www.htmlartistry.com/ that contains updated links to other resources.

4.24

4.24 How the navigation is set apart, yet blended with the interface of the site through color.

CASE STUDY:
JOANIE MCCOLLOM,
BARBELL DESIGN

The San Francisco studio, Barbell Design, demonstrates that simplicity and elegance in design go a long way. We have been keeping tabs on Team Barbell since they burst onto the Web designing scene three years ago. Driven by their experiences in fashion, music, and writing, this design collective expresses a sharp wit and unmistakable personality in their work, which ranges from 'zines and local bands to major research institutes and corporations. The latest version of their site caught our attention simply for their use of color—solid background colors to be specific. We spoke with founding member, designer and site architect, Joanie McCollom, and asked her what kind of role color plays in Barbell's Web site designs.

"Color is one of our primary concerns because of its central role in establishing a look and feel as well as providing a good user experience. Bottom line: we want users to feel comfortable and confident when they visit the site, and we want them to return."

Indeed, Barbell has McCollom's flair for layout, fun illustrations, and sense for color to thank for these playful and carefully designed environments. These elements certainly reflect the team's easy-going and friendly attitude about the business. The Web site proclaims that Barbell strives to "provide quality, innovative Web sites that people can afford. Not a bad plan...." The team members work in an environment that fosters collaboration between each other and with their clients and finding solid design solutions within the capabilities of HTML rather than filling every available pixel on a Web page with the Web technology of the moment.

Space is exactly what makes the Barbell Web site striking and impressive. With an economy of text and images, McCollom designed a site that enables the backgrounds, and therefore the colors themselves, to play a role in the design. The use of solid background colors accentuates the expanse of the space. The visitor can see a harmony between all the elements on the page.

The home page greets the visitor with playful illustrations, text, and links carefully laid out within two HTML frames (see Figure 4.25). The combination of black, white, warm grays, and a slate blue give the Barbell Design home page a clean, simple, professional, yet subdued, gentle, and approachable feel as well.

Surveying the different pages, side by side, there does not seem to be an apparent cohesion between the colors. The colors range from light to dark to warm to cool. From the deep blue of the home page to the white of the information section (see Figure 4.26) to the light green of services (see Figure 4.27) to the deep red of the projects section (see Figure 4.28), we couldn't quite figure out why we responded so strongly and quite positively to the site. We knew that the consistency of the layout made the site intuitive and flow in a natural manner from page to page, despite the fact that the background colors were changing so dramatically. McCollom somehow creates an unusual blend of calm, mellow colors and occasionally injects an element of surprise (see Figure 4.29). We asked McCollom how she goes about choosing a color scheme or palette for a Web site.

"For our own site, we began with my favorite colors! For clients' sites, we begin with their corporate colors, a target audience, or the message they're trying to convey. Then we choose Web-safe colors, which really limits the palette. We further limit the palette to about three colors a page. We're big on simplicity. We believe this highlights content.

We almost always use black text. It is extremely legible and suggests content. I reserve color for highlighting, links, or headers. This is where Barbell is conservative. We rarely use black backgrounds (although Barbell's main navigational frame has a black background!), but when we do, we go with white or light blue text. We tend to use rich colors—deep reds, blues, and oranges—offset by light green and white."

Call it personal preference; call it gut instinct. McCollom's sense of strong and perhaps unusual color combinations enhances the simple layouts and graphics used by Barbell Design. Her selections seem to be right on target because the studio's primary audience is "playful and somewhat unorthodox." Who better to design for than your own demographic!

Like most Web designers, McCollom tries to QA her designs on several platforms, focusing on a PC-based audience. She does, however, choose colors based on their appearance on both.

"This really limits my preferred palette to about ten colors.

I tend to use

These blues: 003366, 336699, and 6699CC; Also 000033 and 000066.

These reds: CC0000, 990000.

These greens: 99CC99, 669966.

This orange: FF99CC.

And, of course, 000000 & FFFFFF."

So, we encourage you to try out McCollom's favorite Web colors, but keep in mind that her designs are about the integration of colors into a strong layout. Interesting colors can only get you so far. And remember that good design is about discretion.

4.25

4.27

4.26

4.28

4.25   Barbell Design home page.

4.26   Barbell Information page.

4.27   Barbell Design Services page.

4.28   Barbell Design Projects page.

The only way you will know is with experimentation. As demonstrated by Barbell Design's Web site, crafted by Joanie McCollom, good design is the synthesis between compelling content, intuitive design, and expressive color. Color communicates the identity of the site or particular section. Color solidifies your design and keeps the information cohesive and consistent. If nothing else, you, too, can create a beautiful and expressive, yet functional, Web site with the use of background colors, simple graphics, carefully layed out with the textual content.

4.29

4.29   Barbell Design's color palette.

Chapter Summary

Working with only 216 colors serves not as a hindrance but a help. With the plethora of variables in designing Web sites, we embrace strict and specific parameters. We have yet to exhaust the possibilities of colors.

Whether dealing with HTML text, graphics, or background colors, focus on the content and select colors that strike a balance between each other, so as not to interfere with the site's message and content. Dealing with the concept of scale in layouts works the same way. Don't design a page full of text with each word set at the same point size because no clear message will come across. You would have no apparent thesis or headline message because each letter and word and sentence would be treated equally. Also, don't make the least significant item the biggest item. The bigger the element, the faster and more surely it will catch people's attention. The smaller the element, the more likely it will get lost in the background.

Likewise, choose the brighter, bolder, hotter colors for the items you want at the forefront. Choose light colors when the background is dark and vice versa. And select one or two accent colors to highlight the important elements of a page.

So far in this book, you learned about the psychology and human factors of integrating the issues of layouts, navigation, typography, and color to communicate in visual form compelling and useful content. As you might have guessed, hard-core discussions about functionality are coming up! The next chapter helps you create opportunities for enhanced dialogues with your audience through HTML. But before you go, don't forget to check out our companion Web site at http://www.htmlartistry.com/ to make use of our online resources for helping you select colors effectively for your Web site.

URLs in This Chapter

- Qpid Valentine Site (original): http://www.akimbodesign.com/qpid/
- Qpid Valentine Site (current): http://www.URL.com/
- SuperFly Fashions: http://www.dhtmlzone.com/tutorials/
- California Pizza Kitchen: http://www.cpk.com/
- The Replacement Killers: http://www.spe.sony.com/movies/replacementkillers/
- Elixir: http://www.dreamweaver.com/ (click on gallery)
- Barbell Design: http://www.barbell.com/
- HTML Artistry Companion Web Site: http://www.htmlartistry.com/

Cross-Browser and Platform Comparison Guide

Property	Browser	Platform	Support
Background colors	Netscape 3,4	Macintosh	Yes
	Netscape 3,4	Windows	Yes
	IE 4	Windows	Yes
	IE 4	Macintosh	Yes
Text, link, vlink, alink colors	Netscape 3,4	Macintosh	Yes
	Netscape 3,4	Windows	Yes
	IE 4	Windows	Yes
	IE 4	Macintosh	Yes
Font colors	Netscape 3, 4	Macintosh	Yes
	Netscape 3, 4	Windows	Yes
	IE 4	Windows	Yes
	IE 4	Macintosh	Yes
Table background colors	Netscape 3, 4	Macintosh	Yes
	Netscape 3, 4	Windows	Yes
	IE 4	Windows	Yes
	IE 4	Macintosh	Yes
English names for color values	Netscape 3, 4	Macintosh	Yes
	Netscape 3, 4	Windows	Yes
	IE 4	Windows	Yes
	IE 4	Macintosh	Yes

INSPIRATIONAL DESIGN MODEL:

Amy Franceschini, Future Farmers

Ever since we glimpsed the pages of Atlas Magazine (www.atlasmagazine. com/) three years ago, we have been bookmarking Amy Franceschini's work like there's no tomorrow. Our admiration has remained steadfast over the years in spite of all the new technologies and special HTML tricks. If she never updated her Web site, we would have tirelessly looked at the same things over and over again. In fact, we didn't realize until meeting with her that she didn't change Atlas for almost a year!

So, of course, Amy Franceschini was an obvious pick as an inspirational designer for us. Her designs—both print and digital—combine surprise and sweetness with daring and confidence. She draws from memories of yesterday and combines them with references to a today and a tomorrow that subsequently produce a unique other-worldliness quality. Undaunted by technological constraints, she manages to transform each project into a work of art.

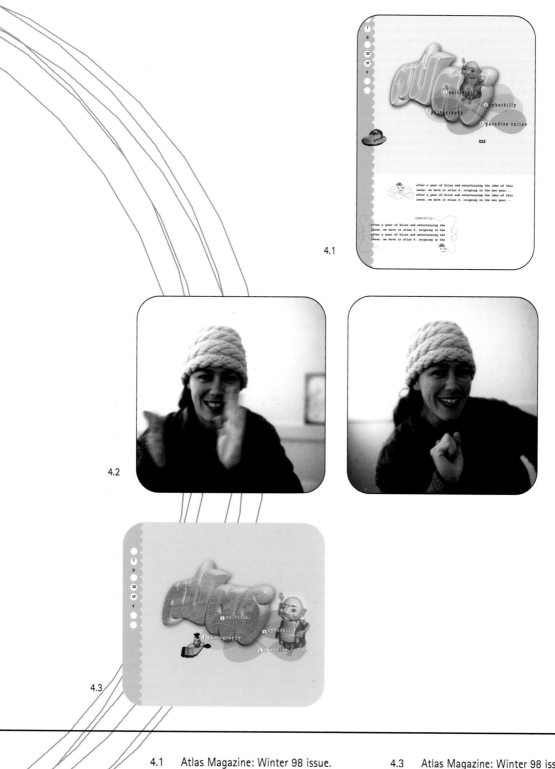

4.1

4.2

4.3

4.1   Atlas Magazine: Winter 98 issue.   4.3   Atlas Magazine: Winter 98 issue.

4.2   Amy Franceschini.

How did you get your start in design?

I studied photography and I wanted to be a photo-journalist. And I got a job at *Photo Metro* photography magazine. I always wanted to work there, and I wanted to get my work in there. So, I got an internship there. The whole magazine was designed and published on a computer. They used Quark and Photoshop, and I couldn't even print out a laser print! They hated me there! But I could type, so they kept me on because I could type pretty fast, so I would transcribe all of the interviews. And in exchange for being an intern, they had Photoshop classes there, and I took a couple Photoshop classes and one Quark class. And then, I said, "Oh, I can do this!"

I already had a degree in art, in photography. So, I got a partial scholarship to CCAC (California College of Arts and Crafts). When I got there, I had all these visions in my head, but I didn't have the tools to make them. I wanted to make posters. My dream was to make public posters and paste them all over the town, and just put weird imagery in the midst of all this advertising. I went there with the intention of doing stuff like that and everyone was so into advertising in their dialogue, design lingo.... A lot of my teachers thought, "You're depressed. You're [screwed] up." We'd have a poster project and everyone else wanted to do Nike, and I wanted to do animal rights. I tried to address issues. To me, that's important, especially in design. It's all about communicating ideas, and why not have it be an educational idea?

When I was there, I was really frustrated because they're really into concept and I spent two years at an art school learning all about concept. I was ready to just learn some tools and techniques. So, I quit and I got a job at this service bureau, and I was like, "I'll do anything! I'll sweep floors. I just want to learn how to use a computer." And then, I learned how to do all the print stuff. The whole offset thing. I learned a lot.

Then I got a job with Post Tool Design for about six to eight months and I learned a lot about interactive media because I had only done print stuff. And we did a couple of interactive pieces.

Then, I did Atlas! Oh yeah! I met Olivier, my partner, at this party, and he came up to me and said, "What do you want to do? What do you want to do with your life?" I didn't even know this guy. "I want to be a photojournalist." And he says, "No, you don't." I didn't know that he himself was a photojournalist. We started talking. He and this friend had this idea to do Atlas, this forum, this online showcase of design and illustration. He asked me to design it. So I did it and I had never seen a Web site before.

So how did you do that? You said you had never seen a Web site before?

Well I had done interactive stuff; we had done CD-ROMs for music. I had helped Post Tool do interactive press kits for bands. We did the kiosks for the Rock-n-Roll Hall of Fame. So, I knew how things worked in an interactive, linear way, but I didn't really understand the concept of a Web site. But I just thought of it as a CD-ROM, and so we did this first issue, but I don't know why, but we entered it in CA (*Communication Arts*) and *Wired* wrote up a little blurb about it, and it just got a lot of publicity and got a lot of hype.

Can you describe how you come up with an image or an idea and how you translate it to a particular medium?

With *Atlas*, it's different because I'm not really thinking of information design, a certain way of navigating through things in a grid fashion. I'm just thinking more about giving each section of our Web site an identity, and having the pieces within that section relate to each other and create its own dialogue but with a flavor for each section. Right now, I'm working on the photography section and this is the same way I worked on the initial issue. Say there are four photographers and they're all doing photojournalistic stories. They're all photographers and I want to use the navigation in a more imagery-based way rather than just buttons, so I want to combine elements. How I usually think about it is creating one structure that kind of weaves together and placing the images within that. And I like using imagery in my pieces. Whenever I go to the Web, it's like "Ah!" (*horrified scream*) squares and buttons.

How do you know when you're finished?

Deadlines! (*laughs*) That's the only thing. I am really bad. I've been working on my own site. And I'll work for a week and create 20 home pages and none of them are right. And the only thing that makes me get things right is the fact that I have to post it at this time. It's the only thing. And I still don't feel that it's right, and then once it goes up and I go, "Oh, it's finished!"

So how much of what you do is dictated by something academic? Something you've learned or intuition?

4.4

4.5

4.6

4.4 Atlas Magazine: Cyberbilly main page.

4.5 Atlas Magazine: Photography main page.

4.6 Printed calendar for Future Farmers.

I think a lot of it is dictated by my childhood. I don't read very much. I've been learning a lot on the Web, and I've been researching biotechnology and I'm interested in that. It stems from my childhood, growing up on a farm. I read about organic farming, just a lot about farming, and I've learned about physics and chemistry from that and I think that gets into my work somehow. I grew up on a commercial farm. My mom was an organic farmer. Those two dynamics have totally shaped my vision. Plus, my mom was married by an Indian swami, so I've been inundated by Indian imagery. I used to hate it as a kid. "Why can't you have normal pictures on the wall?" But it comes back.

How do you reconcile creating something that is of you for corporate clients? Do clients seek you out because you are who you are, and they want something very Amy Franceschini?

They say they are but they're not! I think of projects differently than others. I think of commercial projects like math. I just break it down like a calculus problem. I used to love calculus. There's always an answer.

What is the answer?

I just did AutoDesk's Web site, coming up with a main element that's not just a button or a box. When you go to a home page, it's all there. Everything you're going to see is there. And then when you go to another page, it's a piece of what you've already seen, even if it's a color or a shape that translates into that page. I think that's important. I like to figure that out, how it's going to work.

How does technology come into play in your work?

I want to say that it doesn't dictate my work, but my lack of knowledge of technology does dictate my work. This month, I've taken a lot of time to learning Director more, and Java and Dreamweaver—doing more of what's available to me. Because if you don't, it's kind of like a cop-out. It's so easy to learn, really. I think things become more interesting the more technology you know. You can tell a story a million different ways, in different levels. And, people like to be talked to on different levels. They like to have

subtext and refer. Knowing technology allows you to do that.

How about in print?

The technology doesn't dictate my work in that respect because I like old techniques like die-cutting and perforation. It's not like technology has really changed print. It's more about paper and what you can put on the paper. I just use three tools to create anything in print: Photoshop, Illustrator, and Infini-D, a 3D program.

Do you prefer any medium over another?

That's hard. I love print, and if I had to do one thing, I would do print, but it's so time-consuming. I like to do it all myself. I like to get it all perfect. I like to get this spot color and this overlay. I like to get into the production. It's super time-consuming.

Getting back to the idea of presenting your ideas to corporate clients...looking at your work, it doesn't look like you compromised your art or your design. What other qualities (other than design skills) do you find make you a good designer, especially when working with corporate clients? Is it being a salesperson of your work?

I never thought of being a designer as being a salesperson until I went to work for an ad agency, and I saw how they presented their work. It's a sales pitch! I never knew that. And, I was sickened by that! And they'd even say, "We have to *sell* this idea." And, I'd think, "Ugh! What? That's sick." With one project in particular, it got down to this ugly square thing that I would especially never want to show in my portfolio. It got down to two sketches: one was exactly what they wanted and one was a little better. They wanted one that was like everyone else's Web site, but even worse! I just said, "Okay. I have to defend myself here." So I stood up and said, "Listen. You hired me because I showed you my work. I showed you my portfolio. I showed you the sites. And this is nothing of the sorts. And you hired me because I have knowledge of pushing technology. And if you can't support a Java rollover, then I don't want to finish this project." I had to really defend myself to get in there. And the guy called me after I got back and said, "That's so great! You put them in their place." They went for the one, and it's great. It's up.

Then I realized that what they're hiring me for is for an opinion really. If you're going to just let them push you around, they'll push you around. But if you stand up and say, "Listen. I'm defining what's good and bad. That's what you hired me for," in an eloquent way, which is not what I did, but it worked! Yeah, I think that always being confident that you can solve a problem even though you can't. You never want to say "no" in a meeting. Come up with a solution within your boundaries.

How do you choose your projects? I would never guess that corporate clients like AutoDesk, NEC, or Microsoft, and so on would be up your alley.

I kind of take it as a challenge. I like dipping into different subcultures. It's so cool to go there and see who works there. It's kind of like photojournalism. And also, it feeds me. So I can do work like *Atlas*.

How do you come up with new ideas? Do you keep a sketchbook?

I keep a mental sketchbook. I'm a geek in that I use the computer a lot. I'll sit there and do pattern pattern pattern, shape shape shape. My stepdad published a magazine in the '80s called *Cauldron*. And so we got piles of art in the mail every day. There's amazing stuff! I used to go to the post office and get stacks of stuff and go through all of it and go Wow! Wow! Wow!

People are inspirational to me. To see their accomplishments are inspirational. I seem to surround myself with people, not just Web people, but people who are doing a lot.

I think travel, too. I'm really into hedges right now. I just like these biomorphic shapes.... Then I took pictures of these mattresses. The patterns on the mattresses were really ugly, but I like the flowers. They're beautiful. Elements you can find in trash. I'll totally use that!

Is there ever a point where you feel you run out of ideas?

I go through phases. For producing my own work, I feel like I have a bank that's endless. I go through times when I feel like I'm so burnt out! So burnt out on design. Then I go on a trip and want to be back so bad that I'll want to make stuff.

CHAPTER 5
ADDING SOPHISTICATION AND INTERACTIVITY WITH HTML AND JAVASCRIPT

Visitors will arrive at your site with all sorts of personal quirks, idiosyncrasies, and computer configurations. JavaScript enables you to interact with visitors and to dynamically redesign the site on the basis of what they tell you. You wouldn't sell short pants to a tall guy or serve flounder to someone who hates the smell of fish. Likewise, there is no reason why you should serve the same Web site to every visitor.

This chapter presents many compelling JavaScript techniques that help you develop an artificially intelligent site—a site that responds to individual characteristics. Although it might seem like you need a computer science degree to get through this chapter, the code is actually quite simple. The difficult part involves deciding how to use the code to create smart designs.

Understanding VBScript and JavaScript

Before diving into JavaScript, we should say a word about another well-known scripting language—VBScript. The story begins when Netscape developed JavaScript to aid developers in controlling the elements on a Web page. JavaScript enabled developers to validate forms, set cookies, dynamically switch images, and a whole lot more. Microsoft thought JavaScript was a pretty neat idea, so they came up with VBScript—a proprietary language that can do the same things as JavaScript. They based this language on a familiar (at least to programmers) and older language called Visual Basic. In our humble opinion, the language has little value, as it can be understood only by Internet Explorer 3.0+. Recognizing its limited appeal to Web developers, Microsoft also released a language called JScript, which is essentially Microsoft's version of JavaScript. Luckily, you don't have to do anything for Internet Explorer to understand standard JavaScript.

Controlling the Presentation of Your Site

Although the majority of techniques in this chapter make intelligent use of user information, the first three techniques use more of a brute force approach to customizing the user's experience. They employ JavaScript to reduce the number of variables that you have to deal with when designing a site. By eliminating unknown factors such as window size, browser button visibility, and when images load, you can ensure that your design looks the same and functions reliably across many different browsers and configurations. You don't have to ask yourself questions such as "What happens to my design when the user resizes the window?" or "If the user displays the Location bar, toolbar, and directory buttons, can they still see the bottom of my page?" By using JavaScript, you can configure the user's browser environment to function as you like it.

Opening Browser Windows

To eliminate many unknown factors, you can launch your site in a new browser window. A simple JavaScript routine enables you to open a window of any size and to preset many factors such as scrolling, resizing, and window-option visibility. You can use this window to simply display content or to serve a specific purpose such as a floating navigational bar, as described in "Floating the Navigational Window." later in this chapter. In terms of displaying content, we use this technique quite frequently for our dynamic HTML sites where a kiosk-like presentation would be more effective (see Figure 5.1.). The next section of the book explains the specifics of coding DHTML sites; but for now, without setting the browser window size for these DHTML sites, you would have to create enormous graphical masks to hide some of the layers placed offscreen for animation purposes.

The following code shows how to launch a new window from a normal HTML page. We recommend including information about the window to be launched. For the Replacement Killers site, we made a notation that the launched window was optimized for a 800×600 pixel size window (see Figure 5.2).

```
<HTML>
        <HEAD>
                        <TITLE>window example
</TITLE>
<SCRIPT LANGUAGE="JavaScript">
function launch(){

newWind=window.open("intro.html","newWindow",
"status=yes,toolbar=no,resizable=no,scroll-
bars=no,width=200,height=200")
}
</SCRIPT>
        </HEAD>
<BODY>
<a href="javascript:launch()">launch
window</a>
</BODY>
</HTML>
```

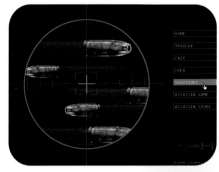
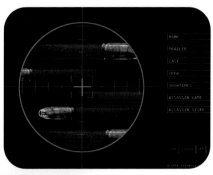

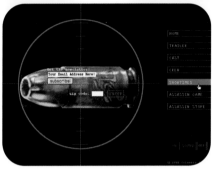

5.1   Opening a window to create a kiosk-like presenta-
        tion.

5.2   Simple HTML page to launch a new window.

This code consists of a page with a link on it. When you click the link, the `launch()` function is called and a small window pops up (see Figure 5.3).

The intro.html file loads within the window. The window itself will be called newWindow and will display a status bar. It will not display a toolbar or scrollbars, however, and it will not be resizable. To customize the code to your needs, you can change any of the parameters. There are also a few more options that you can add to the parameter list:

```
toolbar[=yes|no]
location[=yes|no]
directories[=yes|no]
status[=yes|no]
menubar[=yes|no]
scrollbars[=yes|no]
resizable[=yes|no]
width=pixels
height=pixels
```

The *toolbar* consists of the buttons that include Back and Forward buttons. *Location* is the field that displays the current URL. *Directories* are those Netscape buttons that say People, Search, and so on. The *status* bar is the strip at the bottom of the browser that lets the user know what is loading and from where. We usually set this option to yes because it's quite reassuring to see the progress of a page as it loads. The *menubar* is the list of options at the top of the browser such as File, Edit, View, and so on. If you set *scrollbars* to no, the new window will never display scrollbars, even if the content goes beyond the visible edges of the window. The *resizable* option, when set to no, prevents the user from resizing the window. Finally, the *width* and *height* options determine the dimensions of the new window.

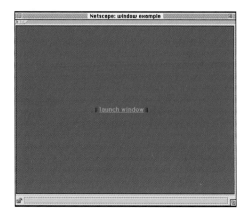

5.3

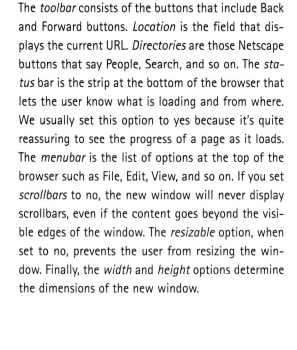

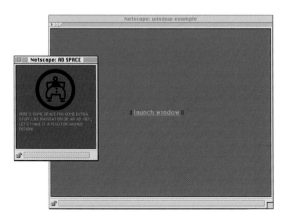

5.3   Simplified version of the pop-window example.

Floating the Navigational Window

One useful application of opening special browser windows is creating a floating navigational window. Bringing your site's navigational elements to a new window frees up each page for content and also provides a distinct, unmistakable place for the site links—a sort of remote control. For instance, you can use this technique if you want to look at a series of pages. Instead of implementing a navigational bar that might distract the viewer's attention from the content on the page, you can create a floating navigational window. In Figure 5.4, a floating navigational window flips between different storyboards.

It's a pretty straightforward task, but to properly target the main window, you need to add a few special lines to your code. Here's an example of the floating navigational window code:

```
<HTML>
<HEAD><TITLE> launcher page </TITLE>
<SCRIPT LANGUAGE="JavaScript">
function launch(){
     window.name="mywin";
     newWind=window.open("floatingNav.html",
"newWindow","toolbar=no,scrollbars=no,
width=200,height=200")
}
</SCRIPT>
</HEAD>
<BODY>
<A HREF="JavaScript:launch()">Launch
Navigation Window</A><BR>
</BODY>
</HTML>

Code for the Navigational Page:
<HTML>
<HEAD><TITLE> nav </TITLE></HEAD>
<BODY bgcolor="#999966" text="#FFFFFF"
link="#333300" vlink="#333366"
alink="#000000">
 [ PROJECT IDEAS: ]

<p>

<b><A HREF="01.html" target="mywin">Example
1</A></b><BR>
<b><A HREF="02.html" target="mywin">Example
2</A></b><BR>
<b><A HREF="03.html" target="mywin">Example
3</A></b>
 </BODY>
</HTML>
```

You might have noticed that there is an extra line in the `launch()` function:

```
window.name="mywin"
```

This line gives a name to the main document (the page from which the new window is launched). Now that it has a name, it can be referred to by any other window.

Preloading Images

Left to its own devices, the browser downloads images as the user requests them. Often, especially in the case of rollovers, you'll want these images to load *before* the user requests them. Without this intelligent loading function, the user has to wait for the browser to retrieve the images when a rollover occurs and the delay looks like an error. By using JavaScript, you can build an intelligent preloading system that retrieves images and loads them into the cache before they are needed. Look at the following example code:

```
<html>
<head><title>image preload</title>
<script language="JavaScript">
     homeRoll=new Image();
     menuRoll=new Image();
      homeOrig=new Image();
     menuOrig=new Image();
     homeRoll.src="chap5_ex3Roll1.gif";
     menuRoll.src="chap5_ex03Roll2.gif";
      homeOrig.src="chap5_ex3Orig1.gif";
     menuOrig.src="chap5_ex03Orig2.gif";
function doRollover(arrayNum,graphicName){
     document.images[arrayNum].src=eval
(graphicName+'Roll.src');
}
function doRestore(arrayNum,graphicName){
     document.images[arrayNum].src=eval
(graphicName+'Orig.src');
}
</script>
</head>
<body>
<a href="home.html" target="main"
onMouseOver="doRollover(0,'home')"
onMouseOut="doRestore(0,'home')">
<img src="chap5_ex3Orig1.gif" width="85"
height="85" border="0" name="home" alt="home
button"></a>
<a href="menu.html" target="main"
onMouseOver="doRollover(1,'menu')"
onMouseOut="doRestore(1,'menu')">
<img src="chap5_ex03Orig2.gif" width="70"
height="85" border="0" name="menu" alt="menu
button"></a>
</body>
</html>
```

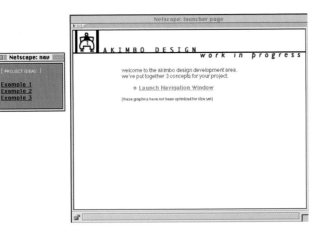

5.4

5.4   Using a floating navigational window to navigate
        between different pages.

The four lines of code immediately following the `<SCRIPT>` tag preload the rollover images into the cache. The line: `homeRoll=new Image();` defines a new image object. The line `homeRoll.src="assets/nav02b.gif"` sets this image object's source property. In English, this means that the browser goes and gets assets/nav02b.gif and loads it into the cache. Use this code to customize the browser's behavior to suit the needs of your design. Refer to Chapter 2, "Designing Intuitive Navigation," to learn more about rollover effects.

Knowing and Responding to Your Audience

The remaining techniques use a bit more finesse to dynamically shape your site according to each user's configuration and personal tastes. The first set of techniques utilizes built-in browser variables, and the second set of techniques enables you to customize your design by interacting with individual users and by tracking their habits.

Using Built-In Information

Each browser contains a host of information that describes the user's platform and the browser environment. You can use this information to customize your site to the user's particular configuration.

Detecting Browser Type

Not all browsers were created equal. Netscape offers many features that are unavailable in Internet Explorer and vice versa. Even when Netscape and Internet Explorer do offer the same functionality, they usually do it in different ways. If you want to offer additional features to users of a particular browser or if you just need to make a function work properly on both browsers, use a browser-type detection script.

For example, Internet Explorer supports a unique feature called Floating Frames. A *Floating Frame* is much like a standard frame, except that you can position it anywhere in your document just like an image. In Figure 5.5, the white box at the center of the page with the JPEG image and HTML text is a Floating Frame. Each time a user clicks on a photo link, this frame is the only area that reloads (see Figure 5.6).

A still image of the Netscape alternative would look exactly the same; however, the actual experience would differ substantially. Each time the user clicks on a photo link in the Netscape example, the entire frame (with the brown background) would have to reload. Floating Frames considerably expand the design possibilities, but, unfortunately, Netscape does not support them. Instead of tossing them out of the realm of possibility, you can detect the user's browser type and give a Floating Frames version of your document to Internet Explorer users and a standard page to Netscape users. The following code shows a browser type detection in action.

```
<HTML>
        <HEAD>
                        <TITLE>browser detect
example</TITLE>
        </HEAD>
<SCRIPT LANGUAGE="JavaScript">
document.write('<FRAMESET ROWS="70%,30%">');
if (navigator.appName == "Netscape") {
        document.write('        <FRAME SRC=
"standard_feature.html" NAME="feature"> ');
}else{
        document.write('        <FRAME SRC=
"floating_frames_feature.html" NAME=
"feature"> ');
}
document.write('        <FRAME SRC="nav.html"
NAME="navigation">');
</SCRIPT>
        <NOFRAMES>
                        No frames site.
        </NOFRAMES>
</FRAMESET>
</HTML>
```

This code writes a frameset to the screen. The JavaScript function dynamically writes the frameset according to the visitor's browser. If the visitor is using a Netscape browser, a page called standard_feature.html is placed in the top frame. Otherwise, a page called floating_frames_ feature.html is placed in the top frame. (See the companion Web site for the comparison at http://www.htmlartistry.com/.)

5.5

5.6

5.5   Floating Frames layout in Internet Explorer.

5.6   Implementing Floating Frames isolates reloading
       to small, specific areas of a page.

Detecting Browser Version

Netscape and Microsoft have made enormous strides in increasing the functionality of their browsers over the past several years. In Utopia, every visitor would have the newest browser version. Unfortunately (and understandably), many people have not invested the time to upgrade their browsers. Because some people still surf with limited browser capability, you should consider designing sites that accommodate these people. By detecting the browser version number, you can go a long way toward making everybody happy.

For example, since Netscape 3.0, it has been possible to implement some neat rollover effects (see Chapter 2). Without version detection, however, a rollover spits up dozens of JavaScript errors on older browsers. Some simple code can prevent these errors and the resulting visitor frustrations. Here's a sample rollover code with version protection:

```
<HTML>
<HEAD>
      <TITLE>simple rollover with version
detect</TITLE>
<SCRIPT LANGUAGE="JavaScript">
      var vers=
navigator.appVersion.charAt(0);
      if (vers >=3){
            homeRoll=new Image();
            homeOrig=new Image();
            homeRoll.src="buttonRoll.gif";
            homeOrig.src="buttonOrig.gif";
      }
function doRollover(arrayNum,graphicName){
      if (vers >=3){
            document.images[arrayNum].src=eval
(graphicName+'Roll.src');
      }
}
function doRestore(arrayNum,graphicName){
      if (vers >=3){
            document.images[arrayNum].src=eval
(graphicName+'Orig.src');
      }
}
</SCRIPT>
</HEAD>
<BODY>
<a href="home.html" target="main"
onMouseOver="doRollover(0,'home')"
onMouseOut="doRestore(0,'home')">
<img src="button.gif" width="85" height="85"
border="0" name="home" alt="button"></a>
</BODY>
</HTML>
```

This code prevents older browsers from attempting to run the rollover code. By preventing this action, visitors with older browsers will see a simple navigational button (see Figure 5.7) and will never know that newer browsers see a rollover effect (see Figure 5.8). For example, Akimbo Design wanted to liven up California Pizza Kitchen's Web site with navigational rollovers, but it did not want to alienate audiences without such capabilities.

The line that reads

```
var vers= navigator.appVersion.charAt(0);
```

assigns the built-in version number variable to a new variable called vers. If the visitor is using Netscape 2.0, vers will be set to 2. If the visitor is using IE3.0, vers will be set to 3 and so on.

All the other JavaScript code is prefaced by a line that reads

```
if (vers >=3){
```

This tells the browser to run the code only if the visitor is using a 3.0 or higher browser version. So when a visitor loads this page with Netscape 4.0, for example, she can use the rollover code, but if she is using Netscape 2.0, she won't see anything unusual.

Knowing this browser version detection technique helps you and your audience when you implement the enhanced dynamic HTML features (discussed in the next section of the book) available only on 4.0+ browsers.

Detecting Platforms

Differences exist not only between browser type and version but also between machines. In the recent past, browser development for the Macintosh platform has slowed compared with that of the PC. By using a platform detection function, you can take advantage of the advances in PC browser development without alienating approximately 10 percent of visitors who use the Macintosh.

While building The Replacement Killers Website (http://www.spe.sony.com/movies/replacementkillers/), we discovered that the Macintosh browser could not reliably support particular combinations of Dynamic HTML effects.

5.7

5.8

5.7   Standard version for older browsers.

5.8   Navigation with rollover effect.

The DHTML version of the cast section presented each cast member's information in an animation that simulated a marksperson surveying an area through a gun site. When the person's bio information was found, the image within the site would focus and "lock" on the image of the character and display the appropriate text (see Figure 5.9). (Due to copyright issues, we swapped Ardith's photo and name into the site interface to illustrate the concept.) Even when Macintosh users had 4.0 browsers, they would get error messages. We had already created two different versions of the site—a "classic" version and a DHTML version—so for Macintosh users, we used the platform detect function to feed them the classic page in lieu of the dynamic page, as shown in Figure 5.10.

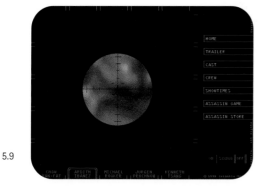

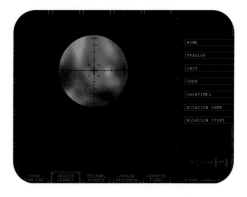

5.9

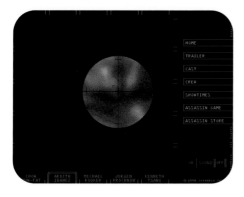

5.9   The animated DHTML version of the cast section.

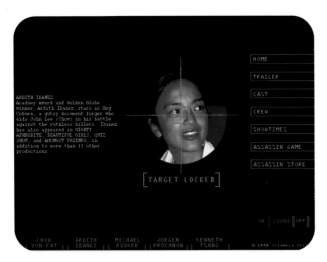

5.10

We condensed and simplified the code to illustrate the technique:

```
<HTML>
<HEAD>
      <TITLE>platform detection
example</TITLE>
<SCRIPT LANGUAGE="JavaScript">
      function routeUser(){
            if
(navigator.appVersion.indexOf("Mac") > 1){
                  location.href="mac_cast.
html";
            }else{
                  location.href="pc_cast.
html";
            }
      }
</SCRIPT>
</HEAD>
<BODY >
 <A HREF="trailer.html"
target="main">Trailer</A><BR>
 <A HREF="crew.html" target="main">>Crew
</A><BR>
 <A HREF="javascript:routeUser()"target=
"main">>Cast</A><BR>
</BODY>
</HTML>
```

This simple navigational page has three links on it. The first two are standard links. When the user clicks on the third link, however, it calls a JavaScript function called routeUser(). This function loads one page if the visitor is using a PC and another if using a Macintosh. You can use this code in many different situations to make sure that both Macintosh and PC visitors enjoy your work.

When combined, the browser type, browser version, and platform detection scripts enable very specific targeting. Although it requires a lot of time and effort, you can create different designs for every possible browser and platform combination from Netscape 2.0 for Macintosh to Internet Explorer 4.0 for Windows. To create a manageable and easy-to-update site, write browser or platform-specific code only when absolutely necessary.

5.10   The static, standard version of the cast section used for Macintosh users on both 3.0 and 4.0 browsers.

Using Date and Time

All browsers ship with a built-in function that returns the date and time on the user's system. Use this function to customize your site to each user's particular situation. For example, you can write a script that changes the site's color scheme and background image, depending on whether it is night or day in the user's location. At 4:30 p.m. PST, Californian visitors can see a bright-day design, while European visitors see a dark-night site. If you design a fashion Web site, the home page might present a sportswear outfit during the day (see Figure 5.11) and feature an evening gown ensemble at night (see Figure 5.12). You can do the same for a restaurant by spotlighting a lunchtime menu item during the day and a dinner item at night. Implementing this technique on a news Web site where timeliness and late-breaking news are crucial is especially important.

```
<HTML>
<HEAD><TITLE> date and time example </TITLE>
</HEAD>
<SCRIPT LANGUAGE="JavaScript">
var date="", time="", timeNum="", spaces=0,
colons=0;
var dateTimeString = new String (new
Date());
for (var i = 0; i < dateTimeString.length;
i++) {
     var letter=dateTimeString.charAt(i);
     if (letter == " "){spaces++}
     if (letter == ":"){colons++}
     if (spaces < 3){date+=letter}
     if (spaces == 3){time+=letter}
     if ((spaces == 3) &&
(colons==0)){timeNum+=letter}
}
if ((timeNum >= 20) ¦¦ (timeNum <=6))
{var night=1}
     if (night){
          document.write('<BODY
BGCOLOR="black" BACKGROUND="stars.gif"
TEXT="white">');
          document.write('Good night.
<BR>The time is ' +time+ ' and the date is '
+date);
     }else{
          document.write('<BODY
BGCOLOR="yellow" BACKGROUND="day.gif">');
          document.write('Good day. <BR>The
time is ' +time+ ' and the date is ' +date);
     }
</SCRIPT>
</BODY>
</HTML>
```

The code parses the date-time variable and then dynamically writes the <BODY> tag and a text greeting to the page. If it's between 8:00 p.m. and 6:00 a.m. in the visitor's region, he sees a page featuring a night design. Otherwise, he sees a day design.

The JavaScript code works as follows: The date-time variable is retrieved from the user's machine and parsed into three different variables. Date holds the current date, time holds the current time in military format (for example, 20:12:32), and timeNum holds just the first part of the military time (for example, 20). Without worrying about how the code works, you can use any of these variables to customize your page.

For example, you can create a version of your site for each month and then use the date variable to automatically switch versions when the month changes. There are also some useful built-in functions that enable you to extract data from the date object such as getMonth(), getDay(), and so forth. Again, you can apply these techniques to something like a news Web site. Look at Netscape's JavaScript user's manual for more information (http://home.netscape.com/eng/mozilla/3.0/handbook/javascript/index.html).

Note:

Beware of a bug in Netscape 3.x that causes unpredictable results when inserting a date within an HTML table. The browser will sometimes not recognize the script, and other times it will display the code!

5.11

5.12

5.11   Daytime version of a Web site.

5.12   Nighttime version of the same site.

Using the Cookie to Track Tastes, Preferences, and Patterns

The most sophisticated and customized sites keep detailed tabs on visitor tastes, preferences, and patterns. They use this data to dynamically customize their sites and to display ads based on each visitor's personality. Some companies such as Firefly (`http://www.firefly.com`) specialize exclusively in making back-end software that builds and manages user profiles. Believe it or not, you can use JavaScript to perform many of the same tracking tasks. Although not as refined as Firefly's software, these functions go a long way toward providing your site's visitors with a personalized Web experience.

The upcoming techniques rely on the *cookie*, which is a file that is stored in your browser directory. JavaScript can write to and retrieve data from this file over time. The code used to set and retrieve cookies is a bit complicated, so we won't go into detail about how it works. Instead, we will show you how to use it. You need to know two basic function: `GetCookie()` and `SetCookie()`. These functions are invoked in the following way:

```
GetCookie(name)
```

where `name` is the name of the cookie that you want to retrieve.

```
SetCookie (name,value,expires)
```

where `name` is the name that you use to refer to this cookie, `value` is the data that you want to put into the cookie, and `expires` is a date that specifies the time at which the cookie should be erased. In all the examples, we've hard-coded the date into the code and put a comment by the line with instructions regarding how to change the date.

The `GetCookie()` and `SetCookie()` functions were written by Bill Dortch of hIdaho Design. We came across his functions about a year ago and have been using them ever since! Bill recommends that you check out the latest version at: `http://www.hidaho.com/cookies/cookie.txt`. His notes describe the cookie functions in detail and also provide a few bug fixes for certain browser versions. You can also read about a few more optional parameters for `SetCookie()`.

Asking Questions

A simple and direct way to probe the user's predilections is to ask! Ask each user to answer a few questions relevant to your site, store the answers in the cookie, and from that point forth, use the data to customize your site to their tastes. For example, say that you manage a site that sells all kinds of clothing. You can ask visitors to choose their favorite type of clothing (sporty, formal, casual, and so on) and to specify their gender. Throughout their visit and when they return to your site at a later date, you can run ads for clothing that matches their gender and tastes.

The code for this example requires two pages. The first page asks the user to fill out a survey (see Figure 5.13).

The second uses a simple script to format itself according to the survey data. The user needs to fill out the survey only one time. After responding to the questions, the answers are stored in the cookie for one year. Here's the code for the survey:

```
<html>
<head>
<title>cookie questions example</title>
<script language="javascript">
//COOKIE FUNCTIONS REMOVED
</script>
</head>
<body>
Please specify your gender and favorite type
of clothes.<BR>
<form name="info">
<SELECT NAME="gender"
```

```
onChange="SetCookie('gender',this.options
[this.selectedIndex].text,expdate)">
<OPTION>Gender
<OPTION>Male
<OPTION>Female
</SELECT>
<SELECT NAME="clothes"
onChange="SetCookie('clothes',this.options
[this.selectedIndex].text,expdate)">
<OPTION>Clothes
<OPTION>Sporty
<OPTION>Formal
</SELECT>
<input type=button value="submit"
onClick="location.href='clothes_main.html'">
</form></body></html>
```

This page features two pull-down menus. When the user makes a selection, her choice is stored in the cookie by using the `SetCookie()` function. The cookie functions have been removed from the script to save space; you can access the complete code at the Web site (`http://www.htmlartistry.com/`). When the user clicks the Submit button, she is delivered to the site's main page called 'clothes _main.html'. Here is the code for this page:

```
<HTML>
        <HEAD>
                        <TITLE> clothes cookie main
page </TITLE>
<script language="javscript">
//COOKIE FUNCTIONS REMOVED
//function that picks proper ad, formats it,
and writes it.
    function writeAd(){
            var gender=GetCookie('gender');
            var clothes=GetCookie('clothes');
            if ((clothes != null) &&
(clothes != "Clothes")
                && (gender != null) &&
(gender != "Gender")){
                    document.write('<img
src=' + gender+clothes+'.gif
alt='+gender+clothes+'>');
            }else{
                    document.write('<img
src="defaultAd.gif" alt="default ad">');
            }
    }
</script>
</HEAD>
<BODY>
CLOTHES MAIN SITE<P>
<script language="JavaScript">
    writeAd();
</script>
</BODY></HTML>
```

As this page loads, it calls a function called `writeAd()`, which reads the data stored in the cookie. If the cookie has been properly set, it creates an appropriate image tag and writes it to the screen. For example, if Female and Sporty have been selected, it writes the following image tag:

```
<img src="FemaleSporty.gif"
alt="FemaleSporty">
```

You can use this image to showcase sporty female sale items or to advertise another company interested in the sporty female demographic (see Figure 5.14). Of course, this script works only if you created images for all the possible variations: FemaleSporty.gif, FemaleFormal.gif, MaleSporty.gif, and MaleFormal.gif. You can add as many fields as you like to the survey, but you have to be sure to create the corresponding images. If you create a new ad image every day, you can constantly supply the user with fresh and customized content.

Tracking Patterns

A more sophisticated way to customize your site involves tracking click-through patterns. You can use the cookie to keep tabs on how often a user visits a specific part of your site or to record the type of information most commonly requested by a particular user. For example, if you manage a music Web site, you might want to track a user's favorite genre. Each time the visitor returns to your site, a JavaScript routine can dynamically arrange the site to suit the visitor's interests.

Although it sounds quite complicated, it's actually easy to set up a tracking system. It requires three steps. This example uses a frames layout (see Figure 5.15). First, you need to add a little code to every link that you want to track. Second, you have to add a script to the <HEAD> of each document in which you want to activate tracking. Third, you have to add a small function to your site's main frameset. Although you can track patterns without framesets, using framesets is the easiest most manageable way.

5.13

5.14

5.13   A simple form survey asking the user questions.

5.14   Customized page based on survey results.

The first step is to modify the links. Decide what you want to track and create categories. In the music example, we're tracking genres, so we create categories according to genre: jazz, rock, techno, and so on. Find all the links that you want to track and add an onClick handler to each of them:

```
<a href="miles_davis_info.html"
onClick="track(jazz)">Jazz</a>
```

The onClick handler specifies the relevant category, jazz in this case. Your navigation buttons might be the best place to add the onClick handler because the visitor will use them repeatedly. The music site's navigational links look like this:

```
<a href="country.html" onClick=
"track('country')" target="main_bottom">
country section</a><BR>
<a href="rock.html" onClick="track('rock')"
target="main_bottom">rock section </a><BR>
<a href="jazz.html" onClick="track('jazz')"
target="main_bottom">jazz section </a><BR>
<a href="rb.html" onClick="track('techno)"
target="main_bottom">techno section </a><BR>
```

The second step is to add this tracking script in the <HEAD> of every document.

```
        function track(categoryName){
            var
cookieValue=GetCookie(categoryName);
            if
(cookieValue==null){cookieValue=0};
            cookieValue++;

SetCookie(categoryName,cookieValue,expdate);
        }
```

All those onClick handlers call this function. When a link is clicked, this function increments the value stored in the cookie for the specified category. For example, when a jazz link is clicked, the total-clicks for the jazz category goes up by one. Please note that this function is preceded by the standard cookie functions. Refer to the Web site for the complete code (http://www.htmlartistry.com/).

The third and final step involves doing the actual customization. We will dynamically generate the site's frameset so that each time the user return's to the site, the main frame consists of a page dedicated to the user's favorite genre. If the visitor checks out the rock section the most, he will be welcomed by the rock main intro page rather than the generic home page for the site (see Figure 5.16).

Of course, all this scripting occurs without the user's knowledge, so the site seems to magically learn the user's tastes. Here is the code for the customized frameset:

```
<HTML>
        <HEAD>
                    <TITLE>tracking example:
frameset</TITLE>
<script language="javascript">
//COOKIE FUNCTIONS REMOVED
//Script that determines most popular
click-through categories
    var allCategories=new Array
("country","rock","jazz","techno");
    var
topCategoryNum=0,topCategoryName="default";
    for (var i=0; i<allCategories.length;
i++){
            var
numClicksThisCategory=GetCookie(allCategories
[i]);
            if (numClicksThisCategory >
topCategoryNum){

topCategoryName=allCategories[i];

topCategoryNum=numClicksThisCategory;
        }
    }
    var topSrc=topCategoryName +
"Feature.html";
</script>
        </HEAD>
<SCRIPT LANGUAGE="JavaScript">
    document.write('<FRAMESET
COLS="150,*">');
    document.write('<FRAME SRC="blank.html"
NAME="navigation">');
    document.write('<FRAMESET
ROWS="70%,*">');
    document.write('<FRAME SRC="'+topSrc+'"
NAME="main_top" >');
    document.write('<FRAME SRC="blank.html"
NAME="main_bottom" >');
</SCRIPT>
                    </FRAMESET>
</FRAMESET>
</HTML>
```

The frameset is dynamically written according to the tracking data. As the page loads, a JavaScript routines loops through all the categories stored in the cookie and finds the most popular. Be sure to replace the array elements in the following line with your own category names:

```
var allCategories=new Array
("country","rock","jazz","techno");
```

You can include as many categories as you like. When the top category is determined, the script creates a filename by using the name of that category. For example, if jazz is the top category, the script creates the following variable: jazzFeature.html. This variable is then used to specify the filename for the top frame. Be sure to create a file for each of the possible filenames. In this example, the filenames will be: countryFeature. html, rockFeature. html, jazzFeature, and technoFeature. html.

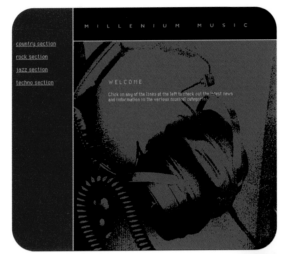

5.15

5.16

5.15   A music Web site that tracks user preferences.

5.16   Welcomed by your favorite genre's section rather than the generic home page.

CASE STUDY:

OLIVIA ONGPIN, FABRIC8

For the past four years, the San Francisco-based Web design studio, fabric8, has created online communities revolving around fashion, music, and, naturally, commerce (see Figure 5.17).

We sat down and spoke with one of the founders, Olivia Ongpin, to hear her views on how they have successfully created beautiful sites that make extensive use of JavaScript.

Our goal is to make Web sites that look good and work well. While there's no real formula to how we go about this, there are patterns. The style we are trying to convey is an important part of the process, and experimentation is key. Our sites end up looking and feeling completely different than we initially imagined because as we work with separate ideas, they begin to blend together with the medium and evolve into something surprising and unexpected.

JavaScript, which is available on most of our audience's browsers, has been a successful way to add low-maintenance interactivity to the fabric8 sites. For example, we used it to develop our client-side ordering system because it's easy to modify and update. Moreover, its immediacy means less of a wait for the customer. It becomes a useful tool for adding a unique, customized site experience, and perhaps an element of surprise.

Over the past two years, JavaScript has become far more reliable as well. Although thorough testing is paramount in any kind of programming, the fact that JavaScript is a relatively new language means there are always unsolved and undocumented bugs. However, these are being resolved at a quick pace and it seems that JavaScript will soon be completely standardized.

In its online ordering system, I-Shoppe, fabric8 combines a compelling and intuitive design with extensive JavaScript functionality (see Figure 5.18). The system keeps a record of all ordered items, checks for browser version, validates form entries, updates navigation, and dynamically generates a checkout item and price list—all without a single trip to the server. It provides a stellar example of how JavaScript can be used to add artificial intelligence to a site.

The main page of the frameset consists of several links. When one of these is clicked, the pull-down navigational menu automatically updates to reflect the current selection. The original script contains dozens of links and spans multiple documents; when the link is clicked in one frame, the pull-down menu is updated in another (see Figure 5.19). fabric8 handily avoids potential confusion by maintaining consistency between frames.

Although a full understanding of the code can only be achieved by looking at the site and source code itself, you can learn a lot by looking at code snippets from the site. We've excerpted and simplified the code that dynamically updates the navigational pull-down menu. To explain the coding more clearly, we combined the elements on one HTML page instead of breaking them out into two different frames (see Figure 5.20).

Here's the code:

```
<HTML>
        <HEAD>
                    <TITLE> Fabric8 I-Shoppe
Example </TITLE>
<SCRIPT LANGUAGE="JavaScript">
function setPulldown(productID) {
        with(document.frmSelect.products) {
                for (var i = 0; i <
options.length; i++) {
                        if
(options[i].value == productID) {
```

```
selectedIndex = i;
                                        break;
                    }
                }
        }
}
</SCRIPT>
            </HEAD>
<BODY>
<a href="pro_PS0100.html"
onclick="setPulldown('PS0100')">starr zip
jacket by penelope starr</a><BR>
<a href="pro_PD0100.html"
onclick="setPulldown('PD0100')">one-of-a-kind
sweater by phobos &amp; deimos</a><BR>
<a href="pro_LA0100.html"
onclick="setPulldown('LA0100')">astarte hemp
coat by labyrinth</a><BR>
<form name="frmSelect" method=post>
<select name="products">
<option value="home" selected>** CHOOSE AN
I-SHOPPE ITEM **:
<option value="PS0100">starr zip jacket by
penelope starr
<option value="PD0100">salvation sweater by
phobos &amp; deimos
<option value="LA0100">astarte hemp coat by
labyrinth
</select>
</form>
</BODY>
</HTML>
```

Thus, the success of their work is grounded in good design sense—expert layouts, skillful typographic treatments, consistent color palettes. The functionality engineered through JavaScript coding is carefully integrated into these aspects of the site. With smart and sassy design, unique products, extensive JavaScript enhancements, and very nicely formatted code, fabric8 shines as a company that successfully balances artistic expression with sophisticated functionality.

Continues on following page

5.17

5.18

5.20

5.19

5.17   fabric8 home page.

5.18   The I-Shoppe main page.

5.19   Synchronized navigational elements.

5.20   Simplified example of fabric8's pull-down menu.

Chapter Summary

You can use JavaScript to build a remarkable amount of intelligence into your site. From setting browser properties, to tracking user tastes and patterns, to fully functional commerce solutions, you can create sites that rival CGI-based applications.

Believe it or not, this is the end of Part I. If you read straight through, you covered a lot of ground and have a very solid foundation upon which to explore Web design and scripting possibilities. Part II dives into Dynamic HTML and the 4.0 browsers where JavaScript assumes a central role in everything from animation to sound control. Enjoy!

Cross-Browser and Platform Comparison Guide

This is a comprehensive list of the techniques used in this chapter and their support on the top two browsers: Netscape 2.0–4.0 and Internet Explorer 3.0–4.0—on both Macintosh and Windows.

URLs in This Chapter

- The Replacement Killers: `http://www.spe.sony.com/movies/replacementkillers`
- Firefly: `http://www.firefly.com`
- Cookie Functions: `http//www.hidaho.com/cookies/cookie.txt`
- Netscape JavaScript User's Manual: `http://home.netscape.com/eng/mozilla/3.0/handbook/javascript/index.html`
- fabric8: `http://www.fabric8.com`
- HTML Artistry companion Web site: `http://www.htmlartistry.com`

Technique	Browser	Platform	Support
Opening Browser Windows	All	Both	Yes
Floating Nav Windows	All	Both	Yes
Preloading Images (preloading code only)	Netscape 2	Both	No
	Netscape 3,4	Both	Yes
	IE 3	Both	No
	IE 4	Both	Yes
Determining Browser Type	All	Both	Yes
Determining Browser Version	All	Both	Yes
Detecting Platform	All	Both	Yes
Using Date and Time	Netscape 3, 4	Macintosh	Yes
	Netscape 3, 4	Windows	Yes
	IE 4	Windows	Yes
	IE 4	Macintosh	Yes
Asking Questions	Netscape 3, 4	Macintosh	Yes
	Netscape 3, 4	Windows	Yes
	IE 4	Windows	Yes
	IE 4	Macintosh	Yes
Tracking Patterns	Netscape 3, 4	Macintosh	Yes
	Netscape 3, 4	Windows	Yes
	IE 4	Windows	Yes
	IE 4	Macintosh	Yes

INSPIRATIONAL DESIGN MODEL:
Emily Oberman and Bonnie Siegler, Number Seventeen

What is Number Seventeen? A room number? A new perfume? Think again. New York-based Number Seventeen, a five-person design studio headed by Emily Oberman and Bonnie Siegler, is on the forefront of design synergizing the world of motion graphics with traditional print. Their work spans the world of television, film, advertising, and print, boasting such clients as ABC, Miramax, "Saturday Night Live," Jane Magazine, and DDB Needham.

Both trained as traditional graphic designers: Oberman worked as senior designer at M & Co. and Siegler was design director at VH1 before they decided to go off on their own to form Number Seventeen. Best friends for about 12 years, you can tell that the success Oberman and Siegler have found together hasn't put a damper on their friendship. They are a team. A dynamic duo. Aside from their busy work schedules, they even find the time to teach once a week at Yale University's Graduate School of Art teaching "Design for TV."

What first caught our eye was the dazzling opening credits to the 23-year-old NBC comedy show "Saturday Night Live." It was a mixture of bold colorful lines and clean type. Oberman and Siegler were given complete creative freedom on the project and decided that in order for the opening sequence to have an updated look, it needed to lose the standard black-and-white shots of New York City at night. "Everyone already knew that it was in New York and that it was live. Through the lines and cool nighttime colors, we wanted to express a frenetic quality—it's a total abstraction of New York City," explains Siegler.

5.1

5.2

5.1　Emily Oberman and Bonnie Siegler.

5.2　A painted postcard portrait of the
Number Seventeen studios in New York.

This wasn't the first time Number Seventeen worked with "SNL." They also lent their sense of humor to produce special parody commercials such as "Crystal Gravy," a jab at clear cola drinks and "Paradox," a spoof on car commercials.

But setting their humor aside, their design skills are in full gear as seen through the simple, classic motion graphic pieces they create for network IDs. One perfect example is their work for ABC daytime, taking the classic ABC logo designed by Paul Rand and adding more movement and transitions. Simple things such as moving from the word "abc" to "day"

by using transitions such as blinds or dissolves create quick identifying moments. They also pay tribute to old musicals by having dancing logos spin and move around each other. The network ID—ABC, the particular focus—daytime TV, and the movement, are all addressed in these 15-second spots.

When you try to pinpoint Number Seventeen as simply motion graphics designers, it turns around and show you that it knows print, and may we add, very well. Number Seventeen's recent advertising

5.3

5.3   Title Sequences and Type Design for "Saturday Night Live."

campaign for the launch of the women's magazine *Jane* was a spoof of the stickers we all know and love, the "Hello, my name is...." Using its sense of humor once again, Number Seventeen takes the basic concept of the sticker and gives it a different twist. "Hello my personal psychic is...JANE" or "My PIN is...JANE" would find its way on billboards and posters all over New York touting this new convention.

We visited Number Seventeen's New York studio and found an environment that was fun, colorful, relaxed, and very organized! It was an eclectic mix that reflected their work and their personality, and one that we found to be most comfortable. Oberman and Siegler could easily be the comedy duo of the '90s with their quick lines that never miss a beat. For now at least, its their designs that are spreading all the humor.

5.4

5.4   ABC daytime ID spot paying homage to old muscials and their kaleidoscope dancers.

Your work spans from print and packaging to motion graphics. How do you separate your thinking? Are there different criteria for designing for these different media?

We don't really separate our thinking. There's always the same problem to solve—'to entertain, to inform, and to communicate.' We can bring a fresh eye to the next project by not working with the same media.

What project has been the most fulfilling in terms of you really connecting with it?

We love all our babies! We usually fall in love with our clients. While we like to step our clients through the process, there's still some spontaneity in the finishing process.

You both are now involved with teaching. What motivated you to become design educators? And what advice would you give to people just now getting their start in design?

When we were in school, we were most inspired by teachers who were out there working. And of course, it's great to get an entirely different perspective on things—from the student's perspective. We see a lot of students who feel like they have to go with their first idea. Advice? Be the project. Get into the Zen of it.

5.5

5.5   ABC daytime ID spot showing simple transitions between "abc" and "day."

5.6

5.6 Promotional advertising campaign for the launch
of *Jane* magazine.

PART 2:

Pushing Your Design with Dynamic HTML

Uh-oh! Dynamic HTML. At first, we regarded it as yet another new bit of technology riding the turbo-speed development of the World Wide Web. We resisted it. We dismissed it as an overrated trend in Web site design and development. Deal with learning more code? For the sake of a minority of viewers using 4.0 browsers? Forget about it! Why bother? We were happy with and proud of our HTML pages composed of tables, frames, animated GIFs, and Shockwave movies.

Then we started to experiment with DHTML, and we saw the light.

All of a sudden we could lay out elements on an HTML page using absolute coordinates. For one thing, there were no more misalignments of graphics between browsers and platforms! Because of absolute positioning between different "layers" of an HTML page, we can create fascinating grid-busting layouts, overlaying different graphics and HTML text. And what's this? Create animations and interactive elements without the use of plug-in technology? Amazing!

In Part 2, we show you how to take the same Web design issues featured in Part 1 to the next level in your design with Dynamic HTML. While discussing the new and expanded possibilities in layouts, typography, interactivity, and animation, we cover specific coding techniques integrated with our methods and approaches to design and visual communication. Chapter 6, "Using Layers, the Building Blocks of Dynamic HTML," provides the foundation for implementing Dynamic HTML code and demonstrates how to make use of absolute positioning and alignment. Chapter 7, "Cascading Style Sheets: Typography Made Simple," covers how to expand the typographic possibilities of your Web site designs by implementing style sheets. Chapter 8, "Interactivity: Making the Most of Your Layers," helps you find ways to enhance the dialogue between you and your users through your Web site and its Dynamic HTML features. Chapter 9, "Creating the Animations of Your Dreams," synthesizes the concepts discussed in the previous chapters—layouts, typography, colors, interactivity—by addressing the use of multimedia experiences to further engage and even entertain your audience.

So yes, only users with 4.0+ browsers can view content created with DHTML. The fact is: Dynamic HTML enables Web designers to build the layouts, the functionality, and the interactivity that they have always wanted and needed in their Web sites for a potentially plug-in-less audience. One day, a majority of users will have the appropriate browsers to view your ground-breaking Web sites created with DHTML. Until then, we highly recommend experimenting with the code. You have the technology at your fingertips.

CHAPTER 6
USING LAYERS, THE BUILDING BLOCKS OF DYNAMIC HTML

The Web changed when the 4.0 browsers shipped. Internet Explorer and Netscape offered so many new features that developers were able to explore entirely new design possibilities and techniques. What has been possible in print, in multimedia applications such as Macromedia Director, and with coding languages such as C and C++, is now feasible on the Web.

At the heart of the 4.0 innovations lies the layer. If you worked with Photoshop 4.0 or any other layer-enabled graphics program, you're probably familiar with the concept. Imagine making a collage out of magazine clippings. You start with a piece of construction paper and then begin gluing clipping after clipping. Some of these clippings overlap each other, which add complexity and richness to the final product. With layers, you can create a similar kind of collage on your Web pages (see Figure 6.1). In addition, you can use JavaScript to manipulate the layers after you place them on the page. This chapter describes the basic code needed to add a layer to your page, as well a few useful techniques to use layers to enhance your design. JavaScript and its relationship to the layer is also briefly discussed.

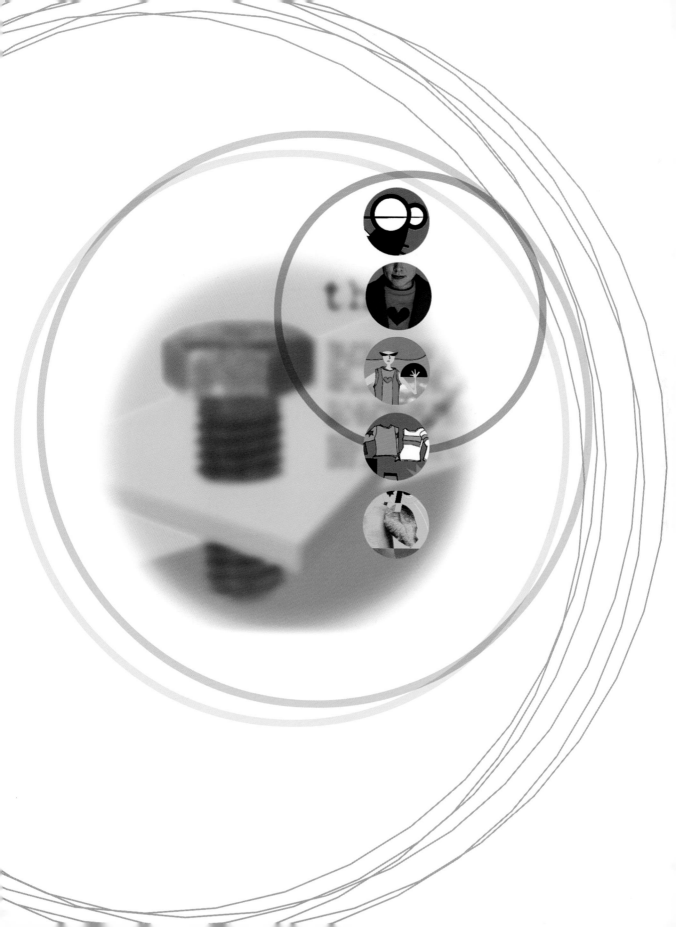

Coding a Basic Layer

In its very essence, a layer is simply a rectangle. You can work with this rectangle in a variety of ways—put graphics and text in it (see Figure 6.2), position it at a precise location on your Web page, make it move, hide it, show it, or show part of it. These advanced capabilities are discussed later in this chapter and throughout the rest of the book. First, you see how to create the most basic of layers.

There are actually two ways to code a layer. One way works in Netscape and the other works in both browsers. Naturally, we favor the second way, but we'll show you how to do both. Place all the following code within your <BODY> tags.

6.1

6.2

6.1 An example of a multilayered page incorporating graphics and HTML text Akimbo Design created for a Macromedia tutorial.

6.2 A single layer containing HTML text, an image, and a link.

Using the <LAYER> Tag

The Netscape-only way to code a layer looks like this:

```
<LAYER ID="myNetscapeLayer" WIDTH="200"
HEIGHT="300">
Some text in a layer.
</LAYER>
```

Here the <LAYER> tag defines the layer. As mentioned previously, this layer is simply a rectangle with a width of 200 pixels and height of 300 pixels. The layer is also identified as myNetscapeLayer. This ID becomes useful when you want to manipulate the layer with JavaScript. The ID can consist of any combination of letters, numbers, and other characters. For the rest of this book, leave the <LAYER> tag behind because it cannot be used in a cross browser environment. Instead, focus on the <DIV> tag.

Using the <DIV> Tag

The <DIV> tag groups related bits of information together, telling the browser that everything after the opening <DIV> tag and before the closing </DIV> tag should be treated as a single entity. You can apply different properties to this entity, such as an ID, color, or position, and the browser formats the entire group according to these properties. In essence, the <DIV> tag enables you to define something very similar to a <LAYER> and works on both browsers. Here is the code needed to define a basic layer with the <DIV> tag:

```
<DIV ID="myCrossBrowserLayer"
STYLE="width:200; height:300;">
Some text in a layer.
</DIV>
```

This code defines a layer with ID, width, and height properties similar to the Netscape layer. The difference is a matter of syntax. With the <DIV> tag, properties are defined in the following manner:

```
STYLE="property name:value; property name:
value;"
```

Width and height are among many properties that you can set.

Placing Content in a Layer

You can place any HTML element in a layer including text, images, tables, and content that requires plug-ins such as Shockwave. Everything that you put in a layer becomes part of a group and is treated as such by the browser. If your layer contains an image followed by some text, and you move the layer to a new location, the image and text moves as a single entity. Here is an example of a layer that contains an image, text, and a link.

```
<DIV ID="myCrossBrowserLayer"
STYLE="width:200; height:300;">
<IMG SRC="boat.jpg"><BR>
Look at my boat. It's neat huh?<BR>
Click <a href="boat.html">here</a> to see a
larger image.
</DIV>
```

Layer Positioning

Knowing how to code a basic <DIV> layer doesn't get you very far in terms of widening the design possibilities—knowing how to position this layer does. Two positioning options are available: relative and absolute.

Relative Positioning

You can tell the browser to place a layer relative to the other elements on your Web page. You are probably already familiar with this concept because all other HTML objects such as images and text are also relatively positioned. If you write some text at the beginning of your page and then add an image, the image will be placed directly after the text; it flows onto your document relative to the existing content.

The same is true for a relatively positioned layer. The browser treats the content in a layer as a single entity, so if you type some text and then add a layer, the entire contents of the layer will be placed directly after the text, just like an inline image. Use relative positioning when it's easier to work with separate HTML elements as a group such as a photo with a text caption. The default positioning for a layer is relative, however, and for clarity's sake, you can add the positioning property to your layer definition:

```
<DIV ID="myCrossBrowserLayer" STYLE="posi-
tion:relative; width:200; height:300;">
Some text in a layer.
</DIV>
```

Absolute Positioning

The more exciting type of positioning is absolute. If you're like most designers, you've been longing to place elements at precise locations on your page. Although tables go a long way toward giving you positioning control, they are still limited. By absolutely positioning a layer, you can place any HTML element including text, images, and plug-ins at an exact location on your page. Here is the code:

```
<DIV ID="layer1" STYLE="position: absolute;
visibility: visible; width:450; height:170;
top: 100px; left: 60px; z-index: 20;">
    text!  text!  and more text in a
layer!  yippee!<br>
    <img src="experiments.gif" width="435"
height="120" border="0"><br>
        <a href="nowhere.html">wow!  a
link.</a>
</DIV>
```

Here the position property changed from relative to absolute. Left and top properties are added, which tell the browser where (in absolute terms) to place the layer. The browser understands the window in which your document is displayed as a grid. The position 0,0 is the top-left corner of your window. Left describes the layer's horizontal (or X) axis and top describes the layers vertical (or Y) axis. This layer's top-left corner will be positioned at 100,60—100 pixels from the left of the browser window and 60 pixels from the top (see Figure 6.3).

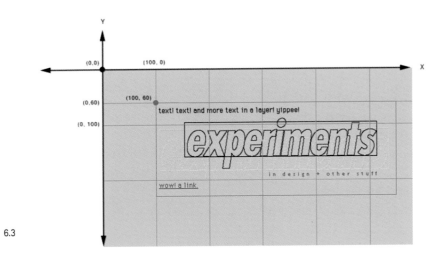

6.3   This diagram shows the browser window's coordinate system. The added red bounding box illustrates that the layer is 450×170 pixels.

Bleeds

If you're not familiar with the term, a bleed occurs when content goes beyond the edge of the page. The content is said to bleed off the page. Print designers use bleeds to create a rich visual presentation.

Prior to layers, it was nearly impossible to achieve a bleed. Although tiled background images do bleed, it is challenging to properly align page contents with them. In addition, they tile, which does not always work with your design. You might also have set a table's width or height to more than 100 percent and thereby created a right or bottom bleed. Layers allow you to create left, right, top, and bottom bleeds.

Remember that position 0,0 represents the top-left corner of your browser window; to create a top or left bleed, just position a layer at negative coordinates. To create a right or bottom bleed, place a layer at a location that you know will extend beyond the window borders. Usually, you will only know the window dimensions if you set them yourself. See Chapter 5, "Adding Sophistication and Interactivity with HTML and JavaScript," for more information on

setting window sizes. Here is the code for a layer that bleeds top and left:

```
<DIV ID="myCrossBrowserLayer" STYLE=
"position:absolute; left:-25; top:-10;
width:200; height:300;">
<IMG SRC="boat.jpg">
</DIV>
```

Defining Layer Properties

In addition to position, width, and height, you can set a wide range of additional properties including visibility, z-index, color, background color, background image, clip, font face, text alignment, and more. Here are some of the most common properties:

- **Position, width, height, left, and top:** You learned about these properties earlier in this chapter.
- **Visibility:** You can set your layer's visibility to hidden, visible, or inherit. When set to hidden, no part of your layer will be visible; this property is very useful in Dynamic HTML. Setting visibility to visible makes your layer appear as if it were previously hidden. You rarely use the inherit property. When a layer's visibility is set to inherit, the layer assumes the visibility property of the "parent" layer that contains it. For example, if you put layer B inside of layer A, layer B has the same visibility property as layer A. Here is an example of a layer with its visibility set to hidden:

```
<DIV ID="myCrossBrowserLayer" STYLE=
"position:absolute; visibility:hidden;
left:-25; top:-10; width:200; height:300;">
<IMG SRC="boat.jpg">
</DIV>
```

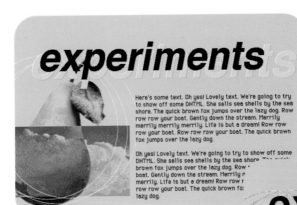

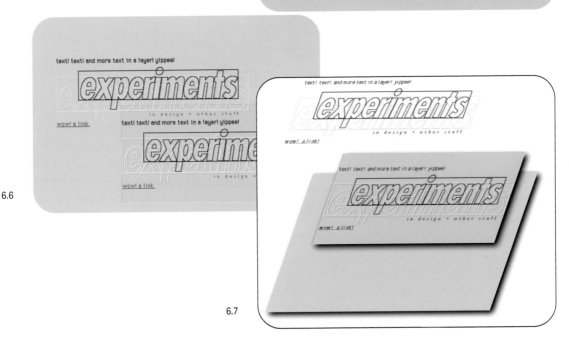

6.4 A simple layer with Helveitca for the HTML text on a Macintosh.

6.6 The layer copied from Figure 6.2 with a background color and a lower z-index value.

6.5 The same layer with Times New Roman on a PC.

6.7 An exploded view of the HTML page with two different z-axis planes. The gray plane represents the background color of the HTML page.

You cannot see this layer unless you use JavaScript to change its visibility property to visible. Using JavaScript with layers is discussed later in this chapter.

- **z-index:** This property assigns a stacking order to your layer. The layer with the highest number is on top. A layer with a z-index of 20 overlays a layer with a z-index of 10 (see Figure 6.6). Here is the code for two stacked layers:

```
<DIV ID="layer1" STYLE="position: absolute;
visibility: visible; top: 100px; left: 60px;
z-index: 20;">
    <table width="100%" height="50%">
        <tr>
            <td>
                    text!  text!  and more
text in a layer!  yippee!<br>
                <img
src="experiments.gif" width="435"
height="120" border="0"><br>
                <a
href="nowhere.html">wow!  a link.</a>
            </td>
        </tr>
    </table>
</div>

<DIV ID="layer2" STYLE="position: absolute;
visibility: visible; top: 200px; left:
200px; z-index: 10;">
    <table width="100%" height="50%">
        <tr>
            <td bgcolor="#FFCC00">
                    text!  text!  and more
text in a layer!  yippee!<br>
                <img
src="experiments.gif" width="435"
height="120" border="0"><br>
                <a
href="nowhere.html">wow!  a link.</a>
            </td>
        </tr>
    </table>
</div>
```

This property assigns a stacking order to your layer. The layer with the highest number is on top. A layer with a z-index of 20 overlays a layer with a z-index of 10 (see Figure 6.7).

You can set many additional properties. To learn more, head to Netscape or Microsoft's Web site, W3C's Cascading Style Sheets recommendation Web site (http://www.w3.org/TR/REC-CSS1), or pick up a book such as *Web Designer's Guide to Style Sheets* by Steve Mulder. There are two properties of note that enable you to set a layer's background color and tiled background image (see Figure 6.8); however, they are buggy in Netscape. Look to Appendix C, "Cross-Browser Dynamic HTML Reference List," to learn how to work around the bugs.

Layers and JavaScript: Dynamic Content

The capability to stack and precisely position layers opens the door to thousands of new design possibilities. If you stop reading this book right now, you can create compelling static pages for the 4.0 browsers. However, you'd miss out on the fantastic new capability to modify a page's content after it has loaded.

Using JavaScript, you can read and change a layer's position, as well as many of its properties. This capability allows you to create intensely interactive Web applications similar to any game or presentation built with traditional programming languages such as C or C++ or with a multimedia application such as Macromedia Director. JavaScript might not be as fast or elegant as a programming language or as easy as multimedia applications, but it's free and works on all recent browsers without a plug-in. Read on for an introduction to creating pages featuring dynamic content.

Changing Layer Properties with JavaScript

One of the simplest and most powerful ways to control a layer with JavaScript is to change its properties. Note that in Internet Explorer you can change properties for HTML elements other than layers such as images and text. However, Netscape doesn't fully support this behavior.

Out of all the properties, you will consistently manipulate the layer visibility property. By hiding and showing layers, you can put a substantial amount of content in one document and then let the user navigate through it without ever having to reload the page. By not reloading the page, the user enjoys a much more instantaneous and consistent experience.

For example, if you want to put your portfolio of five paintings on the Web, you can make five different HTML pages, each featuring one painting and its description. Using layers and JavaScript, you can put each painting and its description in a layer and stack the layers on top of one another. By putting the content into layers, the user does not have to wait for an entirely new page to load each time he wants to see a new painting.

6.8

6.8   Layer with a tiling background.

Here is an example of a page that uses JavaScript to change a layer's visibility:

```html
<HTML>
<HEAD><TITLE> layer property change example
</TITLE>
<SCRIPT LANGUAGE="JavaScript">
    function showLayer(layerName){
        if (navigator.appName ==
"Netscape") {

document.layers["myLayer"].visibility=
"visible";
        }else{

document.all["myLayer"].style.visibility=
"visible";
        }
    }
    function hideLayer(layerName){
        if (navigator.appName ==
"Netscape") {

document.layers["myLayer"].visibility=
"hidden";
        }else{

document.all["myLayer"].style.visibility=
"hidden";
        }
    }
</SCRIPT>
</HEAD>
<BODY>
<form>
<input type=button value="Hide Layer"
onClick="hideLayer()">
<input type=button value="Show Layer"
onClick="showLayer()">
</form>
<DIV ID="myLayer" STYLE="position:absolute;
z-index:20; visibility:visible; left:200;
top:150; width:200; height:300;">
    Text in my layer.
</DIV>
</BODY>
</HTML>
```

This page features two form buttons and one layer called myLayer. When clicked, the Hide Layer button calls the hideLayer() function, which hides myLayer. The Show Layer button calls showLayer(), which makes myLayer visible again.

The showLayer() and hideLayer() functions are described fully in Chapter 8. One thing to note at this point is that these functions check the visitor's browser before running any code. If the visitor uses Netscape, it executes one line. If the visitor uses another browser (presumably Internet Explorer) it runs a different line. As with most JavaScript, the syntax for changing layer properties is different on each browser. With a little fancy JavaScript

footwork, you can write only one line of code. This technique is described later in this chapter.

In addition to modifying properties, you can change a layer's position. By repeatedly changing a layer's position, you can create a simple animation. Chapter 9, "Creating the Animations of Your Dreams," discusses layer animation. Macromedia's new HTML editor, Dreamweaver, makes changing layer properties and positions a breeze. Similar to Flash and Director, it turns the whole process into a graphical experience. Unlike many other HTML editors, it doesn't meddle with your existing code and it also gives you complete access to the code even as you are using the graphical tools.

Cross-Browser JavaScript Tricks

Although they cause an enormous amount of extra work, the differences in JavaScript syntax between the browsers are usually quite small. By adding a little JavaScript code to the beginning of your document, you can avoid double coding in many situations.

To create cross-browser code, you need to define a few global variables. A global variable is a variable that, once defined, can be used throughout your document. It contrasts with local variables that can be used only in the function in which they are defined. Recall that to hide a layer, you needed to write the following code:

```
1.function hideLayer(layerName){
2.  if (navigator.appName == "Netscape") {
3.    document.layers["myLayer"].
visibility="hidden";
4.  }else{
5.    document.all["myLayer"].style.
visibility="hidden";
6.  }
7.}
```

Line 3 is executed by Netscape; line 5 is run by Internet Explorer. You notice two minor syntactical differences between these lines. To refer to a layer in Netscape, you need to write the following code:

```
document.layers["layerName"]
```

In Internet Explorer you need to write the following code:

```
document.all["layerName"]
```

The difference is the matter of a single word: "layers" versus "all." A similar difference occurs later in that same line. Internet Explorer uses the word "style" after the layer name, and Netscape does not use any word at all.

To get around the problem, define global variables. You place different values in these variables depending on the visitor's browser. Then, you can use these variables to replace hard-coded instances of browser-specific code. Here's an example of a script that initializes global variables:

```
1.if (navigator.appName == "Netscape") {
2.    var layerRef="document.layers";
3.    var styleSwitch="";
4. }else{
5.    var layerRef="document.all";
6.    var styleSwitch=".style";
7. }
```

If the visitor is using Netscape, this script executes lines 2 and 3. It runs lines 5 and 6 on Internet Explorer. In both cases, the script initializes two global variables: layerRef and styleSwitch. On Netscape, the string document.layers is assigned to the layerRef variable and nothing is assigned to the styleSwitch variable. On Internet Explorer, the string document.all is assigned to the layerRef variable and the string .style is assigned to the styleSwitch variable.

Now that the global variables are defined, you can use them in your scripts. Replace the words that are different across browsers with the proper variable. When the script is run, the browser reads the proper syntax no matter which browser is used. Take a look at the revised hideLayer() script:

```
function hideLayer(layerName){
  eval(layerRef+'["myLayer"]'+styleSwitch+
'.visibility="hidden"');
}
```

The code is a lot shorter. However, it's also a lot more confusing to read. It starts out by using the eval() function (see Note). The plus signs (concatenation operators) attach the variables to the other parts of

the line.

> **Note:**
>
> The eval() function is built in to both browsers and evaluates everything between its parentheses. For example, it reads the line
>
> ```
> eval(layerRef+'["myLayer"]'+styleSwitch+'
> .visibility="hidden"');
> ```
>
> and replaces the variables layerRef and styleSwitch with the values assigned to them in the initialization script. Then it evaluates the line of code, which sets the layer's visibility property to hidden.

When all is said and done, Netscape reads this line:

```
document.layers["myLayer"].visibility=hidden
```

And Internet Explorer reads this line:

```
document.all["myLayer"].style.visibility=
hidden
```

The syntax is perfect for each browser and the hideLayer() function works without error on both browsers. To look at the initialization code in a full HTML page, check out the code for the next technique.

Creating a Loading Message

If you build a page that takes a long time to download, you can create a layer that blocks all other layers until the page is completely loaded. The visitor will be prevented from seeing a messy jumble of layers and images as your document is in various states of download.

The concept is this: Set up one big colored layer that has a width and height larger than any other layer. You can put an interesting text message or a small graphic in this layer to give visitors something to look at while they wait. When all the images and other elements have finished downloading, hide this layer. Here is an example:

```
<HTML>
<HEAD><TITLE>  loading message example
</TITLE>
<SCRIPT LANGUAGE="JavaScript">
//Initialize Global Variables
if (navigator.appName == "Netscape") {
  var layerRef="document.layers";
  var styleSwitch="";
}else{
  var layerRef="document.all";
  var styleSwitch=".style";
}
//Hide layer function
function hideLoadingLayer(){

eval(layerRef+'["loadingLayer"]'+styleSwitch+
'.visibility="hidden"');
}
</SCRIPT>
</HEAD>
<BODY onLoad="hideLoadingLayer()">
<DIV ID="loadingLayer" STYLE="z-index:15000;
visibility:visible; width:640; height:480;
font-color: white">
    <table width=640 height=480
bgcolor=black><tr><td>
    Hi There. Please wait for this page to
load
        </tr></td></table>
</DIV>
<DIV ID="myLayer" STYLE="position:absolute;
z-index:20; visibility:visible; left:200;
```

```
top:150; width:200; height:300;">
    <IMG SRC="bigImage.gif"><BR>
    Look at this very big picture.
</DIV>
</BODY></HTML>
```

This page consists of just two layers: the loading layer and a layer that contains a large image and some text. The loading layer consists of a big table that fills the screen with black. Look in Appendix C for more information about tables in layers. Another thing to notice about the loading layer is that its z-index is set to a very high number (15000). Always set the loading layer's z-index at a number so high that you never have to worry about it being stacked under any of the other layers. There is also an extra bit of code in the <BODY> tag. When the browser finishes loading document content, it runs the functions specified in the onLoad() handler. In this example, the hideLoadingLayer() function in the onLoad() handler is invoked. After the big image has loaded, this function hides the large black loading layer, which reveals the underlying layer.

6.9

6.9   Using a preloading message for the Elixir demo hopefully minimizes the perceived download time of the site.

CASE STUDY:
SUPERFLY FASHIONS BY
AKIMBO DESIGN

Akimbo Design created the SuperFly Fashions site for Macromedia's DHTML Zone as a demonstration of the power of layers and Dynamic HTML. The site also features a tutorial that explains how to code the techniques used in the demo. We coded the site by hand, before the release of Macromedia Dreamweaver and other Dynamic HTML capable HTML editors that enabled us to become very familiar with Dynamic HTML. We coded and recoded a lot of sections as we learned more about Dynamic HTML's limits, capabilities, and bugs. We developed a lot of techniques for dealing with layers that should come in handy even for smaller efforts.

The site consists of a lot of images, so we set up a loading layer (described earlier in this chapter) to keep the visitor occupied as the site loads (see Figure 6.10).

The site opens with a fly zipping on, around, and off of the screen (See Figure 6.11).

A transparent pull-down menu enables visitors to navigate through a collection of SuperFly garments (see Figure 6.12).

After selecting weather, event, and gender, the outfit planner recommends an outfit. The planner also features moving backgrounds (see Figure 6.13).

Visitors can dress a mannequin by clicking and dragging clothes to the appropriate places (see Figure 6.14).

Credits scroll across the screen just like in the movies (see Figure 6.15).

Although this site employs many advanced Dynamic HTML techniques, it also shows how to make good use of layers. In particular, it demonstrates the value of launching a new window, of defining layers in the document's <HEAD>, and in splitting a large site into frames. It also shows how to construct a unique interface.

Launching a New Window

To access the SuperFly site, you have to click on a Launch SuperFly button, which launches a 640×480 pixel window. The opening windows technique is discussed in Chapter 5. We set the window size so that we would know exactly when a layer would be offscreen and when it would be onscreen. This knowledge was crucial in the case of the fly animation.

The fly starts offscreen left, moves to offscreen right, and then back across the screen to off-stage left, back to offscreen right, and then up from the bottom, and finally down from offscreen top. Much of the animation is based on the fact that the fly will be either partially or fully offscreen. Without setting the window size, we wouldn't have known when the fly would be offscreen.

Defining Layers in the <HEAD>

The site uses 81 different layers. That's a lot of layers. In addition, most layers contain a significant amount of code. Altogether, the code is 57K and

consists of 1,416 lines. Needless to say, the code is a bit overwhelming and confusing at times.

One trick that used to simplify modification was to group all the layer definitions in the document's <HEAD>. We didn't mention it earlier in the chapter, but there are actually two ways to define a layer. The first way is familiar:

```
<DIV ID="myCrossBrowserLayer"
STYLE="width:200; height:300;">
   Some text.
</DIV>
```

The second way involves defining the layer position and properties in the document's <HEAD> like so:

```
<HTML>
<HEAD><TITLE> alternate layers definition
</TITLE>
<STYLE TYPE="text/css">
  #myLayer{position:absolute; width:200;
height:300;}
</STYLE>
</HEAD>
<BODY>
<DIV ID="myLayer">
     Some Text
</DIV>
</BODY>
</HTML>
```

All the STYLE property definitions have been moved to the document's <HEAD>. The name that follows the number sign (#) corresponds to the layer's ID. When all the layer's definitions are defined in one place, it makes modifications and edits to layer properties a lot easier. Here is a snippet from SuperFly's layer definition code:

```
/*DRESSING ROOM LAYERS*/
/*Z-INDEX FROM 39,000 TO 40,000*/
#model {position: absolute;  visibility:
hidden;  z-index: 39010; }
#apparel1 {position: absolute;  visibility:
hidden;  z-index: 39907; }
#apparel2 {position: absolute;  visibility:
hidden;  z-index: 39900; }
#apparel3 {position: absolute;  visibility:
hidden;  z-index: 39898; }
#apparel4 {position: absolute;  visibility:
hidden; z-index: 39899; }
#apparel5 {position: absolute;  visibility:
hidden;  z-index: 39897; }
#apparel6 {position: absolute;  visibility:
hidden;  z-index: 39998; }
#apparel7 {position: absolute;  visibility:
hidden; z-index: 39999; }
#apparel8 {position: absolute;  visibility:
```

Continues on following page

```
hidden;   z-index: 39200; }
#apparel9 {position: absolute;  visibility:
hidden; z-index: 39700; }
#apparel10 {position: absolute;  visibility:
hidden;   z-index: 39908; }
#apparel11 {position: absolute;  visibility:
hidden;   z-index: 39909; }
#apparel12 {position: absolute;  visibility:
hidden;   z-index: 39910; }
#dressingRmBG {position: absolute;
visibility: hidden;  z-index: 39000; }
```

```
/*CREDITS LAYERS*/
#pause {position: absolute; visibility:
hidden; z-index: 29010;  width: 100px;}
#restart {position: absolute; visibility:
hidden; z-index: 29009;  width: 100px;}
#credits {position: absolute; visibility:
hidden; z-index: 29100;  width: 250px;}
#creditsBG {position: absolute; z-index:
29000; visibility: hidden; left: 10; top:
50;}
```

6.10

6.11

6.12

6.10   SuperFly preloading message.

6.11   SuperFly opening animation.

6.12   SuperFly catalogue.

6.13

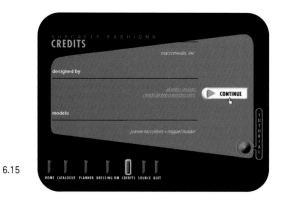

6.14

6.15

6.16

6.13 SuperFly outfit planner.

6.14 SuperFly dressing room.

6.15 SuperFly credits page.

6.16 Cutting up the interface to make the main content clickable.

INSPIRATIONAL DESIGN MODEL:

Howard Brown, Urban Outfitters

For the one place where fashion, music, and design merge, look no further than Urban Outfitters, the popular clothing store that boasts 24 locations in the U.S. and Canada. But step into any Urban Outfitters store and you see that it sells so much more than just clothes. True, it sell pillows, books, lamps, and picture frames. But it also sells a certain trendy, youthful lifestyle that can be seen through its advertising, packaging, and publications. These elements collide and groove together by the innovative vision and design know-how of Art Director Howard Brown.

Leading a team of twenty-something designers, Brown is at the forefront of innovation. Heavily influenced by music, especially the underground variety, and music-related graphic design and designers, notably Art Chantry, Brown uses his traditional design background and creates works that not only sell the goods but also define the culture that buys them. He takes old concepts in printing techniques and makes them new again. The printing process for the "Seventies" poster campaign used the technique of printing and over-printing with 100% process cyan, magenta, and yellow. His design concepts for Urban Outfitter's annual reports that were created in timeframes of a couple weeks or less have won kudos and design awards. The work at Urban Outfitters was fast-paced and the projects were constant.

Despite the heavy workload, Brown was up for any design challenge. In 1994, Brown decided to start a quarterly newspaper called Slant. It was a different kind of newspaper, especially for a corporate fashion house.

6.1

6.2

6.3

6.1 *Slant* cover for issue #9, the "Sports" issue.
Art Director: Howard Brown
Design/Illustration: David Mazzecchelli

6.2 Howard Brown.

6.3 Trocadero night club poster.
One of a five-piece set.
Art Director: Howard Brown
Design: Howard Brown

Slant had feature articles that ranged from "UFO Coverup: The Saucer Conspiracies" to commentaries such as "Pro Athletes Deserve Your Respect." The well-written and often satirical articles combined edgy graphics and a keen sense of humor.

"When we first started *Slant*, none of us that were involved in it had any experience in publishing. We had never layed out an editorial feature or done any editing," Brown remembers. Yes, there were the intermittent Urban Outfitters ads throughout the newspaper, but this was no ordinary corporate advertising publication. It wasn't simply self-promotion. It informed; it dazzled; it was funny; and it was interesting to read. It was a project born out of experimentation that led to success, garnering a "Best Overall Design" award in 1996 from the Society of Publications Designers. *Slant* was distributed for free not only through the Urban Outfitter stores, but through five hundred other retail storefronts as well.

After five years as art director, Brown has since moved on, leaving Urban Outfitters in Philadelphia for Sao Paulo, Brazil to work, on temporary assignment, for DM9.DBB, a Brazilian advertising agency. Upon his return to the U.S., Brown will head to Vermont and a design director position with design firm Jager DiPaola Kemp. Before leaving for South America, we talked more with Brown to find the sparks of his creative genius.

How did you get started in design?

I always loved to draw and was good at it from an early age. However, I was raised in rural Montana, which is not exactly a cultural Mecca. My family initially discouraged me from pursuing a career in art. They encouraged a more pragmatic route; accounting, law, or economics. So, I enrolled as an Economics major my freshman year at the University of Montana and I was miserable.

6.4

6.5

6.4   Urban Outfitters Packaging.
       Art Director: Howard Brown
       Design: Howard Brown, Mike Calkins

6.5   Urban Outfitters 1996 Annual Report
       Art Director: Howard Brown
       Design: Howard Brown, Mike Calkins, Lance Rusoff

In my second semester, I had an open elective and took a drawing class—my first ever. I loved it and that changed everything. Sophomore year, I got a scholarship to attend the University of Arizona where I graduated with a degree in art and design. After college, I spent three months at home in Montana, reworking my portfolio. I didn't want my options to be limited by the few good projects that I was given in school. I created my own projects; an underground publishing company called Culture Weapon that produced music, books, propaganda, and a magazine—ironically the initial concept of *Slant*—and a clothing and outdoors equipment company called GOAT, Great Outdoors Apparel and Tackle. For Culture Weapon, I focused on the record label and conceived a band called Polterkriest, designing a record, 7-inch single, CD, Video, and print campaign.

How did you get your job at Urban Outfitters?

I landed what I considered to be my dream job, my first job after college in 1991 with International News in Seattle, an innovative clothing line that made its name in the mid-'80s with printed silk-screen designs on sportswear. That's where I met Mike Calkins. Mike and I were hired on the same day and worked together for two years until Urban Outfitters, International News' best customer, hired me to be its art director. After I was at Urban for eight months, I hired Mike and he moved to Philadelphia where we worked together for four more years.

Do you use a computer to design?

I have a strong foundation in traditional design and production. I still do a lot of design the old-fashioned way; without a computer. I think the desktop computer revolution has made design very accessible. I feel that a strong design foundation and interest level in design—not computer trickery—coupled with good hand skills are essential to qualify your work. There are many design effects that can't be imitated properly with a computer. For example, I've never limited my typographical solutions to the availability of computer fonts.

6.6

6.6   Fall 1996 "Seventies" poster series.
       Art Director: Howard Brown
       Design: Howard Brown, Mike Calkins

I have hundreds of type books, and if there is a certain style I need I'll cut it out and paste it from a book, and clean it up by hand. Most of our posters and almost all *Slant* work was done with traditional mechanical boards, films, and overlays.

How do you express yourself within the corporate agenda?

At Urban Outfitters, I had a tremendous amount of creative freedom. They hired me in 1993, when I was 25 years old and living in Seattle; living the lifestyle of the Urban Outfitters' customer. They figured I understood the customers' vernacular. They let me do what I wanted, which was to incorporate my own interests into my work for the company. It enabled me to start *Slant* as well as a music and promotions program where I solicited music for in-store play, organized record promotions, and had bands play live in-store, in addition to many other cool endeavors. I incorporate a bit of my own personality into everything I do. That's what keeps it interesting for me. I firmly believe that an intimate connection to your work ensures success.

How do you know when you're done?

It varies from project to project. I do a lot of research. I make an honest assessment of the project's parameters or *the problem*. Then I work toward solving *the problem* or *the solution* while respecting the parameters but not being suppressed by them. I never try to play it safe, you don't stand to gain or learn as much that way. Ultimately, you do the best you can with the realization that failure is always a possibility. And if you screw up, big deal; mistakes are part of life and part of the learning process, not a crime. The only crime is not trying and doing your best.

Is there ever a point where you feel like you run out of ideas?

Never. I have too many ideas. The older I get, the more ideas I have.

From your work we know that the music industry has inspired your design sense a lot. What else inspires you?

Other personal interests. One of the reasons I'm working for Jager DiPaola Kemp in Vermont is that I love outdoor sports. In my spare time, I like to go backpacking, white-water rafting, skiing, camping, snowshoeing, and all that kind of stuff.

Have you ever thought of bringing a publication like *Slant* and transcribing it onto the Web, bringing it to a wider audience?

Of course, that was one of our future goals. One of the things that appealed to me about that would be the challenge because Web sites are so different from traditional publishing mediums. The challenge to me is translating a medium which is organic by nature and functions in a three-dimensional space into a medium which is inorganic by nature and exists in a two-dimensional space. A computer screen and a newspaper are very different realities. Each has its own advantages and disadvantages; they shouldn't be treated in the same way. Instead of being condescending to the medium, you should embrace it.

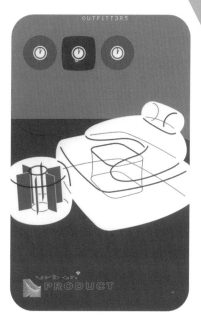

6.7

6.7 Postcards for the 1997 product series.
Art Director: Howard Brown
Design: Howard Brown, Mike Calkins
Illustration: Mike Calkins

Style Sheet Basics

Think of style sheets as a set of rules that tells the browser how to display text and images. Rather than having to code a handful of HTML each time you want to reference a header with a font face of Arial and Helvetica and with a specific font size, with style sheets you can specify it easily. Here's an example:

```
H2 { font-family: arial, helvetica, sans-
serif;
        font-size: 25pt }
```

This code shows that anytime an <H2> header tag appears, it will display with either Arial, Helvetica, or a san-serif font. Also, the font size will display at 25 points. (Finally you can have a better range of font sizes!)

Note:

Although you can experience the power of style sheets with the 4.0 browsers, the 4.0 browsers are far from perfect. There needs to be standards of code between the browsers as well as more support for some proposed style sheet rules that don't seem to work just yet.

The vast design capabilities of using style sheets allows you to create not only works of art, but you can have big design at a small file size. Although previously impossible without the use of graphics, you can now create colorful layered pieces of text that takes seconds to load. Figure 7.1, a screen from the Microsoft Style Sheets Gallery, comes in at only 6K!

Note:

For a background on style sheets, visit the World Wide Web Consortium (W3C) at http://www. w3.org/pub/WWW/TR/REC-CSS1.

What's more important to realize with style sheets is the capability to separate the formatting style from the HTML code. Take a look at Figure 7.2 to get an idea of how style sheets actually work. This flow chart outlines how style sheets are organized.

The rest of this section provides you with the essentials you need to start with style sheets.

Setting Up Style Sheet Rules

To start, you have to know the basics to set up your style sheet rules. A style sheet rule has two parts: the selector and the declaration. The *selector* is the HTML code that links the style to the HTML document, and the *declaration* is the style definition, all the properties and values within the brackets { }.

```
H2 { font-family: helvetica }
```

Here H2 is the selector and font-family: helvetica is the declaration.

You can set up as many style sheet rules as you like to your most commonly used HTML effects to save time from having to handcode them all.

Note:

You might feel weird doing it at first, but if you want to work with style sheets, you need to always close all your paragraphs with the closing </P> tag. This is because as you set up rules for paragraphs, the browser needs to know when the selection ends in order to start the next rule.

7.1

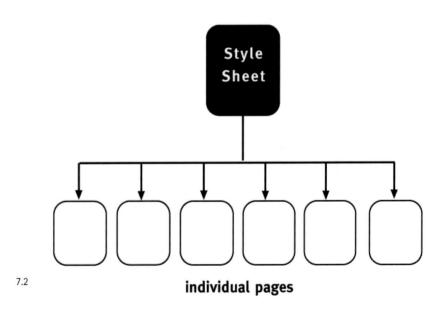

7.2

individual pages

7.1 "Safety in Numbers" from Microsoft's Style Sheet Gallery is only 6K.

7.2 Style Sheet flow chart.

> ## Tip:
> Use the <SPAN> tag when you want to override certain style elements that are in your style sheet. The <SPAN> tag displays only the declaration you specify in your style sheet, as in the following example:
>
> ```
> SPAN { font-family: arial }
> ```
>
> By inserting the <SPAN></SPAN> around the area in your HTML document, you ensure that anything contained within the tags displays in Arial.

Grouping Your Style Sheet Rules

To save space, always group your declarations with their corresponding selectors with a semicolon. Here's an example:

```
H2                      { font-family: Arial;
                        font-weight: bold;
                        font-size: 18pt;
                        color: blue }
```

By separating each declaration on its own line, you can easily go back and edit your styles.

You can also group your rules together:

```
H1, H2, P               { font-family:
helvetica;
                        font-weight: bold;
                        font-size: 24pt;
                        color: blue }
```

What this shows is that for every <H1>, <H2>, and <P> tag, the HTML page displays blue, 24pt, bold helvetica text. By grouping these different HTML declarations, you'll not only find it easier to edit, but you'll save space in your HTML page as well.

Adding Styles to Web Pages

It's very easy to add style sheets to your Web pages. Because style sheets are nothing more than text, they can live in their own document or you can add them straight into your HTML.

Here are some different ways you can add style sheets to Web pages:

- **Inline Styles:** For quick style face lifts where your styles live next to your HTML.
- **Embed:** For a single Web page.
- **Link:** For the most control where your one style sheet is linked to a number of HTML pages.

Inline Styles

If you want a quick fix to your HTML pages, you can add styles inline to your HTML document. It's not the most efficient way of using style sheet properties, but if you just want to add one or two style elements, it's okay.

Here's an example:

```
<P STYLE="color: red; margin-left: 1 in;
margin-right: 1 in">
```

This code replaces one normal <P> tag.

Embedding a Style Sheet

To change the face of a single Web page, you can embed your styles before the HEAD of the HTML document. To begin, add <STYLE TYPE="text/css"> right after the initial <HTML> tag. Next notice the comment code in the following sample code. Browsers that don't support style sheets simply ignore the style sheet rules. Go ahead and set up your rules and close everything with a </STYLE> tag. Here's an example of an embedded style sheet:

```
<HTML>
<HEAD>
<STYLE TYPE="text/css">
<!--
P {font: 8pt "arial" "helvetica"; color:
#003399}
-->
</STYLE>
    </HEAD>
<BODY>
```

As you can see in Figure 7.3, Mr. Showbiz uses embedded styles to enhance its home page with specialized font properties. You can combine your style sheet font rules with your regular old <FONT FACE> tag so that your pages degrade well across browsers.

Linking an External Style Sheet

Linking an external style sheet is one of the most powerful aspects of style sheets. You can create one style sheet and link it to a number of HTML pages thereby creating a sort of style template for your site.

First, create the external style sheet with your code:

```
BODY   { background: black;
         font-family: arial }
```

```
H2      { font-weight: bold;
          font-size: 18pt }
P       { font-size: 14pt }
```

Save this text file with a name and extension .css. Call this document mystyles.css and upload it to your server.

To link this mystyles.css to a Web page, add the following line within the <HEAD></HEAD> tags of your HTML page:

```
<HTML>
<HEAD>
 <TITLE>welcome to style</TITLE>
 <LINK REL="stylesheet" HREF="mystyles.css"
TYPE="text/css">
</HEAD>
```

7.3   Mr. ShowBiz uses embedded styles for its home page.

The great thing about linking to a style sheet is that if you want to change something simple such as the font or background color, all you have to do is modify that in one style sheet file and upload it again. It will save you valuable time from having to go back and handcode every HTML page again.

Classes and IDs

For more flexibility with style sheets, you can further divide them into classes. Sometimes you might find that attributing a style to a <P> tag can get too general. What if you want to change fonts for special paragraphs? You can create different "classes" of <P> tags by separating and naming them in your style sheet and HTML accordingly.

```
<STYLE TYPE="text/css">
 <!--
  P.a   { color: blue;
             font-family: courier }
  P.b   { color: red;
             font-family: arial }
     -->
</STYLE>
```

You can name the classes anything you want. We've named them simply P.a and P.b. From then on, when you want to use the various styles on the page, you simply activate them within the HTML:

```
<P CLASS="a">Class A shows up in blue
Courier.</P>
<P CLASS="b">Class B shows up in red
Arial.</P>
```

By naming the class in the HTML, the style attribute for the specific class tells the browser which variant of <P> to use, as seen in Figure 7.4.

7.4

Class A shows up in blue Courier.

Class B shows up in red Arial.

7.4   Two different classes of <P>.

Another way to set up your own specialized rules is with IDs. IDs are similar to classes in that you can set up certain rules in your style sheet and reference them in your HTML. Here's an example:

```
#100 { color: red;
          font-family: arial }

<H3 ID="100">Red is the most amazing
color.</H3>
```

The Cascade

Style sheets are also called *cascading* style sheets. This is because with all the intricacies associated with creating different style sheets, the browser reads the rules in a certain order. The browser decides which rules in each style sheet are the most important and displays them. This can affect the look of your pages because when the browser finds a conflicting rule, it won't display it the way you want it to look.

This is the order of how styles cascade:

1. **Inline:** Style references within HTML code

2. **Embedded:** Style sheets rules embedded in the HTML page

3. **Linked:** External style sheets referenced in the HTML page

4. **Imported:** Referencing a style sheet within another style sheet with @import

5. **User:** The browser display settings the user has modified

6. **Browser default:** The default browser settings

Unfortunately not all browsers follow this simple order. Navigator 4 and Internet Explorer 4 both have their own kinks when cascading style sheets. As a result, if you find yourself mixing between adding inline, embedded, and linked styles, make sure you test things properly and don't forget the cascading order.

When it comes to simple HTML tags such as FONT FACE, the style sheet tags can override them. This is because the browser reads the HTML tags first before moving on to the style sheet rules. If there are declared rules that match FONT FACE, the style sheet rule wins.

Contextual Selectors

For more options when declaring style sheet rules, you can set up contextual selectors that allow you to have two or more declarations follow the same rule.

```
CENTER B        {color: red }
```

The previous code means that anything that is both centered and in bold appears in red and won't affect other bold text or other centered text. With each declaration separated by a space, you can use contextual selectors not only with HTML tags but also with Classes and IDs.

Style Sheets and Graphics

You've always used graphics and text in your Web pages, but not like this! Now you can create some cool looks by layering text over graphics and even graphics over graphics. With style sheets' capability for absolute and relative positioning, you can achieve some different looks for your Web page. It will also prepare you for animating your site with dynamic HTML.

You'll also find that the precise control over backgrounds such as no tiling and transparent backgrounds will give you a reason to jump out from the standard white background we are all so used to.

Text over Graphics

Magazine layouts seem to fuse graphics and text in creative and artistic ways. It was not possible to do that on the Web with graphics and HTML until now. Relative position enables you to position elements such as HTML relative to the position of another element that is its parent element.

In Figure 7.5 , the HTML text is layered over the duotone graphic in a way that previously was impossible.

First, we create a CLASS named .a to use for the graphic image. For example, here are the rules to position the graphic:

```
.a { position: relative; left: 100 px; top:
50 px }
```

The previous code shows that for the CLASS.a, the element will appear 100 pixels from the left and 50 pixels from the top relative to the paragraph text.

Next we select the positioning and attributes of the paragraph text:

```
P              { position: relative;
                left: 100 px;
                top: -80 px;
                font-face: arial;
                font-size: 10pt;
                z-index: 1 }
```

The z-index number 1 dictates the layering order of the elements. The higher number 1 ensures that the text will always appear on top of the graphic.

Here's the full code for the HTML page:

```
<HTML>
<STYLE TYPE="text/css">
```

```
<!--
BODY       { background: white }
.a             { position: relative;
                left: 100 px;
                top: 50 px }
P              { position: relative;
                left: 100 px;
                top: -80 px;
                font-face: arial;
                font-size: 10pt }
-->
</STYLE>
<HEAD>
<TITLE>text over graphics</TITLE>
</HEAD>
<BODY>

        <SPAN CLASS="a"><IMG
SRC="images/model2.gif"></SPAN>

<P>

design style cool fresh funky free type <BR>
design style cool fresh funky free type <BR>
design style cool fresh funky free type <BR>
design style cool fresh funky free type <BR>
design style cool fresh funky free type <BR>
design style cool fresh funky free type <BR>
design style cool fresh funky free type <BR>
design style cool fresh funky free type <BR>
design style cool fresh funky free type <BR>
design style cool fresh funky free type <BR>
design style cool fresh funky free type <BR>
design style cool fresh funky free type <BR>
design style cool fresh funky free type <BR>
design style cool fresh funky free type <BR>
design style cool fresh funky free type

</P>


</BODY>
</HTML>
```

Besides relative positioning, you can also use absolute positioning to position elements such as text over graphics on a page. Absolute positioning is different from relative positioning in that it is independent of any other element on the page. You can use absolute positioning to position elements anywhere you want. Relative positioning depends upon another element for its position.

In Figure 7.6, the example shows a graphic positioned absolutely on the page.

As you resize the browser window, the graphic stays in place as seen in Figure 7.7.

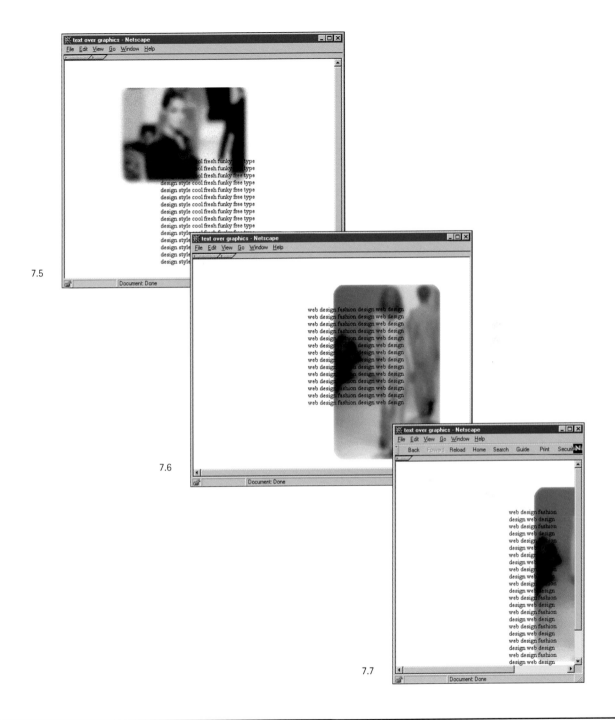

7.5   HTML text layered over a graphic.

7.6   Overlapping text over graphics with absolute positioning.

7.7   Resizing the browser window with absolute positioning.

The code works much the same as relative positioning, except here everything works independently of each other because they are absolute.

```
<HTML>
<STYLE TYPE="text/css">
<!--
BODY      { background: white }
.a            { position: absolute;
              left: 300 px;
              top: 50 px }
P         { position: absolute;
              left: -50 px;
              top: 50 px;
              font-face: arial;
              font-size: 10pt;
          z-index: 1 }

-->
</STYLE>
<HEAD>
<TITLE>text over graphics</TITLE>
</HEAD>
<BODY>


<SPAN CLASS=a><IMG
SRC="images/model.gif"></SPAN>

<P>

web design fashion design web design    <BR>
web design fashion design web design    <BR>
web design fashion design web design    <BR>
web design fashion design web design    <BR>
web design fashion design web design    <BR>
web design fashion design web design    <BR>
web design fashion design web design    <BR>
web design fashion design web design    <BR>
web design fashion design web design    <BR>
web design fashion design web design    <BR>
web design fashion design web design    <BR>
web design fashion design web design    <BR>
web design fashion design web design    <BR>
web design fashion design web design
</P>


</BODY>
</HTML>
```

Graphics over Graphics

After you learn how to layer text over graphics, layering graphics over graphics is a breeze. The addition

of the z-index declaration enables you to program the layering order with the highest number as the element on top.

We will start with two graphics, Figure 7.8 and Figure 7.9, that we will layer on top of each other.

With the logo as CLASS .a and the background graphic as CLASS .b, we'll find a position that works for the logo to fit nicely within the outline green circles.

```
<HTML>
<STYLE TYPE="text/css">
<!--
BODY      { background: white}

.a            { position: absolute;
                  left:10px;
                  top: 10px;
                  z-index: 1 }

.b            { position: absolute;
              left: 300px;
              top: 150px;
              z-index: 2 }

-->
</STYLE>
<HEAD>
<TITLE>-- retro -- design and style</TITLE>
</HEAD>
<BODY>

    <SPAN CLASS="a"><IMG
SRC="images/bluesquare.gif"></SPAN>
<BR>

<SPAN CLASS="b"><IMG
SRC="images/retro.gif"></SPAN>

</BODY>
</HTML>
```

Because the z-index of the circle is 2, which is higher than the z-index of the large blue graphic, the retro logo appears layered above the larger graphic (see Figure 7.10).

To incorporate another element into the Web page, you can add text with a z-index of 3 so that it appears on top of the larger graphic.

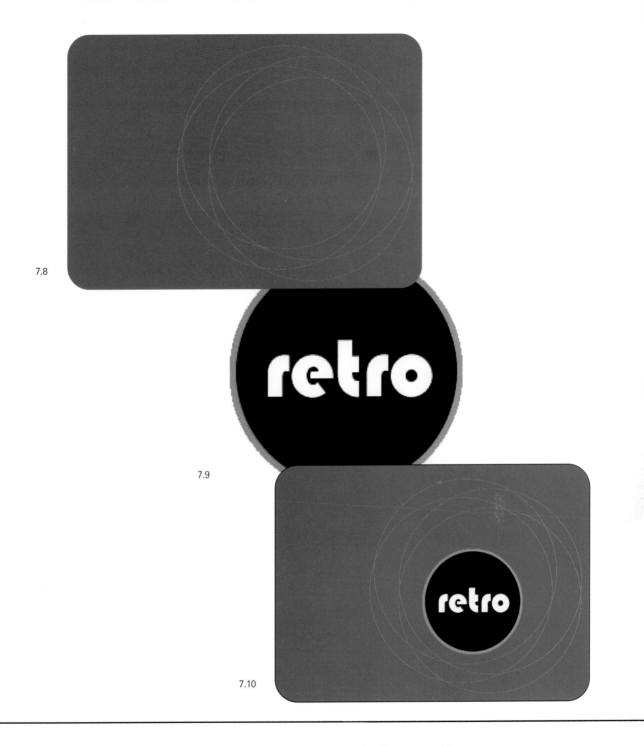

7.8

7.9

7.10

7.8   The large background graphic.

7.9   Logo graphic.

7.10   Graphics over graphics.

```
<HTML>
<STYLE TYPE="text/css">
<!--
BODY      { background: white}

P              { position: relative;
                 left: 50px;
                 top: 150px;
                 z-index: 3}

.a             { position: absolute;
                   left:10px;
                   top: 10px;
                   z-index: 1  }

.b             { position: absolute;
                 left: 300px;
                 top: 150px;
                 z-index: 2 }

-->
</STYLE>
<HEAD>
<TITLE>-- retro -- design and style</TITLE>
</HEAD>
<BODY>

<P>
<B>design and style on the web</B> <br>
You won't want to miss all the <br>
exciting things that are happening<br>
this season.  Get ready to head to<br>
the beach where we'll show you some<br>
new styles in swimwear.  Dont' forget<br>
your sunscreen!<br>
In music, we'll review who's the hottest<br>
new young artist that's tearing up the
charts.<br>
Finally, where do you like to get your cof-
fee?<br>
Write us and tell us where your favorite
hangout<br>
cafe is.
</P>

<SPAN CLASS="a"><IMG
SRC="images/bluesquare.gif"></SPAN>
<BR>

<SPAN CLASS="b"><IMG
SRC="images/retro.gif"></SPAN>

</BODY>
</HTML>
```

What's great is that z-index works perfectly in both Netscape and Internet Explorer browsers. You can see and compare the final results for Netscape in Figure 7.11 and for Internet Explorer in Figure 7.12.

Backgrounds

You know that background images tile when referenced the traditional HTML way of <BODY BACKGROUND="image.gif">. But did you know that with style sheets you can turn tiling off for backgrounds you only want to repeat once?

Here are the properties to use for background:

- background-color : To specify the background color with color name, RGB, or hex code
  ```
  H2 { background-color: red }
  H2 { background-color: 204,255,102}
  ```

- background-image: To insert a background graphic
  ```
  BODY       { background-image:
  url(shapes.gif) white }
  ```

Adding a default background color like white ensures that a background will be there should the image take a while to load or doesn't appear.

- background-repeat: To determine tiling of the background graphic
  ```
  H2     { background-image: url(colors.gif);
                     background-repeat:
  repeat-x }
  ```

Note:

Some browsers such as Internet Explorer 3 don't support the multiple background properties. In that case you can use the shortcut background property instead of background-image or background-color.

We'll work with background-repeat because this is the newest effect you can use on your Web pages. There are several attributes associated with the background-repeat property:

- no-repeat: background image appears just once and doesn't tile
- repeat: background image tiles
- repeat-x: background image tiles only horizontally
- repeat-y: background image tiles only vertically

In Figure 7.13, we have a simple black background that is a rectangular shape with rounded edges. We want to create a modular look without having the background tile and repeat.

Here's the code:

```
<HTML>
 <STYLE TYPE="text/css">
 <!--
  BODY { background: url(images/bike.gif);
               background-repeat: no-repeat }
-->
 </STYLE>
<HEAD>
 <TITLE>backgrounds</TITLE>
</HEAD>
<BODY>

</BODY>
</HTML>
```

You can compare a normal tiling background in Figure 7.14 and our no-repeat background image in Figure 7.15.

You can also get better control over your backgrounds with background-attachment and the background-position. Background-attachment can make backgrounds fixed in place rather than scroll along with the page, so you'll always have the image perfectly aligned in the browser window.

```
BODY { background-image: url (images/
background.gif);
        background-attachment: fixed }
```

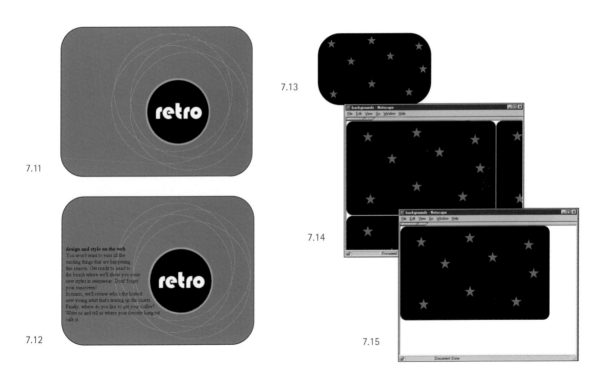

7.11

7.12

7.13

7.14

7.15

7.11   Text incorporated with layered graphics in Netscape.

7.12   Text incorporated with layered graphics in Internet Explorer.

7.13   The background image.

7.14   Tiling the background image.

7.15   Background image that doesn't tile.

CASE STUDY:
SIMON DANIELS, DESIGNER, MICROSOFT

You've probably seen all his work currently on the Microsoft Typography site and also in the Style Sheets Gallery. His innovative use of style sheets has inspired many designers to try style sheets. We got a chance to talk to Simon and see what techniques he uses for style sheets as well as what his projections are for Web design in general.

*One of his classic creations is the **Space Gun Magazine** example (http://www.microsoft.com/typography/css/gallery/slide7.htm) that can teach you how to create some great type layering. **Space Gun Magazine** combines cool colors with awesome layering type effects (Figures 7.16 and 7.17). The multilayer effect of the type creates the illusion that there are graphics but the whole page is only 7K!*

To achieve the special Space Gun typography, there are multiple layers of the same text that are then separated into layers. Each layer is defined and differentiated by their margin placement, size, and color.

Background-position can position the background to the browser window via keywords, length, or percentage.

```
BODY { background-image: url (images/
background.gif);
      background-position: top center }
```

Here's an example showing the layers for the "Space Gun Magazine" type.

```
<HTML>
<HEAD>
<TITLE>SpaceGun Magazine</TITLE>
<STYLE>

BODY { background: darkorange }

.layer1 { color: black; margin-top: -15px;
margin-left: 20px; font-size: 150px; font-
family: Impact, Arial, helvetica, sans-serif
}
.layer2 { color: black; margin-top: -170px;
margin-left: -40px;       font-size: 150px;
font-family: Impact, Arial, helvetica, sans-
serif }
.layer3 { color: white; margin-top: -190px;
margin-left: 0px; font-size: 150px; font-
family: Impact, Arial, helvetica, sans-serif
}
.layer4 { color: white; margin-top: -183px;
margin-left: -20px;       font-size: 150px;
```

```
font-family: Impact, Arial, helvetica, sans-
serif }
.layer5 { color: red; margin-top: -190px;
margin-left: -10px; font-size: 150px; font-
family: Impact, Arial, helvetica, sans-serif
}
```

In the HTML, each of the layers are specified by their CLASS, for example:

```
<DIV ALIGN=CENTER CLASS=layer1>SpaceGUN</DIV>
<DIV ALIGN=CENTER CLASS=layer2>SpaceGUN</DIV>
<DIV ALIGN=CENTER CLASS=layer3>SpaceGUN</DIV>
<DIV ALIGN=CENTER CLASS=layer4>SpaceGUN</DIV>
<DIV ALIGN=CENTER CLASS=layer5>SpaceGUN</DIV>

<DIV ALIGN=CENTER CLASS=layer1>Magazine</DIV>
<DIV ALIGN=CENTER CLASS=layer2>Magazine</DIV>
<DIV ALIGN=CENTER CLASS=layer3>Magazine</DIV>
<DIV ALIGN=CENTER CLASS=layer4>Magazine</DIV>
<DIV ALIGN=CENTER CLASS=layer5>Magazine</DIV>
```

"The advantages of using 'live text' instead of bitmaps for text are well documented and accepted. However, some of these advantages also apply where graphics are used for nontextual purposes, such as ornament, illustration, a user interface, or game type graphics.

7.16

7.17

7.18

7.16   Space Gun Magazine.

7.17   More Space Gun Magazine.

7.18   Typographic Ornament.

In most of the embedding demos, I've used symbol and custom dingbat fonts where one would normally use bitmaps—I think the Ornament (see Figure 7.18) and Worms and Turns (see Figure 7.19) demos are the most graphic illustrations of this." Not only are they graphically pleasing, the files Daniels creates end up being the smallest of files.

For working with style sheets, Daniels suggests to use the CLASS attribute to distinguish between various types of content. "Definitely consider setting up your site so that it is able to serve up a different linked style sheets depending on which browser the reader is using," he adds. On embedded fonts, such as the "A Blot on the Cookbook" demo he created (see Figure 7.20), Daniels believes that designers shouldn't be concerned with the two different font embedding standards that are out there now. "Both can co-exist in the same page/site quite happily. Think of TrueDoc as like a JPEG graphic—achieving high compression at the expense of quality. OpenType embedding doesn't achieve as high a compression level, but it is lossless," says Daniels. He also notes, "If you use poor quality fonts to begin with, you'll get poor quality results when they are displayed on the user's computer."

For Daniels, working on the edge of new technology is something he's used to. But does he see anything out there now that he likes? "I admire sites that are brave enough to use technology such as DHTML and CSS to add to the site visitor's experience. I'm opposed to using bitmap graphics to display text, but I admire those Web designers who take the time and effort to make their bitmapped text as legible as possible," Daniel concludes. Without the work of Daniels, most of us would never know the new technologies and design techniques that lie just ahead for us in the horizon.

7.19

7.20

7.19   Worms and Turns.

7.20   "A Blot on the CookBook" embedded fonts demo.

Conclusion

With style sheets, designing for the Web takes on a whole new direction, giving you more flexibility and control. These simple commands make organizing your site and HTML pages a breeze. Embedded fonts that you create can bring your style sheet typography to the next level without having to depend on the user's system fonts. Although style sheets are far from perfect, the 4.0 browsers bring some powerful design capabilities giving us the first look at the possibilities of design on the Web.

Cross Browser and Platform Comparison Guide

Please note that with style sheets all the examples in this chapter work on both Netscape 4 and Internet Explorer 4. Internet Explorer 3 for Windows and Macintosh also support some style sheet properties but their range of support for them is limited. Netscape 3 on both Windows and Macintosh do not support style sheet properties.

URLs in This Chapter

- Microsoft Style Sheets Gallery: www.microsoft.com/truetype/css/
- Microsoft Typography: www.microsoft.com/typography/
- Mr. Showbiz: www.mrshowbiz.com

Property	Browser	Platform	Support
font-family,	Netscape 4	Macintosh	Yes
font-size,	Netscape 4	Windows	Yes
font-color	IE 3, 4	Windows	Yes
	IE 3, 4	Macintosh	Yes
background-image,	Netscape 4	Macintosh	Yes
background-repeat,	Netscape 4	Windows	Yes
background-attachment,	IE 4	Macintosh	Yes
background-color,	IE 4	Windows	Yes
background-position			
background	IE 3	Windows	Yes
	IE 3	Macintosh	Yes
Class,IDs	Netscape 4	Macintosh	Yes
	Netscape 4	Windows	Yes
	IE 3, 4	Windows	Yes
	IE 3,4	Macintosh	Yes

INSPIRATIONAL DESIGN MODEL:

Steve Zehngut, Zeek Interactive

Warped. Sick and twisted. A little bit tweaked. Those are just a few of the comments people make about the interactive Web games created by the guys that make up ZeeK Interactive (www.zeek.com). But talk to president and Senior Programmer Steve Zehngut and you hear that behind everything ZeeK does there is a business to be run creating memorable and fun experiences on the Web. These experiences, in turn, have become some of corporate America's biggest marketing advantages on the Web.

Zehngut started ZeeK Interactive at the tender age of 24. Three years later, ZeeK Interactive has created some of the top games on the Web for Columbia TriStar Pictures, Toshiba, Aiwa, and even the U.S. Post Office.

What's its secret to interactive success? "We try to take the context of what we are doing and build something around that," says Zehngut. The Toshiba Web project (www.officemangaer.com/game.htm), designed in collaboration with Internet Outfitters, gave Zehngut and his crew an exciting challenge. How do you create an exciting game for a company that sells mostly copy machines and faxes? Never fear, ZeeK ended up creating a game in pure shoot 'em up style as a parody of the popular game Doom. Armed with wads of copy paper, you stroll through the office and shoot down other employees before they shoot you. Before the game, the site averaged 1,000 hits per week. After the game got exposure, within a week the hits started soaring to 150,000 hits a week. Not a bad way to get some brand recognition and have fun at the same time.

Zehngut's film background might come into play as ZeeK has created some of the most memorable online games for movie Web sites. One of the ZeeK classic games is Punch the Clown from our all-time favorite movie site, Multiplicity (www. spe.sony.com/Pictures/SonyMovies/ movies/multiplicity/stress/ sor.htm).

7.1

7.3

7.2

7.1   Big Shot for Columbia TriStar
        Television.

7.2   The Toshiba Copier Game designed in
        collaboration with Internet Outfitters.

7.3   Steve Zehngut.

In the game, a bobbing clown shouts "Loser," taunting you to punch him until he's a deflated mess. Another favorite is Big Shot (www.spe.sony.com/bigshot/), created for Columbia TriStar Television to promote various television shows. Big Shot's key to success was creating an intricate story with various games in which you, as the player, move up the studio system from mailroom clerk to studio head. Both of these games still receive many hits even though they are considered relatively geriatric for being over a year old. Other movie sites ZeeK has designed games for are "Anaconda," "High School High," and "The Man Who Knew Too Little."

We talked to Zehngut over lunch in early January during the MacWorld conference in San Francisco. His experience, creativity, and sheer honesty can help inspire any designer to create cool games for the Web. In addition, he's on his way to becoming the best business model for success for Generation X.

How did you get into doing what you are doing now?

I went to film school. I went to Cal State Northridge. I never studied computers. I was always kinda just into it. I worked as a production assistant in a post-production facility on a lot of films, and multimedia wasn't even a word yet, but I knew something was coming.

What attracted you to computers when the film industry seemed to be thriving?

I saw this new media as up and coming, so I left the film industry to get a production artist job. I worked there for two years and learned the Mac inside and out. While I was there, I picked up [Macromedia] Director and said "This is it!" The things that inspired me early on were stuff by Rvision. For the '94 Lollapalloza, they did an interactive press kit. So when I first was going to get into this, we were thinking two things—games and interactive press kits. I worked at Hollywood Online for two months before quitting and doing my own thing.

What made you want to work on your own?

Many things. I just wanted to be my own boss and try it. Before I started this job, I had about 25 jobs from being a teenager all the way up through college. I skipped around from job to job like every few months. I guess I just figured out that the only way I'd work steadily was to be my own boss and give it a shot. When I left my job to do my own thing, I was already pretty well versed in Director. I'm a totally self-taught programmer. I've never taken any programming classes. Really the only reason I became a Lingo programmer was because we needed someone to do that in our company. When we first started out, no one wanted to be the tech geek; everybody just kinda wanted to be the creative. Somebody had to do it, and since I knew what I was doing, I guess it defaulted to me. But half my job is programming and half is driving new business.

How did you get your ideas to create such different interactive pieces?

We take our inspiration from a lot of stuff. When we first started, we were a games company. The games were always there. That's how we spent a lot of our free time. When Shockwave came out, that was a natural for us because we were already creating Director games for IPK's (interactive press kits). The last CD-ROM we worked on was The New Adventures of Johnny Quest for Virgin Sound and Vision and that was summer '96. We don't do much CD-ROM stuff anymore. We just did a [presentational] kiosk recently. I'm seeing a lot of that come back now. It seems to me that corporations are now waking up to how powerful a well-designed CD-ROM sales kit can be. It's much easier than carrying around a bunch of brochures. You can do a lot of demonstrations [on your laptop].

So tell us more specifically about inspirations for your Web games.

As far as the games go, we get a lot of our inspirations from '80s arcade games. Have you ever seen MacMAME [on www.emulation.net]? It's an arcade game emulator. It has 185 games from the '80s. We get a lot of inspiration from that and play those a lot and look to that a lot for good ideas and good game play because in the '80s there really weren't any graphics. Everything was just line-art stuff. What was important was the game play. That's the reason why those games were so addicting. In the '80s, good game play ruled because they didn't have any graphics to deal with.

The game provides the visitor with a large amount of information in a very small space. It also responds quickly to user input by playing sounds and by instantly making changes to the display as the visitor moves the mouse across the screen. Moreover, we implemented text-switch messages instead of alert boxes to keep the interface consistent and focused the user's attention on the site. When the "assassin" fills out the form and clicks "assassinate," a text message appears to indicate whether or not the assassination was successful (see Figure 8.10) or whether or not the code name has been used (see Figure 8.11). The message provides instant feedback to the user. In sum, the Replacement Killers assassin game demonstrates how simple techniques such as hideLayer() and showLayer() can be used to create very complex and visually interesting designs that interact with the user in a direct and instantaneous way.

8.8

8.9

8.8 Using layers enabled us to free up the main frame for content only when activated by buttons or rollovers.

8.9 Being able to hide and show layers enabled us to provide a considerable amount of information in a limited space.

8.10

8.11

8.10   Using a text switch for messages in the interface
        eliminates the need for alert boxes.

8.11   An "error" message no longer looks like an "error"
        message when incorporated into the interface
        with a text switch. It's a call for attention, not a
        cause for alarm.

Chapter Summary

The fundamental challenge with design is to engage your audience in the design of the message that you are communicating with text and images and, perhaps, even animation. We discussed three general areas involving interactivity to help you make that transition from simply designing an aesthetic interface to designing an active, dynamic, and usable interface—by displaying information interactively and enabling the user to manipulate the content.

Cross-Browser and Platform Comparison Guide

The following table is a comprehensive list of the techniques used in this chapter and their support on the top two browsers—Netscape 2.0–4.0 and Internet Explorer 3.0–4.0—on both Macintosh and Windows.

URLs in This Chapter

- The Replacement Killers: http://www.spe.sony.com/movies/replacementkillers
- SuperFly Fashions: http://www.dhtmlzone.com/tutorials
- HTML Artistry companion Web site: http://www.htmlartistry.com/

Technique	Browser		Platform	Support
Switching Layers	Netscape 2,3		Both	No
	Netscape 4		Both	Yes
	IE 3	Both	No	
	IE 4	Both	Yes	
Text Switch	Netscape 2,3		Both	No
	Netscape 4		Both	Yes
	IE 3	Both	No	
	IE 4	Both	Yes	
Forms and Layers	Netscape 2,3		Both	No
	Netscape 4		Both	Yes
	IE 3	Both	No	
	IE 4	Both	Yes	
Click and Drag	Netscape 2,3		Both	No
	Netscape 4		Both	Yes
	IE 3	Both	No	
	IE 4	Both	Yes	

INSPIRATIONAL DESIGN MODEL:

Stephen Doyle, Doyle Partners

We were fans of Stephen Doyle's work before we even knew we were fans of Stephen Doyle's work. Over the past 13 years, his studio, Doyle Partners (formerly Drenttel Doyle Partners), has produced consistently compelling design pieces ranging from packaging to installations to book designs to posters to film titles. Sometimes irreverent, other times tender and graceful, but always witty, conscientious, engaging, simple, and smart, his creations demonstrate a love for graphic design and visual communication.

What we discovered in our conversation and interaction with Stephen at his New York studio was that not only is he a talented designer working with various media, but he is a warm, generous person, a proud father and husband, and a terribly funny guy! Ever ready with a quip or friendly advice, he freely shared a wealth of stories about his career as a designer and his role as a visual communicator. In that one morning, he reminded us that good design transcends a "look" or technological sophistication. Good design is about driving the message home to its audience. Undoubtedly easier said than done, he has proven his success as a designer by taking on a range of projects rather than limiting himself to a particular medium. No gimmicks or gloss, Stephen Doyle approaches his projects with an intense sense of humor, confidence, and charisma. We hope you enjoy the following dialogue half as much as we enjoyed participating in it!

8.1

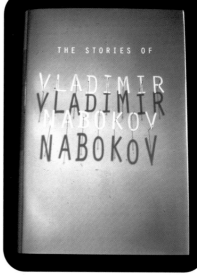

THE STORIES OF VLADIMIR VLADIMIR NABOKOV NABOKOV

8.3

8.2

8.1   Project: Bluebird Soap
       Client: Champion International
       Creative Director: Stephen Doyle
       Designers: Stephanie Rehder

8.2   Stephen Doyle.

8.3   Project: The Collected Stories of Vladmir Nabokov
       Client: Knopf
       Creative Director: Stephen Doyle
       Designer: Stephen Doyle

What are your most favorite projects and why?

That's hard to pin down. I love designing books because they are something like nothing else that will in some way live beyond us, if only for the idea of them. I love being an intermediary between something written and an audience. It's like being a host at a dinner party saying, "C'mere. I want you guys to meet." It's gratifying. You send somebody off with this thing, or you get him to read something that he wouldn't otherwise have done. I also have been enjoying doing film titles because it's really fun to work in space and time, to get the type to move across a picture, instead of the usual static relationship between images and text.

It looks like you're having fun.

It - is - a - blast! I can't believe that they pay people to do this! It's just too much fun. I have friends who are architects, and they work until midnight, and they struggle, and they've gotta get paid, and they get no respect, and they have to go to the site, and the contractors are mean to them. We're just graphic designers. Design is like having this great little hey-day where we're working at a plateau that's about ideas. I have proved that we're good for commerce because I've seen packaging being tested in stores, and I've seen sales increase basically 20 percent because the package is different. No price difference. No product difference. Nothing different but the packaging. So 20 percent on a multimillion dollar industry is an incredible amount of money. So that's really great. I feel confident about it. It's just a blast and a half! And, we get to do all different kinds of stuff. And the strangest people call. You wonder, "God, who's gonna call today?" What could be more fun?

Note:

Figure 8.7: HarperCollins College Outlines are designed to appeal to two distinct audiences: First the bookstore buyers, then the consumer. Traditionally, College Study Guides are books you would be embarrassed to be seen with—they look juvenile and remedial.

This series of books was designed as a sort of "college fashion accessory," something that is great to be seen with as well as something that sheds a human and often humorous light on the subject at hand. Before long, the booksellers were shelving these books as face-outs, and HarperCollins reported record sales.

8.7

8.7   Project: HarperCollins College Outline to Abnormal
       Psychology
       Client: HarperCollins Publisher
       Creative Director: Stephen Doyle
       Designers: Agnethe Glatved
       Photographer: Walter Wick

CHAPTER 9
CREATING THE ANIMATIONS OF YOUR DREAMS

We live in an age where we thumb our noses at stoney, text-only Web pages. We, as Web designers and users, expect Web sites to be alive with information. We want to see rich graphics and extraordinary animations in addition to the neatly formatted textual information.

Thanks to animated GIFs and Shockwave technology, the seduction and temptation of animation for animation's sake has been ever-possible and ever-present. Whereas some animate images and text simply because they can (Ever seen a rotating 3D logo? Hey, how about ten spinning icons on one Web page?), others implement animations to teach, clarify, and articulate ideas that in any other medium would fall short of the intended result. This multimedia approach to presenting information on the Web through animation empowers you and your audience to share and understand information more easily and more compellingly.

This chapter focuses on creating such animations with Dynamic HTML technology where you build on the advanced layout features discussed in Chapter 6, "Using Layers, the Building Blocks of Dynamic HTML." Imagine creating CD-ROM-like animations on the Web, but this time, without requiring users to download a special plug-in! You will also see real-world applications of the techniques, as well as interesting case studies on how some expert Web designers have imple-mented animations with the help of DHTML technology.

The chapter wraps up with a look at Kyle Cooper of Imaginary Forces in Los Angeles and his thoughts on animation in his opening movie credit titles.

Creating a Basic Animation

A basic animation involves using JavaScript to move a layer across the screen along a set of coordinates. These x and y coordinates plot points on an invisible grid, like a Cartesian plane, on your browser window (see Chapter 6). The position of the layer is marked by the upper-left corner of the layer. Moving a layer simply means repeatedly changing its top and left coordinates. With JavaScript, you might animate a layer straight up and down, left and right, diagonally, and along a customized path. Your animation might start onscreen or offscreen, as it might end onscreen or offscreen.

Moving a Layer from Point A to Point B

The most basic type of animation involves moving a layer from point A to point B. Be sure to pay careful attention when using this function because you will need it again to create some of the other animations in this chapter. This function moves a layer only once, which doesn't make for jaw-dropping animation and is most commonly called from another function.

```
1.      function
moveLayerTo(layerName,left,top){
2.
eval(layerRef+'["'+layerName+'"]'+styleSwitch
+'.top=top');
3.
eval(layerRef+'["'+layerName+'"]'+styleSwitch
+'.left=left');
}
```

To invoke this function, you need to write a line such as the following:

```
moveLayerTo(ÒmyLayer",324,211);
```

This function call asks `moveLayerTo()` to move the layer called "myLayer" to the coordinates 324,211.

- **Line 1:** Defines the function `moveLayerTo` and its parameters. These parameters include the name of the layer to move (`layerName`), the new left ("left") coordinate, and the new top ("top") coordinate. The `moveLayerTo` function moves the layer from Point A (where the layer is before you call this function) to Point B (the coordinates defined by the "left" and "top" parameters).
- **Line 2:** Sets the layer's top coordinate to the "top" number that was passed in as a parameter (324 in the example function call). (All that `eval(layerRef)` stuff, explained in Chapter 6, makes the function work across Netscape and IE.)
- **Line 3:** Sets the layer's left coordinate to the "left" number that was passed in as a parameter (211 in the sample function call). By setting the left and top coordinates, the layer moves to that position.

To make a layer animate, you need to call the `moveLayerTo` function over and over again, moving the layer to different positions on the screen. Each time you call it, you have to pass it a new set of coordinates. A real-world example is presented later in this chapter.

Moving a Layer Along a Straight Path

Moving a layer along a straight path (from left to right or from top to bottom) is the most straightforward type of animation because the x or the y coordinates are more mathematically predictable and mathematically more straightforward (see Figure 9.1).

9.1

9.1   Animation moving straight from left to right.

Animating from Bottom to Top

Begin with an example of a layer that contains standard HTML text moving from the bottom of the window to the top. At the beginning of the SuperFly demo, we used the bottom-to-top motion for the SuperFly character to appear as though he had snuck up on the viewer (see Figure 9.2).

Here's the moveLayerUp function that you would define within your <head> tags:

```
function moveLayerUp(layerName){
    if (eval(layerRef+'["'+layerName+'"]'+
styleSwitch+'.top != topStopPoint')){
        currTop-=4;
        eval(layerRef+'["'+layerName+'"]'+
styleSwitch+'.top = currTop');

setTimeout('moveLayerUp("'+layerName+'")',50)
;
    }
}
```

- **Line 1:** Defines the moveLayerUp function and its parameter, which is the name of the layer to move.
- **Line 2:** Does a comparison between the layer's current top coordinate and the variable specified as the top stop point. In English, it says that "If the layer's top coordinate is not equal to the top stop point, then continue on to Lines 3–5." Again, the eval(layerRef) stuff is used to make sure that the code is formatted in a way that is readable to both Internet Explorer and Netscape. To learn more about the eval() function and the layerRef stuff, refer back to Chapter 6, " Using Layers, the Building Blocks of Dynamic HTML."
- **Line 3:** If Line 2 proves true, we get to Line 3, which decreases the variable currTop by four. This is the variable that keeps track of the layer's top coordinate.

9.2

9.2   Animation moving straight from bottom to top.

- **Line 4:** This line says, "Set the layer's top coordinate to currTop." In Line 3 we subtracted 4 from currTop, so when we set the layer's top coordinate to currTop, it moves up by 4 pixels! This is where all the movement actually takes place.

> **Note:**
> You can write cleaner code by combining Lines 3 and 4 into something like the following:
>
> ```
> eval(layerRef+'["'+layerName+'"]'+styleSw
> itch+'.top-=4);,
> ```
>
> But IE can't seem to handle this type of equation, so we're stuck with two lines.

- **Line 5:** This line calls the `setTimeout()` function, which does just that; it tells the computer to chill out for a few milliseconds. The second parameter, in this case 50, specifies the number of milliseconds. The first parameter tells the computer what to do after its break is over. In this example, we are telling the computer to call the `moveLayerUp()` function again. Basically, the `moveLayerUp()` function runs every 50 milliseconds, continually moving the layer up by 4 pixels until the layer's top coordinate is equal to currTop. A function that calls itself over and over again is called a *recursive* function. The `moveLayerUp()` function is a good example of recursion in action. Note that we are also repassing the name of the layer to wipe to the `moveLayerUp()` function. The computer needs to be reminded of what layer it is moving each time that the function is called.

Here is the code in its entirety. Notice the additional global variables defined in the initialization routine. Global variable initializations are described in Chapter 6. You can modify a few lines of this code to make `moveLayerDown`, `moveLayerLeft`, and `moveLayerRight` functions. Check out the companion Web site for these examples.

```html
<html>
<head>
<title>scrolling up</title>
<script language="javascript">
//init lobal variables
var layerRef="null",layerStyleRef="null",
styleSwitch="null";
var topStopPoint=-700;
var backupTopStopPoint=topStopPoint;
var currTop=200;
var pxSwitch="null";
if (navigator.appName == "Netscape") {
    layerStyleRef="layer.";
    layerRef="document.layers";
    styleSwitch="";
    pxSwitch="";
}else{
    layerStyleRef="layer.style.";
    layerRef="document.all";
    styleSwitch=".style";
    pxSwitch="px";
}
function moveLayerUp(layerName){
    if (eval(layerRef+'["'+layerName+'"]'+
styleSwitch+'.top != topStopPoint')){
        currTop-=4;
        eval(layerRef+'["'+layerName+'"]'+
styleSwitch+'.top = currTop');

setTimeout('moveLayerUp("'+layerName+'")',50)
;
    }
}
</script>
</head>
<body onLoad="moveLayerUp('myLayer')">
<DIV ID="myLayer" STYLE="z-index: 10;
position: absolute; top: 200; left: 150px;
width: 250px;">
    <table width=150 height=200><tr><td
bgcolor=black>   </td></tr></table>
</DIV>
</body></html>
```

> **Note:**
> This code would be better if you could say, "Move the layer up until its top coordinate is greater than `topStopPoint`." However, IE has trouble evaluating < and > equations, so we have to use !=. This fact means that you have to decrease `currTop` by a multiple of `topStopPoint`, otherwise the layer's top coordinate will never be equal to `topStopPoint` and the layer will keep on moving up.

Moving a Layer Along a Customized Path

Animating a layer in straight lines is perfect for some purposes such as a ticker tape. However, sometimes you just want to break out of the straight and narrow and make your layer go any which way.

Luckily for you wilder folks, we've written a function called `animate()` just for this purpose. The function enables you to animate along a customized path. To give the SuperFly fly some character, we animated him along some crazy paths across and beyond the boundary of the browser window (see Figure 9.3).

9.3

9.3   Customized, curved path animations.

To do this, first, you have to create the layer that you want to animate. Then initialize some global variables and define the path that you want. Finally, write the simple code that animates the layer along a path and then you're ready to go. Here is how to do it step by step.

Create the Layer That You Want to Animate

This task is easy enough. Simply create a layer, fill it with whatever you want and then position it on your page.

Initialize Global Variables

Initializations should be old hat to you by now (see Chapter 6 to refresh your memory). Initiate the standard globals plus an additional one called "counter." Set counter equal to 0. We'll use this variable to track the layer's current position. Look at the code below to see how it's done.

Create a Path

Okay. Here's where we get into new territory. An array must be created that holds coordinate pairs. An *array* is a variable that can hold lots of different pieces of data. Each coordinate pair defines a location for the animation. Here's what the code looks like to define a path:

```
1.smallArray=new Array (250);
2.var coords="10,22, 12,34, 30,43, 54,20,
60,12, 90,3, 120,-10, 200,-30, 320,-5,
240,24";
3.var numPairs=10;
4.smallArray=coords.split(",");
```

- Line 1: This line defines a new array with 250 spaces for variables (we'll give it some room to grow just in case).
- Line 2: This line fills the array with coordinate pairs. You can put in as many pairs as you like; there is no limit. It can be a curved,

crooked, or diagonal line, and so on. This is the path that your layer takes. Look at the "Determining Coordinates" tip for an easier way to create a path than by trial and error.
- Line 3: The variable numPairs should equal the total number of coordinate pairs in your path. In this example, there are 10 pairs of coordinates.
- Line 4: This line puts the list of coordinates into the array that you defined in line 1. This is a convoluted way to put values into an array, but it avoids a bug in IE. (IE has a problem with direct array assignment.)

Tip:

When you animate a layer along a path, it can be a pain in the neck to figure out every single coordinate by trial and error. We created a tool that enables you to draw and save a path using your browser. This tool works only on Netscape 4.0+.

The tool is available on the Web at (http://www.htmlartistry.com/), and it comes with directions. Some tips on usage are as follows: The tool doesn't record your path if you move the mouse into the text box (see Figure 9.4). If you want to draw a path where the text box is, just make it smaller or move it to another location on the page.

If you want to create a path that begins off of the page, you can change the following lines:

```
currx=e.layerX;
        curry=e.layerY;
```

To make a path that starts off the page by 100 pixels to the left and right, modify the preceding code to the following:

```
currx=e.layerX-100;
        curry=e.layerY-100;
```

This modification subtracts 100 pixels from each pixel set in your path.
That's it. Have fun with it.

Create the animate() Function

We've created the layer that we want to animate, and have initialized the global variables so that the animations work properly on both platforms, and we've created our path. Now the good stuff. The code for animating along a path moves the layer to the first set of coordinates in your path, takes a little break, and then moves the layer to the second set and so on until there aren't any more coordinates in your path. Here's the code:

```
function animate(layerName){
    if (counter < numPairs*2){

moveLayerTo(layerName,smallArray[counter],
smallArray[counter+1]);
        counter+=2;

setTimeout('animate("'+layerName+'")',30);
    }
}
```

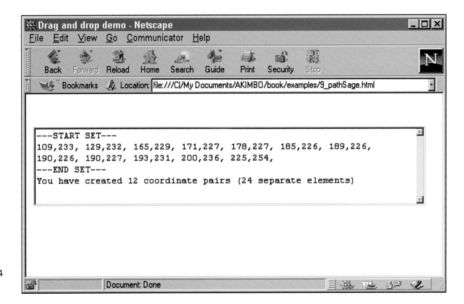

9.4

9.4   Our tool for determining coordinates easily.
       (Note: For Netscape 4.0 and on PC only.)

- **Line 1:** Defines the `animate()` function and its parameter, which accepts the name of the layer to animate.
- **Line 2:** Tells the computer to do the remaining three lines until the counter is equal to twice the number of pairs. Basically, the computer loops through each coordinate pair until none remain. In this example, it loops 9 more times, until the counter is equal to 20.
- **Line 3:** Calls the `moveLayerTo()` function (defined earlier in this chapter) to move the layer to the first two coordinates in the array. The syntax that you see there allows the computer to get to the values stored in the array.
- **Line 4:** Increments the counter by 2. It's incremented by two so that it starts next time at the next coordinate pair.
- **Line 5:** Calls the `setTimeout()` function, which tells the computer to take a break for 30 milliseconds. After the break, the routine calls itself again, executes the animation along the defined path, and then takes another break. This routine loops until the counter is equal to 20.

That's it. Take a look at the complete code that follows to get a better feel for how the `animate()` function works.

```
<HTML>
<HEAD>
        <TITLE>Simple Anim along a path
Example</TITLE>
</HEAD>
<SCRIPT LANGUAGE=JAVASCRIPT>
//GLOBAL VARIABLES INITS
var counter=0;
if (navigator.appName == "Netscape") {
    layerRef="document.layers";
    styleSwitch="";
}else{
    layerRef="document.all";
    styleSwitch=".style";
}
//define path for this layer
    smallArray=new Array (250);
    var coords="10,22, 12,34, 30,43, 54,20,
60,12, 90,3, 120,-10, 200,-30, 320,-5,
240,24";
```

```
    var numPairs=10;
    smallArray=coords.split(",");
function animate(layerName){
    if (counter < numPairs*2){

moveLayerTo(layerName,smallArray[counter],
smallArray[counter+1]);
        counter+=2;

setTimeout('animate("'+layerName+'")',30);
    }
}
function moveLayerTo(layerName,left,top){

eval(layerRef+'["'+layerName+'"]'+styleSwitch
+'.top=top');

eval(layerRef+'["'+layerName+'"]'+styleSwitch
+'.left=left');
}

</SCRIPT>
<BODY onLoad="animate('mylayer')">
<div id="mylayer" style="position: absolute;
visibility: visible; top: 200px; left:
200px; z-index: 10; width: 640; height:
480;">
        <table width=150 height=200><tr><td
bgcolor=black>   </td></tr></table>
</div>
</BODY></HTML>
```

Creating a Wipe Transition

Creating a wipe makes just about everybody and their mothers scream, "Wowie, that's cool." We used a wipe effect on a transparent pull-down menu in the SuperFly Catalogue (see Figure 9.5). The basic concept behind a wipe is that you will be "clipping" the edges of a layer until the entire layer is gone. It looks as if the layer has been wiped away, just as if you were wiping away words from a blackboard or steam on a bathroom mirror.

The first thing that you need to do is to create a layer. After that, you can initialize some global variables so that the clipping works on both browsers. Then all you need to do is write a short routine that does the clipping on the layer of your choice. When all the code is written, simply call the `wipe()` function and enjoy! Here is how to do it step by step.

9.5

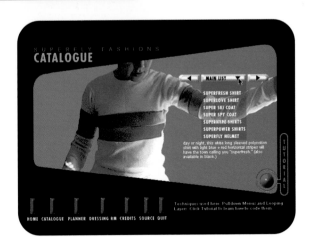

9.5   Wipe effect in action.

Create the Layer That You Want to Wipe

This first part is easy. Simply create a layer and position it anywhere on your page. In this example, you will wipe the layer left or clip the right side of the layer until the layer is entirely clipped. In this example, the layer contains a big black table so that you can see the motion of the wipe more clearly. However, you can put whatever you want in your layer: images, text, and so on. In your pull-down menu example, you used a transparent graphic (see Figure 9.7). You might want to look at the code that follows the step-by-step breakdown to get a better feel for what you're about to do.

Initialize Global Variables

Actually, in this case, there are no global variables to initialize because you'll see an example that only works in Netscape. We developed a wipe that works in Internet Explorer. However, it's still quite buggy and nonmodular. We'll be working on it and will put the in-progress version on the companion Web site. Perhaps you can help us develop a neat and clean cross-browser wipe?

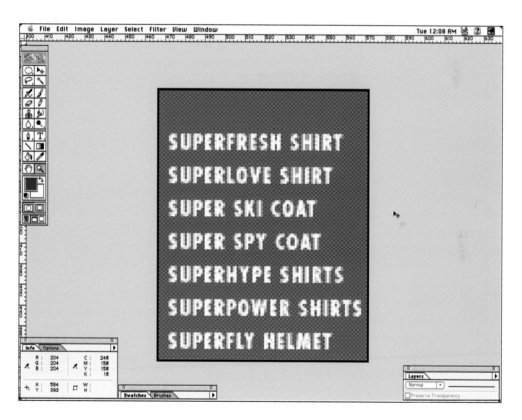

9.6

9.6   A close-up of the pull-down menu layer used for the wipe effect. Notice that we used the transparent checkerboard described in Chapter 4 to create a see-through menu.

Write the Code That Clips the Layer

Now you are ready to write the code that handles all the action. Let's jump right into it.

```
1.     function wipeLeft(layerName,speed){
2.         if
(document.layers[layerName].clip.right > 0){
3.
document.layers[layerName].clip.right-=speed;
4.            setTimeout('wipeLeft("'
+layerName+ '",' +speed+ ')',40);
5.         }
6.     }
```

- **Line 1**: Defines the `wipeLeft` function and its parameters, which are the name of the layer to wipe and the speed with which to wipe. You can send this function the name of any layer that you want to wipe. For speed, enter any number you want and then watch the results until you're happy. Start with a number such as 10. You can also wipe in other directions. The code is included in the following full example.
- **Line 2**: Says "If the layer's width is greater than 0, then execute the next three lines." Basically, if the layer is still visible on the screen (if it hasn't been wiped away yet), do the next three lines. The `eval()` function call simply makes sure that the global variables previously defined will be read properly.
- **Line 3**: Subtracts 10 pixels from the layer's width. This is where the "clipping" takes place. By trimming 10 pixels from the layer's right edge, the layer looks like it is wiping left. In the example, we clip by 10 pixels. You can change this number to 1, 20, 145, or to however many pixels you want. The higher the number, the faster the layer will wipe.
- **Line 4**: This line calls the `setTimeout` function, which tells the computer to chill out for a few milliseconds. The second parameter, in this case 20, specifies the number of milliseconds. The first parameter tells the computer what to do after its break is over. In this example, we are telling the computer to call the `wipe()` function again. Basically, the

`wipe()` function runs every 20 milliseconds, continually subtracting 10 from the width until the width is equal to 0—until the layer is completely wiped away. A function that calls itself over and over again is called a *recursive* function. The `wipe()` function is a good example of recursion in action. Note that we are also repassing the name of the layer to wipe to the `wipe()` function. The computer needs to be reminded of what layer it is wiping each time that the function is called.

Start the Wiping

Now everything is set up for a clean wipe. You just need to call the `wipe()` function to make it happen. You can call `wipe()` from a button or in the onLoad handler as we do in the following example. Check out the code to see how it all fits together. Actually, in the example, we made it even easier for you by adding a function called `runWipe()`, which enables you to run a wipe in any direction. The `runWipe()` function accepts three parameters: the name of the layer to wipe, the speed, and the direction in which to wipe (left, right, up, or down). A call to `runWipe()` looks like this:

```
runWipe('bg',20,'left')

<HTML>
        <HEAD>
                <TITLE> Wipe Test </TITLE>
<SCRIPT LANGUAGE="JavaScript">

    function runWipe(layerName,speed,
direction){
        document.layers[layerName].
visibility="visible";
        if (direction == "down"){
            var stopPoint=document.
layers[layerName].clip.bottom;

document.layers[layerName].clip.bottom=0;

wipeDown(layerName,speed,stopPoint);
        }else if (direction == "up"){
            wipeUp(layerName,speed);
        }else if (direction == "right"){
            var stopPoint=document.
layers[layerName].clip.right;
```

```
document.layers[layerName].clip.right=0;

wipeRight(layerName,speed,stopPoint);
            }else if (direction == "left"){
                wipeLeft(layerName,speed);
            }
        }
        function
wipeDown(layerName,speed,stopPoint){
            if
(document.layers[layerName].clip.bottom <
stopPoint){

document.layers[layerName].clip.bottom+=speed
;
                setTimeout('wipeDown("'
+layerName+ '",' +speed+ ',' +stopPoint+
')',40);
            }
        }
        function wipeUp(layerName,speed){
            if
(document.layers[layerName].clip.bottom > 0){

document.layers[layerName].clip.bottom-
=speed;
                setTimeout('wipeUp("'
+layerName+ '",' +speed+ ')',40);
            }
        }
        function
wipeRight(layerName,speed,stopPoint){
            if
(document.layers[layerName].clip.right <
stopPoint){

document.layers[layerName].clip.right+=speed;
                setTimeout('wipeRight("'
+layerName+ '",' +speed+ ',' +stopPoint+
')',40);
            }
        }
        function wipeLeft(layerName,speed){
            if
(document.layers[layerName].clip.right > 0){

document.layers[layerName].clip.right-=speed;
                setTimeout('wipeLeft("'
+layerName+ '",' +speed+ ')',40);
            }
        }
</SCRIPT>
</HEAD>
<BODY BGCOLOR="black" TEXT="yellow"
onLoad="runWipe('bg',20,'left')">
<div id="bg" style="position:absolute;
left:0; top:0; width:302; height:285;
z-index:200;; visibility:hidden">
        <IMG SRC="../assets/rh_ex1.GIF"
WIDTH=510 HEIGHT=391 BORDER=0>
</div>
</BODY>
</HTML>
```

Making Your Layers Scroll

You might run into some situations where you think, "Geez, I wish I could put a scrollbar in that layer." Say that you have some kind of story that you want to put in a single layer behind a customized mask. You need to create some sort of scrolling mechanism for your viewers to see the entire story (see Figure 9.7). Although it's not possible to put the standard scrollbars in a layer, you can simulate a scrolling effect with a bit of simple code. Please note that we haven't been able to make this technique work in IE yet, but we're working on it. The function in progress will be up on the companion Web site (http://www.htmlartistry.com/).

The basic concept is that you will create up and down (or left and right) buttons. When clicked, the layer in question moves up or down a little bit—just as if it were being "scrolled." The first thing that you need to do is to create a layer and a couple of buttons. After that, you can initialize some global variables so that the scrolling works on both browsers. Then all you need to do is to write a routine to do the scrolling.

Here is how to do it step by step.

Create Scrolling Layer and Button

Go ahead and create the layer that you want to scroll. Place it anywhere on your page. Now create a couple of buttons that say "up" and "down." You can put these buttons in any layer except for the one that you want to scroll. If you put them in that layer, they would scroll off the page!

Initialize Global Variables

In order for this function to work, you need to run the standard initialization script as defined in Chapter 6, or you can just look at the code in the example that follows the step-by-step instruction.

Write the Function That Makes the Layer Scroll

The `moveLayerBy` function can be used to move the layer up, down, left, right, or diagonally in any direction, and it moves the layer relative to its current position. The `moveLayerBy` function accepts three parameters: the name of the layer to move, the number of pixels by which to move the layer's left coordinate and, finally, the number of pixels by which to move the layer's top coordinate. The direction of the layer is determined by the values sent in as parameters.

9.7

9.7   Example of scrolling layer in action.

```
function
moveLayerBy(layerName,leftPix,topPix){
    var
topCoord=eval(layerRef+'["'+layerName+'"]'+
styleSwitch+'.top') + topPix;
    var
leftCoord=eval(layerRef+'["'+layerName+'"]'+
styleSwitch+'.left') + leftPix;

eval(layerRef+'["'+layerName+'"]'+styleSwitch
+'.top='+topCoord);

eval(layerRef+'["'+layerName+'"]'+styleSwitch
+'.left='+leftCoord);
}
```

- **Line 1**: The first line creates a new variable for the layer's top coordinate by adding the layer's current top coordinate to the value sent in as a parameter. This parameter number can be a positive or negative number. A negative number makes the layer move up on the page. A positive number makes the layer move down.
- **Line 2**: The second line creates a new value for the layer's left coordinate in the same manner.
- **Line 3**: This line sets the layer's top coordinate to the new number created in line 1.
- **Line 4**: This line sets the layer's left coordinate to the value created in line 2.

That was easy. Now all you need to do is add onClick() handlers to your buttons and the layer can move around in any which way. Check out the code that follows to see how it's done.

Note:

This does not yet work in IE because IE won't give up layer positioning data.

```
<HTML>
<HEAD>
        <TITLE>Simple scrolling
Example</TITLE>
</HEAD>
<SCRIPT LANGUAGE=JAVASCRIPT>
        //GLOBAL VARIABLES
            var
layerRef="null",layerStyleRef="null",
styleSwitch="null";
```

```
        var widthClipSwitch="null";

    function init(){
        if (navigator.appName ==
"Netscape") {
            layerRef="document.layers";
            styleSwitch="";
        }else{
            layerRef="document.all";
            styleSwitch=".style";
        }
    }

function
moveLayerBy(layerName,leftPix,topPix){
    var
topCoord=eval(layerRef+'["'+layerName+'"]'+
styleSwitch+'.top') + topPix;
    var
leftCoord=eval(layerRef+'["'+layerName+'"]'+
styleSwitch+'.left') + leftPix;

eval(layerRef+'["'+layerName+'"]'+styleSwitch
+'.top='+topCoord);

eval(layerRef+'["'+layerName+'"]'+styleSwitch
+'.left='+leftCoord);
}

</SCRIPT>
<STYLE TYPE="text/css">
    #mylayer {position: absolute;
visibility: visible; top: 200px; left:
200px; z-index: 10; width: 640; height:
480; }
</STYLE>
<BODY onLoad="init();">

<div id="mylayer">
        <table width=150 height=200><tr><td
bgcolor=black>   </td></tr></table>
</div>
<a href="javascript:moveLayerBy('mylayer',0,
-10)">Scroll Up</A><BR>
<a href="javascript:moveLayerBy
('mylayer',0,10)">Scroll Down</a><BR>
<a href="javascript:moveLayerBy('mylayer',
-10,0)">Scroll Left</A><BR>
<a href="javascript:moveLayerBy
('mylayer',10,0)">Scroll Right</a><BR>

</BODY>
</HTML>
```

Moving Backgrounds

Moving backgrounds are probably the greatest innovation since the blink tag. That's sarcasm in case you didn't notice. No, seriously folks, you can make a really cool effect with a moving background. In the SuperFly Outfit Planner, when you select a rainy day outfit, (see Figure 9.8) the background simulates falling rain, whereas a sunny day outfit produces clouds moving along a blue sky (see Figure 9.9).

The basic concept is that you create a huge layer that extends past the edge of the visible screen. You then create a huge table within this layer and set its background image to some sort of tiling graphic similar to a normal background graphic.

Then initialize some global variables and write the code to make the layer move in the direction of your choice. This function is very similar to the animate-left function except that you need to put in an extra line that resets the animation before it scrolls off the page. (If you want, you can let the animation run off the page, but we think that it looks funny.) The following sections take you through the steps.

9.8

9.9

9.8   Example of moving backgrounds to create the effect of falling rain.

9.9   Another example of moving backgrounds in action. This time with a horizontal movement, suggestive of how clouds move.

Create a Background Layer

Create a layer with a z-index of 0 or 1 and top and left coordinates of 0, and put a table with a tiling background (a small image that, when repeated, creates a seamless larger image) inside it. Make your table very wide so that it completely covers the screen at all times, even as it moves left or right. We set ours to 1280, double the width of our target screen size of 640x480 (see Figure 9.10).

The height doesn't have to be any larger than the height of the screen because the table won't be moving up or down. It's useful to explicitly set the window size for this technique so that you know exactly what its dimensions are. Opening windows is described in Chapter 5, "Adding Sophistication and Interactivity with HTML and JavaScript."

```
<DIV ID="movingBG">
    <TABLE WIDTH="1280" HEIGHT="480"
BACKGROUND="backgroundTile.gif">
        <TD>
            <TD>
                 
            </TD>
        </TR>
    </TABLE> </DIV>
```

Be sure to put a nonbreaking space ( ) in the TD, or the table won't show up in Netscape.

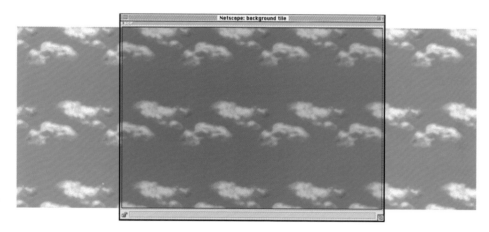

9.10

9.10   A moving background layer should extend
        beyond the browser window boundaries.

Create and Initialize Global Variables

Before you can write the function that performs the actual movement, you need to define a few global variables and initialize one of them in the initialization routine as described in Chapter 6.

```
Line 1: var leftStopPoint="null";
    Line 2: var currLeft=0;
    Line 3: if (navigator.appName ==
"Netscape") {
    Line 4: leftStopPoint=-640;
    Line 5: }else{
    Line 6: leftStopPoint="-640px";
```

- **Line 1**: The variable `leftStopPoint` defines the x coordinate at which the background will stop moving left.
- **Line 2**: The variable currLeft keeps track of the layer's current left coordinate. Remember that in the CSS definition of the layer, we set the coordinates to 0,0. So here we set the current left coordinate to 0 as well.
- **Lines 3-6**: This is the initialization routine that we call at the beginning of every technique to ensure that it will work on both IE and Netscape. The only difference between the browsers in this case is the "px." IE gives faulty answers if you attempt to evaluate numbers without "px" attached to them. See the note in Appendix C, "Cross-Browser Dynamic HTML Reference List."

Write the Function That Moves the Background

This function does the same thing as the `moveLayerLeft` function, except that when it reaches its ending point, it resets and starts all over again. It loops until the user loads a new page or closes the browser window.

```
Line 1: function moveLayerLeft(layerName){
Line 2:    if
(eval(layerRef+'["'+layerName+'"]'+
styleSwitch+'.left != leftStopPoint')){
Line 3:        currLeft-=2;
Line 4:
```

```
eval(layerRef+'["'+layerName+'"]'+styleSwitch
+'.left = currLeft');
Line 5:
setTimeout('moveLayerLeft("'+layerName+'")',
20);
Line 6:        }else{
Line 7:        currLeft=0;
Line 8:
eval(layerRef+'["'+layerName+'"]'+styleSwitch
+'.left = currLeft');
Line 9:
setTimeout('moveLayerLeft("'+layerName+'")',
20);
Line 10:        }
Line 11: }
```

- **Line 1**: Defines the `moveLayerLeft` function and its parameter (the name of the layer to move).
- **Line 2**: If the layer's left coordinate is not equal to leftStopPoint, then continue on to lines 3–5. The `eval()` function is for compatibility between IE and Netscape and is described in Chapter 6.
- **Line 3**: Decrements `currLeft` by two.
- **Line 4**: Sets the layer's left coordinate to `currLeft`. This is how the movement happens.
- **Line 5**: This line calls the `setTimeout()` function, which is described earlier in this chapter.
- **Line 7**: Resets currLeft to 0 once the layer has moved all the way to `leftStopPoint`.
- **Line 8**: Moves the layer back to where it started (0,0).
- **Line 9**: As in Line 5, calls the `moveLayerLeft()` function, which starts the whole process over again.

Set an Event Handler to Call the moveLayerLeft() Function

We set our background to start moving as soon as the page loads.

```
<body bgcolor=black text=white
onLoad="moveLayerLeft('myLayer')">
```

If you want to see this technique in action, you can look at a simplified example, the code for which follows. By changing a few operators along with the table's dimensions, you can make the layer move up, down, right, and diagonally.

```html
<html>
<head>
<title>moving backgrounds</title>
<script language="javascript">

        //global variables
        var leftStopPoint="null";
        var
layerRef="null",layerStyleRef="null",
styleSwitch="null";
        var currLeft=0;

        function init(){
        if (navigator.appName == "Netscape")
{
                layerStyleRef="layer.";
                layerRef="document.layers";
                styleSwitch="";
                leftStopPoint=-640;
        }else{

layerStyleRef="layer.style.";
                layerRef="document.all";
                styleSwitch=".style";
                leftStopPoint="-640px";
                }
        }
        function moveLayerLeft(layerName){
                        if
(eval(layerRef+'["'+layerName+'"]'+
styleSwitch+'.left != leftStopPoint')){
                                currLeft=2;

eval(layerRef+'["'+layerName+'"]'+styleSwitch
+'.left = currLeft');

setTimeout('moveLayerLeft("'+layerName+'")',
20);
                        }else{

currLeft=0;

eval(layerRef+'["'+layerName+'"]'+styleSwitch
+'.left = currLeft');

setTimeout('moveLayerLeft("'+layerName+'")',
20);
                        }
        }

        function showLayer(layerName){

eval(layerRef+'["'+layerName+'"]'+styleSwitch
+'.visibility="visible"');
        }

        function hideLayer(layerName){

eval(layerRef+'["'+layerName+'"]'+styleSwitch
+'.visibility="hidden"');
        }

</script>

<STYLE TYPE="text/css">
#movingBG{position: absolute; z-index: 10;
visibility: visible; left: 0px; top: 0px;}
</STYLE>
</head>

<body bgcolor=black text=white
onLoad="init();moveLayerLeft('movingBG');">

<!--background-->
<DIV ID="movingBG" >
<table border=1 width="1280" height="480"
background="../../images/main/reversed.gif">
        <tr>
                <td>
                 
                </td>

        </tr>
</table>
</DIV>

</body>
```

> **Note:**
>
> It's possible to create a timeline function in JavaScript that controls animations, layer property changes, and sound. The code for the timeline is quite complicated. It is described fully in the SuperFly tutorial. However, the best bet for making a truly robust timeline is to pick up a copy of Macromedia's Dreamweaver and to use its graphical timeline tool.

CASE STUDY:
ELIXIR MOVIE TRAILER BY AKIMBO DESIGN, "CREATING A CINEMATIC WEB EXPERIENCE"

Macromedia approached Akimbo Design to create a trade-show demonstration and Web site by using its new HTML editor called Dreamweaver. We came up with a concept for a fictitious movie called "Elixir." Having been film buffs for years, we were excited to have the opportunity to create our own movie site. To create the trailer animation in DHTML, Akimbo Design looked to actual movie trailers in theaters and movie rentals for inspiration. Although the objective for the project was to show off the capabilities of Macromedia Dreamweaver, Akimbo wanted to wow visitors with a stunning combination of edgy, eye-catching graphics, adrenalin-pumping music, sound effects, voice-overs, and convincing animations in a 28-second, well-edited movie trailer optimized for the Web, weighing in at 150K.

We began the project by starting with a plot idea. Our cynical minds devised the following: A medical school student invents an elixir that, when ingested, ends drug addiction; the government and some powerful industry allies want to destroy the formula and the researcher before her elixir cuts into their profits and kickbacks.

`</html>`

Our design grew out of the plot and Macromedia's need for an attention-grabbing presentation. We storyboarded a site with three sections: trailer, cast, and story (see Figure 9.11). The trailer would showcase Dreamweaver's Dynamic HTML animation capabilities, the cast would show interactivity, and the story would demonstrate text formatting.

After spending hours looking through PhotoDisc's stock photography catalogs, we selected a look and hundreds of photos that could be used in the site. We pared these images down, refined the look and feel, and started designing the site. We chose a cold, blue-black-ish color palette to reinforce the gloomy, paranoid and hi-tech feeling of the plot.

A movie trailer, whether on a little monitor or large movie screen, must tell a story in practically a heartbeat. All aspects—images and sound—must be carefully selected and fine-tuned to deliver a message clearly, concisely, and memorably.

Akimbo Design made sure that all the imagery used would make a strong graphical impact on viewers. Brightly backlit slides of amorphous cellular matter, quick stolen glimpses of the "bad guys" and "good guys" through surveillance camera lenses, the hero and heroine speeding away on a motorcycle, an extreme close-up of a mysterious and menacing surgeon—a small sampling of the images used to tell the story of a gutsy grad student who is on the run from unknown assassins for her revolutionary discovery of a cure for all drug addiction.

At the beginning of every project, we create a series of sketches. For the Elixir animation sequence, putting our thoughts down on paper first helped us to visualize how the story was to unfold in the trailer, to figure out how to incorporate type and sound, as well as to determine the transitions

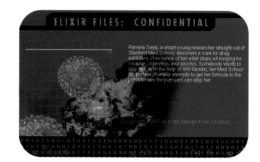

9.11

9.11   Elixir site sections.

between the different frames of the animation (see Figure 9.12).

Regardless of the technology—DHTML or Shockwave—this storyboarding phase is crucial in nailing your story. We decided upon quick cuts and constant motion to enhance the breakneck and frenzied pace. After we figured out these different scenes, we had to plan how to do it technically.

Every scene combines different DHTML techniques to create as much motion as possible. For example, in the opening scenes, there are small transparent GIFs of cells moving sporadically back and forth—animation along a path—while the background swaps between different layers of images (see Figure 9.13).

Another way to suggest movement was to make use of two overlapping layers moving in opposite directions. In the get-away motorcycle scene, we used a blurred moving background tile, moving from right to left, while a transparent GIF of the motorcycle traveled from left to right. With only the motorcycle moving, the motion would look two-dimensional and unconvincing (see Figure 9.14). The combination of two layers moving in opposite directions enhanced the motion of the motorcycle. We used the same type of effect in the scene where a mysterious man with a briefcase is scurrying away

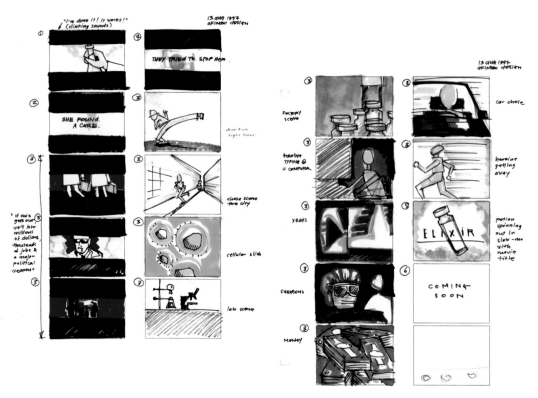

9.12

9.12   Storyboard example of the Elixir trailer.

(see Figure 9.2). Again, we have a blurred image moving in one direction while the figure moves in an another.

Of course, no movie trailer animation is complete without sound. We made a soundtrack in Flash and used JavaScript to play sounds when needed. While a techno loop plays throughout the duration of the movie, specific sounds occur in synch with specific frames. For example, at the very beginning of the animation, a voice-over of the medical student proclaims, "I've done it! It works!" and jumps into the techno beat. At the end, when the image of a gun appears suddenly, you hear a gunshot, and as the name of the movie comes up, you hear an eerie, hi-pitched, almost alien sound.

We found that in creating a complex animation sequence in dynamic HTML, we could deliver simple, action-packed, exciting, and low K movies without the use of plug-ins. It enabled us to achieve some of the interactivity of Director with some of the anima-

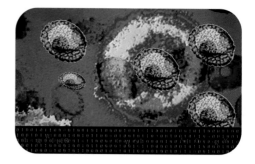

9.13

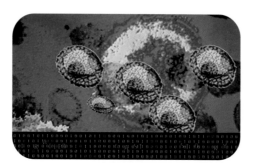
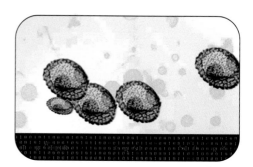

9.13   One set of layeres animating along a path while
        background layers swap.

9.14

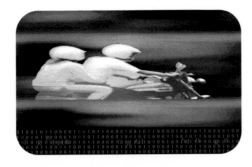

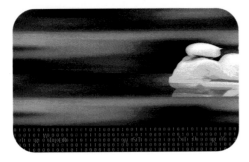

9.14   Two moving layers to accentuate the motion and
speed of the motorcycle.

tion capabilities of Flash without any extra software. We found Dynamic HTML technology to be a great asset in creating professional Web sites.

A chapter about enhanced Web animation would be incomplete without mention of Shockwave technology. From such arcade-like games as mentioned earlier in our discussion with Zeek Interactive to animated movie trailer-esque presentations as Akimbo Design's home page Flash animation (http://www. akimbodesign.com/) (see Figure 9.15), Web designers and developers have enthusiastically created "plugged" versions of their sites to provide rich, multimedia experiences. In Chapters 5 and 8, we present how to achieve sophisticated interactivity without plug-ins or fancy CGI scripts; and earlier in this chapter, we guide you through the process of creating full-blown animations all with just HTML.

9.15

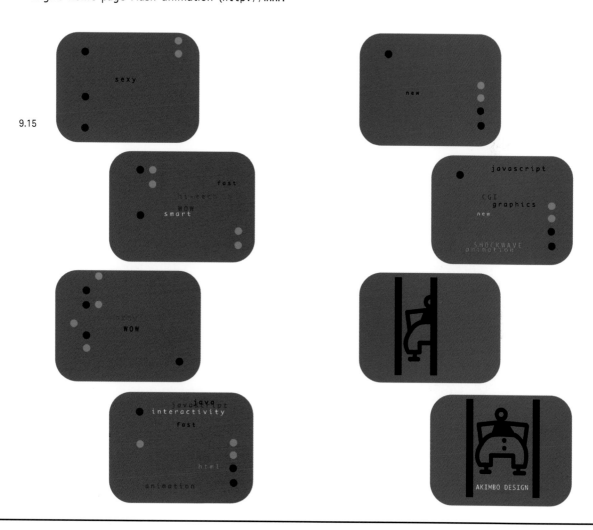

9.15   An example of Flash animation.

CASE STUDY:
INCORPORATING SHOCKWAVE WITH DHTML—KARL ACKERMANN, 415 PRODCUTIONS

We were initially drawn to the Solar System site created for Macromedia's DHTML Zone (`http://www.dhtmlzone.com/swdhtml/` and then click on "Solar System") for the rich illustrations and humorous animations (see Figure 9.16). Its creator, Karl Ackermann, is an artist who is undaunted by computer technology. His unique, organic, and loose drawing style, in fact, has been defined by using a mouse to create his computer illustrations. His past work includes the award-winning Love Disk '95 interactive CD-ROM created in Macromedia Director. It's no surprise that Karl's design work on the Web is paving the way for the rest of us.

So why try to integrate Shockwave Flash movies into a Dynamic HTML Web site? At the moment, Internet Explorer 4.0 for Windows 95 is the only browser that supports this feature at all. Although it seems like a limited audience, Netscape users will soon enjoy this type of functionality. But what's the point? Well, you've seen how popular Flash has become. Web designers have been enjoying the scaleability, editability, and small file sizes of these vector art movies. And of course, their audiences have been enjoying the quick downloads for such rich animations.

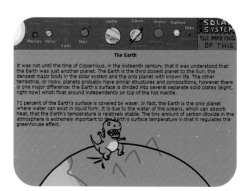

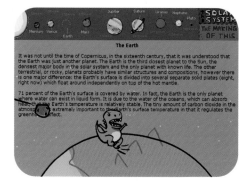

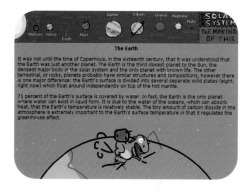

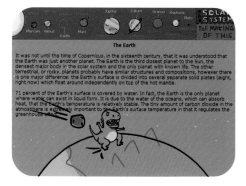

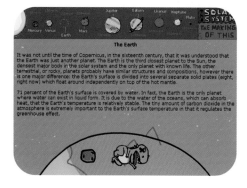

9.16 Bright colors, expressive illustrations, and funny animations caught our attention.

Thanks to an online demo designed and programmed by Karl Ackermann of 415 Productions, we discovered that the combination of the two technologies can be quite exciting.

Now, thanks to a new feature in the Shockwave Flash control, the movies can be transparent, and therefore be incorporated seamlessly into a multilayered Web environment.

The Solar System content lends itself to this type of feature. When you click on a planet in the navigation, it appears to zoom onto the foreground of the page over the HTML text (see Figure 9.17). Each of the nine planets and the sun is a separate Flash movie in its own layer. When a planet zooms in or out, JavaScript is actually changing its size and location on-the-fly. This scaling effect gives the site depth as well as motion. The planets lined up in a row along the top of the window appear further in the background while each close-up version brings the textual context to the forefront of the viewer's attention. By using Flash vector art technology, Karl can create a drawing of a planet once and it can scale flawlessly at any size—big or small (see Figure 9.18).

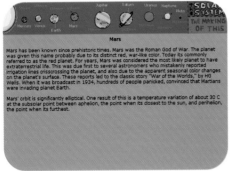

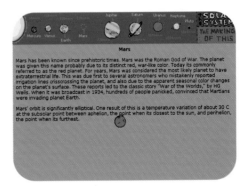

9.17

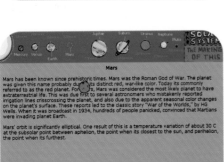

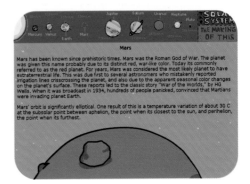

9.17 Planets in a Flash movie zooming over the HTML text.

Fun and entertaining, the site also engages the user on an educational level. The different illustrations provide clear distinctions between the planets. The site is simple, intuitive, and easily navigable. A new planet in the foreground signals that the HTML text has changed. Karl wisely chose regular HTML text for the written content for its easy updatability and of course, for you to "select and copy it from this demo and paste into your science homework due next Tuesday." What a guy!

Certainly, his sense of humor was a major factor in getting him through the project. When we met with him, Karl struck us as someone who truly has fun with what he's doing. From the conceptual stages of the project, he seems to enjoy letting his imagination run wild exploring the possibilities (see Figure 9.19). He usually creates his storyboards in Flash right away to see the relationships between elements and to plan how the animation will work.

Karl organized the 20 separate overlapping layers into four major groups—invisible tables, Flash movies, HTML text, and background images (see Figure 9.20). The topmost level of layers contains invisible areas defined as tables in the HTML. According to Karl, "They react to movement and clicks from the mouse to initiate actions like calling a JavaScript function to begin zooming a planet." Each of the nine planet movies is in its own layer so that the JavaScript might call upon the planets individually. Again, the Flash movies do not obstruct the HTML text or images because of the new control that makes the movie transparent. All the information about the planets is contained in regular HTML text that rewraps according to the browser window size. And last but not least, the background is composed of a few layers of GIFs and colored tables.

Note:

For more information on the code, please check out the demo itself (http://www.dhtmlzone.com/swdhtml/ and click on "Solar System"). We won't go into it here because Internet Explorer for Windows is the only browser and platform that supports it.

So, a sense of humor combined with fun graphics, clever animations, and a keen awareness for the capabilities of Web technologies created a strong presentation of useful information about the Solar System. Without any one of those factors, the site would have fallen flat. It wasn't about pretty pictures. It wasn't about shapes moving across the page randomly. Nor was the site just about HTML. It took a strong personality, organizational skills, Web savvy, and design sense to pull the content together in a cohesive and engaging presentation. Karl Ackermann's multidisciplinary involvement in a Web project as a designer and programmer breathes life into the content in a fuller, more enhanced capacity.

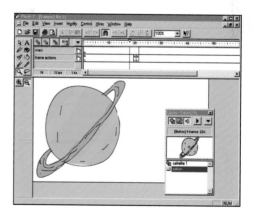

9.18

9.18   Drawing of Saturn in progress using the Flash animator.

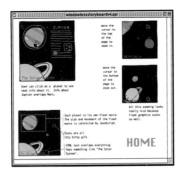

9.19

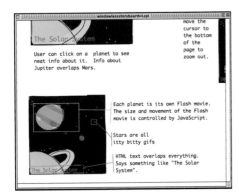

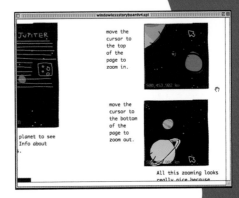

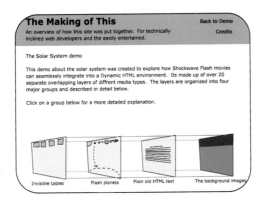

9.20

9.19   Online storyboards created in Flash.

9.20   Exploded view of the layer organization of the
        demo.

Chapter Summary

So this is it. You've reached the end of the beginning. Web design will never be the same. Because now, you have the technology all within HTML to create mouth-dropping, beat-bopping animations. We have reached full circle. This part of the book began by discussing absolute positioning with layers, enhanced typography with cascading style sheets, and implementing advanced interactive features. Hopefully this last chapter has empowered you to take all the information and create the designs of your dreams—designs literally set into motion.

Cross-Browser and Platform Comparison Guide

This is a comprehensive list of the techniques used in this chapter and their support on the top two browsers Netscape—2.0-4.0 and Internet Explorer 3.0-4.0—on both Macintosh and Windows.

URLs in This Chapter

- SuperFly Fashions: `http://www.dhtmlzone.com/tutorials`
- Elixir: `http://www.dreamweaver.com/` (click on gallery)
- Akimbo Design: `http://www.akimbodesign.com/`
- Solar System: `http://www.dhtmlzone.com/swdhtml/` (click on "Solar System")
- HTML Artistry companion Web site: `http://www.htmlartistry.com/`

Technique	Browser	Platform	Support
Straight Path Animation	Netscape 2,3	Both	No
	Netscape 4	Both	Yes
	IE 3	Both	No
	IE 4	Both	Yes
Customized Path Animation	Netscape 2,3	Both	No
	Netscape 4	Both	Yes
	IE 3	Both	No
	IE 4	Both	Yes
Wipe Transition	Netscape 2,3	Both	No
	Netscape 4	Both	Yes
	IE 3	Both	No
	IE 4	Both	No
Scrolling Layers	Netscape 2,3	Both	No
	Netscape 4	Both	Yes
	IE 3	Both	No
	IE 4	Both	No
Moving Backgrounds	Netscape 2,3	Both	No
	Netscape 4	Both	Yes
	IE 3	Both	No
	IE 4	Both	Yes

INSPIRATIONAL DESIGN MODEL:

Kyle Cooper, Imaginary Forces

When it comes right down to it, we go to the movies to design better web site animations and get inspired to experiment with typography! These days, we applaud the opening credits of a movie just as much as we do for the movie itself. With more and more movies coming out with artful opening scenes, we find ourselves effectively transported from real life to the life of the movie.

Enter Kyle Cooper and his 75-person studio, Imaginery Forces. Popularized for their title work for the suspense film "Seven" (New Line Cinema), they have been busy designing pieces for print and broadcast media, on top of main title design, which composes only 35% of their work load. Already featured in numerous publications across the globe, Kyle graciously granted us a telephone interview on a Saturday afternoon from his home to share his theories on and approaches to design.

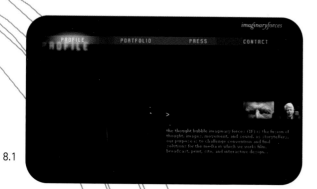

8.1

8.1

8.1

8.2

8.1   Horizontally scrolling Profile section of the Imaginary
       Forces web site (http://www.imaginaryforces.com/).

8.2   Kyle Cooper (photo by Eric Tucker).

Tell us about how you got into film title design, or design in general?

I've always been interested in film, and I've always wanted to design main titles, but my training is in graphic design and fine art. I don't really think about it as "main title design." I meet with the director, producer, and whoever else is involved at the time. I always think of this process as a problem to solve. The solution may be to come up with a metaphor, but not necessarily. It might also be introducing the movie's back story. The problems and solutions are always different. I designed a lot of posters when I was in graduate school at Yale. Posters to magazine spreads to movie titles are all similar exercises with different parameters. Web work is the same. In college I really liked graphic design. Because it was very immediate, someone could look at something I made and they could "get it."

What is your role in the creative process of a project?

Depending on what the job is, other people in the company will do the graphics, and I might do something that involves live action, or I might just focus on the main title work. No matter what, the challenge is always to reconcile all the seemingly unrelated opinions and ideas and try to make everyone happy, including me. An example is going into a meeting and having Tom Cruise (executive producer and starring actor) say, "I don't want this main title sequence for 'Mission Impossible' to be like a movie teaser or trailer; I don't want to see scenes that I will recognize later." While Brian DePalma (director) wants to see some suggestion of the original "Mission Impossible" T.V. show open which consists of numerous shots from the show.

Does that frustrate you?

It doesn't frustrate me at all. They have their set of priorities and I have my own criterion. How I put the two together and make them mesh is what excites me. Sometimes it doesn't work, but on "Mission Impossible"—they were both happy. So I like being able to reconcile contrary expectations and still do good work.

How do you stay so innovative? What inspires you?

Movies inspire me. Directors inspire me. Other graphic design inspires me. Everything inspires me! Anything. Sometimes when I have a deadline and we're getting down to the wire, I haven't really had an idea, I have hundreds of things that I could look at to be inspired but I have no time. I start to get overwhelmed by thinking I need to look at all these things. So, I just grab one book, or take a walk, or drive somewhere and say, "OK, I'm going to open this book and see what inspires something and just go with it."

How do you come up with a distinctive look for a project?

I hadn't seen anything like the spiking type [seen in] "Island of Dr. Moreau" but that was totally borne out of the content. I wanted things metamorphizing, everything changing, men turning into animals and being caught inside the body during the transformation. I think when we run into trouble is when we have a look, but we don't really have a concept, and we don't have a story. On a smaller scale, for a Web page design or a poster design, I always ask "What's the story?" Everything's measured by this. When we did the "Donnie Brasco" title, there was a time when they wanted me to go shoot Johnny Depp in London, but we just didn't have the resources to do that. We thought, this movie is about surveillance, why don't we use the production photos shot by the still photographer on the film. This existing resource solved our problem and supported the idea of surveillance. I think I'm good at looking at a lot of things and saying, "This will work. This won't work or hey, there's something in here."

Is there a pressure to keep on top of emerging technology in what you do?

I think so. Once we have framed the problem, we can ask "What's the best way to get this done? Should we do a traditional film optical?" We just worked on a main title, which was relatively simple, for a movie called, "Fallen." It's type over the scene per se, but I wasn't happy with just type over the scene because there's isn't any content in that. So I tried to think of a way to have the type become like a spirit moving from one body to the next because the film was about demons which travel from one body to another. How could we do that typographically? We could do it as a traditional film optical with an optical printer. It turned out that we couldn't get the gradations needed in the smokey type. After the composite, the smoke was very contrasty. We couldn't really get the lighting subtleties of the smoke. So we had to do it with a digital film compositing system instead. If we didn't know the technology was available to us, we would have failed.

Would it have been an option to surrender that idea and go with something else that could have been done more simply?

Not to me [chuckles]. I always start with the idea and then figure out how to get it done. "Seven" was done as a traditional film optical, and it looks like it. It looks more organic than the Island of "Dr. Moreau," which had to be done digitally because there were so many film clips from different sources. With traditional opticals we wouldn't have been able to control the color for every shot. I used to say that the idea drives the design and technology doesn't matter. But with new tools we're able to do much more much faster. I have to keep on top of technology because I'm trying to use anything I can to make the idea work. The technology allows me a broader base of production resources to support my ideas.

Tell us how you go about creating animations—putting graphic design in motion.

I look at any graphic design and I think of it as a moment in time. Maybe this is inspired by the asymmetric compositions of Paul Rand's posters and book covers. He always captured a moment in time. There's a formal relationship that it appears like it's in space, or there's depth to it. That's always been very interesting to me. You give the moment motion when you add time to the equation. I think every single frame in the sequence has to be like a moment in itself. A test for me is to stop at any frame of a title sequence and pull that frame out, and I ask if that is a nice frame in it's own right? Would that be a good spread for a magazine or a poster if that was it's own image? Another test is if you look at a motion sequence over and over again, a hundred times, is the movement smooth? Does it make sense? Is it dynamic? Most people aren't scrutinizing on that level. It's hard to do. For the last 11 years, I've been hiring people that I think are talented, that come from graphic design backgrounds, that don't have any motion graphics or film experience. I try to hire people who have what I think is a good design sense, and teach them about motion. What we do at Imaginary Forces is a whole other series of disciplines on top of typography. We take designers who are pretty good with graphics and encourage them to integrate live action, animation and sound.

What else can I tell you?

Whatever you want to share with aspiring designers out there.

I guess I have my gripes... I don't like it when someone says that the main title is better than the movie. I think it's an irrational measurement. If the title is successful, it should feel like a part of the movie. I understand that if you start a company, the tendency is wanting to talk to one person, but I have two partners, Peter Frankfurt and Chip Houghton, a computer graphics department, a design department, an editorial department, a production department and a live action division. We're doing a lot of other things besides what I do, and I like it when people mention our vision of what the company is and our goal of creating content for any medium, any format screen, at any length, one to one million frames. The company is a lot larger than me. So I like when the articles recognize that we're a company with an excellent staff. (Which is not to say that I don't work my butt off!)

Conclusion to Book
Appendix A

HTML REFERENCE LIST

This is a handy reference chart of HTML tags organized by function so that you can keep this as a reference tool next to your computer. These are not all of the HTML tags but the ones that are the most frequently used.

Main Tags

Element	Description
\<HTML\>\</HTML\>	Start/End tags of the HTML document
\<HEAD\>\</HEAD\>	Identifies the document head
\<META\>	Meta-info about document (lives in head)
\<META HTTP=EQUIV="name"\>	Binds element to HTTP response header
\<META HTTP=EQUIV="Refresh" CONTENT="n"\>	Refreshes content every n seconds
\<META HTTP=EQUIV="Refresh" CONTENT="n; URL"\>	Refreshes content in n seconds by jumping to URL
\<TITLE\>\</TITLE\>	Denotes title of HTML page
\<BODY\>\</BODY\>	Specifies body of document
\<BODY BACKGROUND="URL"\>	Background Texture
\<BODY BGCOLOR=="#RRGGBB" or "colorname"\>\</BODY\>	Background Color
\<BODY TEXT="#RRGGBB" or "colorname"\> \</BODY\>	Text Color
\<BODY LINK="#RRGGBB" or "colorname" \>\</BODY\>	Link Color
\<BODY VLINK="#RRGGBB" or "colorname" \>\</BODY\>	Visited Link Color
\<BODY ALINK="#RRGGBB" or "colorname" \>\</BODY\>	Active Link Color

Type Related

Element	Description
\<Hn\>\</Hn\>	Heading (n=1-6 with 1 as the largest heading)
\<Hn ALIGN=LEFT|CENTER|RIGHT|NOWRAP|CLEAR\>\</Hn\>	Aligns heading 3.0
\<CODE\>\</CODE\>	Text in monospace computer code
\<TT\>\</TT\>	Teletype Font
\<PRE\>\</PRE\>	Preformatted Text
\<FONT SIZE=n\>\</FONT\>	Font Size (n ranges from 1-7; default is 3)
\<FONT COLOR=="#RRGGBB" or "colorname"\>\</FONT\>	Font Color
\<FONT FACE="fontname"\>\</FONT\>	Specify Font (usually common system fonts)

continues

Appendix B

STYLE SHEET REFERENCE LIST

Here are all of the Style Sheet properties in one location for quick and easy reference for you to look up!

Length Units:

- px: pixels
- in: inches (1in=2.54cm)
- cm: centimeters (1cm=10mm)
- mm: millimeters
- pt: points (1pt=1/72in)
- pc: picas (1pc=12pt)
- em: height of elements font
- ex: x-height, height of letter "x"

Property	Values	Description	Example
		Fonts	
font-family	font name font family name generic family name	Sets font face	P { font-family: "arial," sans serif }
font-style	normal italic	Sets font style	P { font-style: italic }
font-variant	normal small-caps	Sets font display	P { font-variant: small-caps }
font-weight	normal bold bolder lighter	Specifies font weight 100-900 (displayed in 100 increments with 100 as lightest and 900 as darkest)	P { font-weight: 700 }
font-size	length percentage absolute-size relative-size	Sets font size	H2 { font-size: 12pt }
absolute-size	xx-small x-small small medium large x-large xx-large	font-size attribute	H2 { font-size: small }
relative-size	larger smaller	font-size attribute	H2 { font-size: larger }
font	font-style font-variant font-weight font-size line-height font-family	Shorthand for font properties	P { font: 12pt Times bold }

continues

Property	Values	Description	Example
Colors & Backgrounds			
color	color name hexidecimal code RGB value	Determines color of an element	H2 { color: red }
background-color	color name hexideximal code RGB value transparent	Sets background color	BODY { background-color: white }
background-image	URL none	Sets background image	BODY { background-image: url (images/lines.gif) }
background-repeat	repeat repeat-x repeat-y no-repeat	Determines how background image is repeated	BODY { background: url (lines.gif); background-repeat: repeat-x }
background-attachment	scroll fixed	Determines scrolling or fixed nature of background	BODY { background: url (lines.gif); background-attachment: scroll }
background-position	length percentage {1, 2} top|center|bottom left|center|right	Gives initial position of background image	BODY { background: url (lines.gif); background-position: left, center }
background	background-color background-image background-repeat background-attachment background-position	Shorthand for the background properties (better supported)	P { background: url (lines.gif) blue fixed }
Text & Images			
word spacing	length normal	Defines space between words	H2 { word-spacing: 5pt }
letter-spacing	length normal	Defines space between letters	H2 { letter-spacing: 2px }
text-transform	capitalize uppercase lowercase none	Changes case of text	H2 { text-transform: uppercase }
text-decoration	none underline overline line-through blink	Text enhancements	H2 { text-decoration: underline }
text-align	left right center justify	Align text	H2 { text-align: center }

Property	Values	Description	Example
text-indent	length percentage	Defines indentation	P { text-indent: 1in }
line-height	normal number length percentage	Sets the baseline spacing	P { line-height: 5px }
margin-top	length percentage auto	Sets top margin of element	P { margin-top: 1in }
margin-right	length percentage auto	Sets right margin of element	P { margin-right: 20% }
margin-bottom	length percentage auto	Sets bottom margin of element	P { margin-bottom: 5px }
margin-left	length percentage auto	Sets left margin of element	P { margin-left: 40% }
margin	length percentage auto {1,4}	Sets all margins of element by specifying 1-4 values	P { margin: 5px } P { margin: 1px, 2px, 3px, 4px }
vertical-align	baseline sub super top text-top middle bottom text-bottom percentage	Controls vertical alignment of text and images	H2 { vertical- align:top }
padding-top	length percentage	Determines space between top border and element	P { padding-top: 30% }
padding-bottom	length percentage	Determines space between bottom border and element	P { padding-bottom: 30% }
padding-right	length percentage	Determines space between right border and element	P { padding-right: 2in }
padding-left	length percentage	Determines space between left border and element	P { padding-left: 2in}
padding	length percentage {1,4}	Shorthand property, Set all together at once in order padding-top, right, bottom, and left	P { padding: 10px, 20px, 30px, 40px }
float	left right none	Float text and images	H2 { float: left }

continues

Property	Values	Description	Example
clear	left right both none	Unwraps text	P { clear: both }
position	absolute relative static	precision or relative positioning of text and images	P { position: absolute }
left	length percentage auto	An attribute of position, controls horizontal position	P { left: 1in }
top	length percentage auto	An attribute of position, controls vertical position	P { top: 1in }
clip	shape auto	Control visible areas of text/images	H2 { clip: rect(20px 25px 30px 35px) }
overflow	clip scroll none	Control visibility of overflowed text/images	H2 { overflow: scroll }
z-index	integer auto	Control layering order of text/images	H2 { z-index: 3 }
visibility	visible hidden inherit	Decides initial display	H2 { visibility: hidden }
display	block inline list-item none	Decides how text/image is displayed	P { display: inline }
whitespace	normal pre nowrap	Control browser white space	P { white-space: normal }
border-width	length thin medium thick {1,4}	Specifies the width of elements border between 1-4 values	H2 { border -width: 1in }
border-color	color name hexideximal code RGB value {1,4}	Sets the border color up to four values for left, right, top, and bottom	H2 { border-color: blue } H2 { border-color: blue, blue, red, red }
border-style	none dotted dashed solid double groove ridge inset outset {1,4}	Sets border style	H2 { border-style: dashed }

Property	Values	Description	Example
border	border-width border-style color	Shorthand for setting border width, style, and color	H2 { border: dashed red }
width	length percentage auto	Sets width of element	IMG.a { width: 20px, height: 40px }
height	length auto	Sets height of element	IMG.a { width: 20px, height, 40px }
list-style-type	disc circle square decimal lower-roman upper-Roman lower-alpha upper-alpha none	Specifies display of list items	LI.square { list-style-type: square }
list-style-position	inside outside	Determines indentation of item in reference to first item	LI { list-style-position: outside }
list-style-image	URL none	Uses specified image as customized bullet	LI { list-style-image: url(images/button.gif) }
list-style	keyword position URL	Shorthand for list-style-type, list-style-image, and list-style-position	OL {list-style: lower-Roman inside}

APPENDIX C
CROSS-BROWSER DYNAMIC HTML
REFERENCE LIST

You've spent untold hours debugging your Web sites. Nothing matches the frustration of looking at the same five lines of code for three hours and finally figuring out that the browser simply can't do what you need it to do because of a bug. To save you from some degree of this frustration, we've compiled a smattering of the bugs, idiosyncrasies, and hard to find answers to seemingly simple questions. If you happen to stumble into a situation where you're about to throw rocks at the monitor, remember to look at this appendix and you might just find a solution.

Netscape Bugs

The Netscape Web site (www.netscape.com) contains copious documentation about its browsers. When you're in a jam, it's the best place to start looking for a solution. When working with Dynamic HTML, we read about two neat features only to find that they didn't work in Netscape 4.0. However, with some experimentation, we found workarounds. Read on to learn how to make background images and colors for layers function properly.

Background Images for Layers

The background-image property kind of works in Netscape for the Macintosh and doesn't work at all on Windows. The following code is *supposed* to produce a layer with a background image:

```
<div id="divLayer" style="position:absolute;
visibility:visible; left:36px; top:46px;
width:338px; height:79px; z-index:1;
background-image: url(objhier.gif)">
   <font color="#CC3300"><b>Some Text</b>
</font>
</div>
```

The code works fine in Internet Explorer, but in Netscape, you only see the background image in the areas where you have text. A way to solve this problem is simply to put a bunch of
s in the layer like so:

```
<div id="divLayer" style="position:absolute;
visibility:visible; left:36px; top:46px;
width:338px; height:79px; z-index:1;
background-image: url(objhier.gif)">

   <font color="#CC3300"><b>Some Text</b>
</font> <BR><BR><BR><BR><BR><BR><BR>
</div>
```

Background Colors for Layers

The same problem that occurs with the background-image tag also happens with the background-color tag, however, the <BR> fix doesn't work in this case. Instead, you have to insert a table with a background color that stretches to the edges of the layer. Here's the code for the background-color fix:

```
<div id="divLayer" style="position:absolute;
visibility:visible; left:36px; top:46px;
width:337px; height:52px; z-index:1;">
  <table width=337 height=52
bgcolor="#00FF00"><tr><td>
      <font color="#CC3300"><b>Put all of
your content in the table</b> </font>
  </tr></td></table>
</div>
```

Netscape Only Features

Although we try to make every Web site work exactly the same across browsers, there are some features that are too good to pass up. The following feature only works in Netscape.

Setting Layer Source

Netscape enables you to set the source (URL) for individual layers. Unfortunately, you can't set the source of a <DIV> layer. However, it's possible using the <LAYER> tag. Here's a <LAYER> with the source set to an external file:

```
<layer id="searchEngine" left="50" top="63"
width="286" height="127" z-index="1"
visibility="SHOW" src="http://www.excite.com"
clip="200,200">
</layer>
```

Here's the code for programmatically setting <LAYER> source with JavaScript:

```
document.layers["searchEngine"].src=
"http://www.yahoo.com";
```

Internet Explorer Only Features

Although Netscape has been making a fair number of browser innovations, Microsoft has been busily inventing some astounding features itself. One of these advancements is called Multimedia Controls. These are described next.

Multimedia Controls

Microsoft built in these pretty neat controls into 4.0. They enable you to create a bunch of different effects. The following list offers descriptions of these controls:

- **Mixer Control:** Enables you to dynamically mix multiple WAV files.
- **Path Control:** Similar to a JavaScript time-line, this control enables you to animate the position of objects on your page over time.
- **Sequencer Control:** Lets you control various behaviors in your document. For example, you can use it to call a script or to manage ActiveX controls and methods.
- **Sprite Control:** Enables you to add still and animated images to your document with control over frames per second, forward or reverse playback, or the dynamic reading of source files.
- **Structured Graphics Control:** Adds vector graphics to your document and lets you scale, rotate, and apply effects to these graphics.
- **Transitions Control:** Lets you apply effects like a fade to an object.
- **Visual Filters Control:** Also enables you to apply effects to objects on your page such as a reverse-out.

Try a search on www.microsoft.com for "multimedia controls" if you want more information. We haven't used them much because, although they're neat, they only work on IE.

Differences Between Netscape and IE

Most of the frustrations and time-sucking bug fixes result from syntax differences between Internet Explorer and Netscape. Some of these difference are spelled out here and cover the following topics:

- Programmatically referencing layers
- Programmatically referencing layer properties
- Referencing the layer visibility property
- <LAYER> versus <DIV> tags
- Dynamic font control
- Moving a layer
- Click and drag

- Programmatically accessing HTML text
- Array assignment
- Playing sounds
- Referencing pixel coordinates

Programmatically Referencing Layers (document.all Versus document.layers)

Netscape and IE employ different syntax to refer to layers. To reference a layer called "foolsLayer" in Netscape, you write the following:

```
document.layers["foolsLayer"]
```

To access the same layer in IE, you write the following:

```
document.all["foolsLayer"]
```

To get around this problem, you can do a simple initiation routine that defines a variable according to which browser is being used.

Programmatically Referencing Layer Properties (.style)

Netscape and IE also differ in their syntax for accessing layer properties. To reference the *visibility* property of a layer called tooHot in Netscape, write the following:

```
document.layers["tooHot"].visibility
```

To access the same property in IE, write the following:

```
document.all["tooHot"].style.visibility
```

To get around this problem, you can do a simple initiation routine that defines a variable according to which browser is being used.

Referencing the Layer Visibility Property

Netscape enables you to use many different words to set the visibility property of a layer. You can use any of the following words: "hidden" or "hide," "visible" or "show," and "inherit." For example, both of the following layer definitions work in Netscape:

```
<div id="Layer1" style="position:absolute;
visibility:hide; left:38px; top:58px;
width:237px; height:66px; z-index:1">
   TEST LAYER
</div>

<div id="Layer1" style="position:absolute;
visibility:hidden; left:38px; top:58px;
width:237px; height:66px; z-index:1">
   TEST LAYER
</div>
```

However, only the second layer definition works in IE. If you want to make cross browser code, stick with "hidden" and "visible" to define or set the visibility of your layers.

<LAYER> Versus <DIV> Tags

The differences between these two tags are described in detail in Chapter 6, "Using Layers, the Building Blocks of Dynamic HTML."

Dynamic Font Control

With the coming of 4.0 browsers, developers can control the font in which the HTML text appears. Netscape features a proprietary TrueDoc technology along with some new HTML extensions that allow you to display your HTML text in a variety of fonts, and they *do not* have to be installed on the visitor's machine. Instead, the font is downloaded, like an image, and then dynamically installed. (Chapter 7, "Cascading Style Sheets: Typography Made Simple," describes the technique in detail in.) The only problem with this technology is that it takes a while to download each font and, when active, it makes scrolling quite slow—it reduces the browser's redraw to a crawl. In addition, this type of font formatting only works in Netscape. Go to www.bitstream. com/world/ or http://home.netscape.com/ comprod/products/communicator/fonts/index.html for more information.

It looks like IE might be moving toward a similar font technology (at least at the time of this writing). IE might implement a feature that lets a visitor download a font (if it is not available on his system) and

then display HTML text in that font. The specs for this technology are available at http://www.w3. org/TR/WD-font.

At the moment, both IE and Netscape enable you to use CSS or a simple <FONT> tag to define the font used to display HTML text, as long as the font is already installed on the visitor's computer. If the font that you specify is not installed, the browser displays the text normally.

Here's the code for defining a font face with the <FONT> tag:

```
<font face="arial,helvetica">Greetings
Earthlings</font>
```

Here's the code for defining font face using CSS:

```
<div id="fontTest" style="position:absolute;
left:200px; top:100px; z-index:1;
font-family:arial,helvetica;">
   Greetings Earthlings
</div>
```

Chapter 3, "Type Effects: Enhancing Your Interfaces with Stunning Typography," describes font face usage in detail.

Moving a Layer

You know the expression—there is more than one way to skin a cat! Well, it applies quite well to moving a layer. Not only do Netscape and IE have different syntax for moving a layer, but Netscape has many special methods that enable you to move only the <LAYER> type of layer. The following code moves a layer in Netscape:

```
document.layers["myLayer"].top=400;
document.layers["myLayer"].left=322;
```

In IE, rewrite the code to the following:

```
document.all["myLayer"].style.top=400;
document.all["myLayer"].style.left=322;
```

The differences are mainly a matter of document.all and .style variations. To accommodate the differences in syntax, you can do a simple initiation routine that defines a variable according to which browser is being used.

Netscape also features many methods that let you move a <LAYER> (but not a <DIV>) in many different ways. Unfortunately, these methods don't work in IE. Here are the methods as described by Netscape:

- moveBy(x,y)—Changes the layer position by applying the specified deltas, measured in pixels.
- moveTo(x,y)—Changes the layer position to the specified pixel coordinates within the containing layer.
- moveToAbsolute(x,y)—Changes the layer position to the specified pixel coordinates within the page (instead of the containing layer).
- resizeBy(width,height)—Resizes the layer by the specified height and width values (in pixels). This method has the same effect as setting the clip.width and clip.height.
- resizeTo(width,height)—Resizes the layer to have the specified height and width values (in pixels).
- moveAbove(layer)—Stacks this layer above the layer specified in the argument, without changing either the layer's horizontal or vertical position.
- moveBelow(layer)—Stacks this layer below the specified layer.
- load(sourcestring,width)—Changes the source of a layer to the contents of the file indicated by sourcestring and simultaneously changes the width at which the layer's HTML contents will be wrapped. The first argument is a string indicating the external filename and the second is the width of the layer as a pixel value.

Click and Drag

IE and Netscape have so many differences in their event syntax that creating a cross browser click-and-drag effect becomes quite difficult. It is described fully in Chapter 8, "Interactivity: Making the Most of Your Layers."

Programmatically Accessing HTML Text

Although the code is simple, it's difficult to find the proper syntax for programmatically accessing and changing HTML text. Luckily, we have a handy reference for you.

In Netscape, you can change the HTML text in a layer using the following code:

```
document.layers["myLayer"].document.write("hi
there");
document.layers["myLayer"].document.close();
```

In IE, the code looks like this:

```
document.all["myLayer"].innerHTML= "hi
there";
```

Array Assignment

One of the more obscure bugs or limitations that you might run into has to do with array assignment in IE. The weird thing is that the bugs seem only to occur on some occasions, so ignore this note unless you have a problem with array assignment.

Normally, you can assign values to an array like so:

```
var myArray= new Array (6,221);
```

This type of array assignment works wonderfully on both browsers until you try to assign a lot of values to the array. We haven't quite figured out what the limit is, but it does seem to exist (sometimes)—and there is a way around it. Here's the code to get around the bug:

```
var myArray=new Array (250);
var coords="6,221,etc…";
myArray=coords.split(",");
```

If you put the data into a string and then assign it to the array, the problem goes away.

Playing Sounds

IE and Netscape use different syntax to play sound. Actually, IE's syntax is more of a hack to get a sound file to play. Here's a function that plays sound on both browsers:

```
function play_sound(sound_name) {
  if (navigator.appName == "Netscape") {
    eval('document.' +sound_name+
'.play(false)');
  }else{
eval('document.'+sound_name+'.FileName=
  document.'+sound_name+'.FileName');
  }
}
```

Netscape uses the `document.sound.play()` method to play a WAV or AU file that has been previously embedded in the document. In IE, you need to reassign the source of the sound file by resetting the `FileName` property. Very strange, but it works.

Here is a list of other hack-ways to control sound in IE:

`document.sound_name.CurrentState`
> (0=stopped, 1=paused, 2=playing) read only

`document.sound_name.CurrentPosition`
> (runtime counter)

`document.sound_name.SelectionEnd`
> (length of song) read only

`document.sound_name.FileName`
> (URL of song)

`document.sound_name.FileName ="shout.mid"`
> (how to get a sound file to play)

`document.sound_name.CurrentPosition=`
> `document.sound_name.SelectionEnd;`
> (how to stop sound play)

In Netscape, you can use the following methods and state indicators to control and test sound:

```
play('TRUE¦FALSE', 'URL of sound')
stop()
pause()
start_time(int_seconds)
end_time(int seconds)
setvol(int percent)
fade_to(into to_percent)
fade_from_to(int from_percent, int to_per-
cent)
start_at_beginning() - Override a
start_time()
stop_at_end() - Override an end_time()
IsReady() - Returns TRUE if the plug-in has
completed loading
IsPlaying() - Returns TRUE if the sound is
currently playing
IsPaused() - Returns TRUE if the sound is
currently paused
GetVolume() - Returns the current volume as
a percentage
```

Referencing Pixel Coordinates

In the past, you might have had some problems referencing pixel coordinates in IE. We think that the problems are fixed on the latest browser release, but if you ever run into any problems related to programmatically accessing and altering pixel coordinates, you will know how to solve them.

The problem results from the fact that IE prefers to read pixel coordinates with a `px` attached to the number. For example, you might be running into errors when trying to scroll a layer to the left, such as in the following function:

```
1.      var currLeft=300, leftStopPoint=0;
2.      function moveLayerLeft(layerName){
3.          if (currLeft != leftStopPoint){
4.              currLeft-=2;
5.                  eval(layerRef+'['+
layerName+'"]'+styleSwitch+'.left =
currLeft');
6.                  setTimeout('moveLayerLeft
("'+layerName+'")',30);
7.          }
8.      }
```

IE used to throw up errors because it couldn't properly compare `currLeft` with `leftStopPoint` because in line 5, currLeft is set on the basis of the layer's position. If the layer were at the location 270,100, IE set currLeft to 270px instead of just 270. That extra little `px` made it impossible for IE to do a proper comparison because it was trying to compare 270px to 0 and these are different data types. The fix for the problem involves defining an extra initialization variable and adding that variable to the code:

```
//INITIALIZATION
if (navigator.appName == "Netscape") {
pxSwitch="";
leftStopPoint=0;
currLeft=300;
        }else{
pxSwitch="px";
currLeft="300px";
leftStopPoint="0px";
}
//FUNCTION
function moveLayerLeft(layerName){
if (currLeft+pxSwitch != leftStopPoint){
    currLeft-=2;

eval(layerRef+'['+layerName+'"]'+styleSwitch
+'.left = currLeft');

setTimeout('moveLayerLeft("'+layerName+'")',
30);
}
}
```

Notice that the variable `pxSwitch` was defined in the initialization routine and used in the first line of the function. We also defined `currLeft` and `leftStopPoint` just to make everything consistent.

INDEX

A